LAW AND THE WHIRLIGIG OF TIME

For over 30 years, first as a QC, then as a judge, and latterly as a visiting professor of law at Oxford, Stephen Sedley has written and lectured about aspects of the law that do not always get the attention they deserve.

His first anthology of essays, *Ashes and Sparks*, was praised in the *New York Times* by Ian McEwan for its 'exquisite, finely balanced prose, the prickly humour, the knack of artful quotation and an astonishing historical grasp'. 'You could have no interest in the law,' McEwan wrote, 'and read his book for pure intellectual delight.'

The present volume contains more recent articles by Stephen Sedley on the law, many of them from the *London Review of Books*, and lectures given to a variety of audiences. The first part is concerned with law as part of history—Feste's 'whirligig of time'; the second part with law and rights. The third part is a group of biographical and critical pieces on a number of figures from the legal and musical worlds.

The final part of the book is more personal, going back to the author's days at the bar, and then forward to some parting reflections.

Law and the Whirligig of Time

Stephen Sedley

·HART·

OXFORD · LONDON · NEW YORK · NEW DELHI · SYDNEY

HART PUBLISHING

Bloomsbury Publishing Plc

Kemp House, Chawley Park, Cumnor Hill, Oxford, OX2 9PH, UK

HART PUBLISHING, the Hart/Stag logo, BLOOMSBURY and the Diana logo are trademarks of Bloomsbury Publishing Plc

First published in Great Britain 2018

A catalogue record for this book is available from the British Library.

Library of Congress Cataloging-in-Publication data

Names: Sedley, Stephen, author.

Title: Law and the whirligig of time / Stephen Sedley.

Description: Portland, Oregon : Hart Publishing, 2018. | Includes bibliographical references and index. | Description based on print version record and CIP data provided by publisher; resource not viewed.

Identifiers: LCCN 2018002794 (print) | LCCN 2018002881 (ebook) | ISBN 9781509917112 (Epub) | ISBN 9781509917099 (hardback : alk. paper)

Subjects: LCSH: Law—Great Britain.

Classification: LCC KD358 (ebook) | LCC KD358 .S435 2018 (print) | DDC 349.41—dc23

LC record available at https://lccn.loc.gov/2018002794

ISBN: HB: 978-1-50991-709-9
           ePDF: 978-1-50991-710-5
           ePub: 978-1-50991-711-2

Typeset by Compuscript Ltd, Shannon
Printed and bound in Great Britain by CPI Group (UK) Ltd, Croydon CR0 4YY

To find out more about our authors and books visit www.hartpublishing.co.uk. Here you will find extracts, author information, details of forthcoming events and the option to sign up for our newsletters.

To my children
Jane, Ben and Sarah
and my stepchildren
Rachael and Nathan

I have laboured to make a covenant with myself, that affection may not press upon judgment; for I suppose there is no man that hath any apprehension of gentry or nobleness but his affection stands to the continuance of so noble a name and house, and would take hold of a twig or twine-thread to uphold it.

And yet time hath his revolution: there must be a period and an end of all temporal things, ... an end of names and dignities and whatsoever is terrene; and why not of De Vere? For where is Bohun? Where's Mowbray? Where's Mortimer? Nay, which is more and most of all, where is Plantagenet? They are entombed in the urns and sepulchres of mortality.

> Sir Ranulph Crewe, chief justice of the King's Bench, March 1625, giving the advice of the judges to the House of Lords on claims to the inheritance of the earldom of Oxford. Crewe was dismissed by Charles I a year later for holding enforced loans to the Crown to be unlawful.
>
> (Rolle 173; 82 ER 50)

Preface

I had the luck during my years as a barrister and, later, as a judge to be asked from time to time to lecture and write about the law. It meant, inevitably, steering clear of party political issues, but it compelled me to think about law's place in the wider world. It also required me to write intelligibly for non-lawyers; and it allowed me to comment fairly freely on the history and the reality of the legal system of England and Wales.

In 2011, when I retired from the bench, a collection of these writings was published under the title *Ashes and Sparks*. In the years that followed, as a visiting professor at Oxford University, I delivered a series of lectures on the history of English public law, published in 2014 as *Lions Under the Throne*. And I continued to write the reviews and occasional pieces for the *London Review of Books*, and to give the public lectures, which form the substance of the present book. To them have been added some earlier pieces which may still be of interest.

As before, I do not make any large thematic claim for my work. Most of it is reactive—little more than coats hung on other people's pegs, though I hope that they all have something of interest in their pockets. That some points may be made more than once should not matter if, as I would expect, the book is dipped into rather than read sequentially. If it has a unifying thread it is simply that, as Feste remarks towards the end of *Twelfth Night*, the whirligig of time brings in his revenges.

I am grateful to those publishers who are listed in the acknowledgments for permission to reproduce work which they first published, to Bill Asquith of Hart Publishers for his advice and encouragement, and to those institutions where my lectures were delivered for their agreement to publication here.

I am also indebted to Keith Grant, whose painting *Icebergs Drifting Seawards, Ilulissat* graces the book cover, and to Chris Beetles, whose gallery has for many years represented him, for their permission to use one of Keith's many fine works. Time's whirligig has played its part here too. Fifty years ago the three of us lived or worked within half a mile of each other in the London Borough of Camden. Chris was my GP before he exchanged the vagaries of human frailty for the certitudes of the art market. Keith, from whom I bought one of his early acrylics, had his studio down the road before he moved to Norway, which is now his home. The three of us met again in 2010 when Chris mounted a landmark exhibition of Keith's recent work. Not long afterwards Keith became painter in residence at Keble College, a stone's throw from my home in Oxford. The whirligig keeps spinning.

Stephen Sedley
Oxford
November 2017

Acknowledgements

Chapters 1 and 3 were delivered as lectures at the invitation of the institutions mentioned at the head of them. Chapter 1 was published in *Judicial Review* and appears here with the agreement of the publisher, Taylor & Francis. Chapter 3 was published in the *Edinburgh Law Review* and appears here with the agreement of Edinburgh University Press.

Chapter 17 is included by permission of the *Financial Times*, in whose edition of 28 January 2017 it was first published, in shorter form, as an op-ed article.

Chapters 27–31 were written for the *Oxford Dictionary of National Biography* and are published here with the permission of Oxford University Press. Chapter 34 was written for the *Guardian*'s obituary page.

All the remaining chapters, with the exception of Chapter 36 (which was written for *Tribune*), and Chapters 38 and 40 (which have not previously been published), were written either as reviews or as articles for the *London Review of Books*, to whose editor, Mary-Kay Wilmers, and her deputy Jean McNicol I owe an enduring debt of gratitude.

Contents

History

1

Law as History

This paper was given in March 2016 (with the agreement of both institutions) first as the Sir David Williams memorial lecture in Cambridge and then as the All Souls Neill lecture in Oxford—a form of bigamy that I admit having practised in the past[1] but do not commend.

L IKE MOST UNDERGRADUATES in the Cambridge English school in 1960, I used to attend Dr Leavis's lectures. They veered between penetrating insights into texts, splenetic assaults on his critics and grand generalisations about literature and culture. One of these generalisations has stayed in my mind:

'There is no literary history,' said Leavis, who himself had once been a historian. 'There is only literature.'

Albert Venn Dicey, although he too knew a great deal of history, was similarly anti-historicist when it came to understanding law.

'Let us eagerly learn all that is known, and still more eagerly all that is not known, about the Witanagemót,' he wrote.[2] 'But let us remember that antiquarianism is not law, and that the function of a trained lawyer is not to know what the law of England was yesterday, still less what it was centuries ago, or what it ought to be tomorrow, but to know and be able to state what are the principles of law which actually and at the present day exist in England.'

On he goes:[3]

'The struggles of the seventeenth century, the conflict between James and Coke, Bacon's theory of the prerogative, Charles's effort to substitute the personal will of Charles Stuart for the legal will of the King of England, are all matters which touch not remotely upon the problems of actual law.'

---

[1] 'The four wise monkeys visit the marketplace of ideas', *Ashes and Sparks*, Ch 38, was delivered in Cambridge and then Dublin.
[2] *The Law of the Constitution*, 5th edn (1897) p 14.
[3] ibid pp 16–17.

Tom Bingham, with characteristic charity, was prepared to blame at least some of Dicey's obscurantism on the fact that the Oxford law school had only recently been separated from the modern history school, leading Dicey to try to stake out a distinct terrain for the study of law. But even Bingham felt compelled to call Dicey's approach 'not only anti-intellectual but plainly misguided'.

> 'A lawyer without history, as well as literature,' Bingham wrote,[4] quoting Walter Scott, 'is a mechanic, and probably' he added 'not a very good mechanic at that.'

I want here to explore a little of the terrain between an anti-historicism which denies the law's past any role in its present or future, and what has been called the imperialism of the present—the pressing of yesterday into the service of today without regard to the passage of time.

A recurrent example of the latter, highlighted recently on the 800th anniversary of Magna Carta, is the urge of many lawyers and some historians to co-opt the limited undertakings extracted by a group of aggressive barons from a beleaguered feudal monarch into the modern constitutionalisms of Britain and the United States. But this is a long way from saying, as Dicey's myopic historiography would have said, that Magna Carta has no bearing on our own legal culture. If, instead of squinting at the document through the prism of modernity and discerning what appear to be the underpinnings of jury trial and legal aid, one looks at what has happened over the intervening eight centuries, a different function of Magna Carta begins to emerge: the nourishment of a deep-lying and long-term consensus that no power stands outside law and that there exist fundamental rights which no government, whether monarchical or elective, has power to deny.

To say this is, of course, to say both everything and nothing: everything, because in one grand sweep it encapsulates the entirety of the rule of law; nothing, because until you know what power, and what law, and what rights are meant, you are talking in a void. It has been the historic task of the common law to fill this insatiable maw, never forgetting Bacon's admonition that the judges, although they may be lions, are lions under a throne occupied in his time by a monarch but since the revolutions of the seventeenth century by a legislature whose sovereignty the judges have—at least so far—not disputed.

---

[4] 'Dicey revisited', *Lives of the Law*, p 44.

In looking now at some of the ways in which the law of England and Wales has over the centuries reinvented itself, I am not speaking of anything as self-conscious or self-serving as the invention of tradition. In his introductory essay to *The Invention of Tradition*,[5] Eric Hobsbawm made a worthwhile distinction between tradition and custom.

'Custom,' he wrote, 'is what judges do; tradition (in this case invented tradition) is the wig, robe and other formal paraphernalia and ritualised practices surrounding their substantial action.'

THE *ANISMINIC* SAGA

Let me try to illustrate the adaptability, the inventiveness, of common-law custom—of 'what judges do'—by looking first at a legal doctrine which has conditioned my working lifetime: the amenability of all administrative bodies, tribunals or decision-makers to the supervisory jurisdiction of the High Court for errors of law, whether substantive or procedural and whether jurisdictional or not.

By the 1960s judicial review of administrative acts had become entangled in a web of subtle and largely impressionistic distinctions.[6] One was between those acts which were quasi-judicial and those which were merely administrative. The former, broadly speaking, were open to challenge for procedural impropriety; the latter in general were not. Over and above this distinction lay the difference between errors of law which went to jurisdiction and those which had occurred in the exercise of a properly assumed jurisdiction. This was a meaningful distinction which had developed over the course of the nineteenth century from cases decided in the eighteenth and seventeenth centuries, as Parliament sought to protect its proliferating administrative bodies by means of privative or preclusive clauses—provisions forbidding judicial review of their decisions. To this the judges had responded by holding that a decision made without jurisdiction was no decision at all and hence was not shielded by these clauses. The decision in the *Anisminic* case, handed down by the law lords in December 1968,[7]

---

[5] Ed EJ Hobsbawm and T Ranger (Cambridge, 1983).
[6] See my *Lions Under the Throne*, Ch 1 'Lions in winter'.
[7] *Anisminic Ltd v Foreign Compensation Commission* [1969] 2 AC 147 (HL). See in particular the speeches of Lord Pearce and Lord Wilberforce.

added nothing to this well-established rule of the legal game. What it did instead was move the goalposts.[8]

The Foreign Compensation Act 1950, under which a commission of 10 lawyers had held that Anisminic Ltd was not entitled to compensation for the loss of some of its assets in the 1956 Suez crisis, laid down in black and white in s 4(4):

'The determination by the commission of any application made to them under this Act shall not be called in question in any court of law.'

It was difficult to see why the Commission's determination that neither Anisminic Ltd nor its Egyptian successor was eligible for payment out of the Foreign Compensation Fund, even if it was wrong, was not precisely the kind of determination which s 4(4) was designed to keep away from the courts. That was certainly how it had looked to a unanimous Court of Appeal which included Lord Justice Diplock,[9] and how it still looks to a number of commentators.

But the law lords by a majority characterised the finding of ineligibility as an error going to the panel's jurisdiction and rendering its determination void. There were—indeed there still are—sharp intakes of academic and professional breath at the intellectual legerdemain of Lord Reid's reasoning to this effect. But there was nothing of obviously historic consequence in the decision itself: indeed it had been anticipated by the neglected first-instance judgment of Mr Justice Browne.[10] What created legal history was what the profession itself, both bench and bar, set about making of the law lords' decision.

It would have been neither forensically unacceptable nor intellectually dishonest for Treasury counsel in the years after 1968 to submit, and for the courts to hold, that the *Anisminic* decision was confined to a single, arcane statutory régime, bounded by the Foreign Compensation (Egypt) (Determination and Registration of Claims) Order 1962, within which the law lords had positioned a well-established test of justiciability—the jurisdiction test—in an unexpected place. The question is why this is not what happened.

What happened was that it became the experience of counsel (of whom I was one) appearing during the 1970s in judicial review

---

[8] Counsel for the appellant company were Roger Parker QC (who was not the greatest public lawyer of his generation) and Patrick Neill QC (who arguably was); for the Commission, Sydney Templeman QC and the Treasury devil Gordon Slynn.

[9] [1968] 2 QB 862: the argument took 13 days in Jan–Feb 1967, Sydney Templeman QC leading Nigel Bridge (Slynn's predecessor as Treasury devil) for the Commission.

[10] [1969] 2 AC 147, 223.

cases against government departments or official bodies to be told by Treasury counsel that no point was to be taken on the applicability of *Anisminic*. In other words, if the applicant could establish an error of law, it was not going to be argued by the Crown that it was justiciable only if it vitiated the decision-maker's jurisdiction. It was accepted in effect that if the tribunal's error in *Anisminic* truly went to its jurisdiction, as the law lords had decided it did, then the old divide between jurisdictional and non-jurisdictional error had collapsed. The goalposts had become the corner flags.

This was not a *trahison des clercs*. It was a recognition that the orderly development of public law required a comprehensive approach to arguable abuses of power in place of the hair-splitting distinctions which had come to disfigure the law in the inter-war years; and it should be placed on record that it was from the successive standing counsel to the Treasury—first Gordon Slynn,[11] then Harry Woolf,[12] then Simon Brown,[13] then John Laws[14]—that these initiatives came.

Lord Woolf in his 1989 Hamlyn Lectures noted without rancour that the string of celebrated public law cases which he lost as Treasury counsel over little more than a year—*Tameside*,[15] *Congreve*,[16] *The Crossman Diaries*[17] and *Laker Airways*[18]—had (in his words) all contributed to the development of administrative law. One of the great strengths of public law in my years both at the bar and on the bench was that Treasury counsel would if necessary put the development of a principled body of public law ahead of the need to win a particular case. It happened in *R v Greater Manchester Coroner, ex parte Tal*,[19] where Simon Brown as Treasury counsel supported my submission that a recent authority[20] refusing to apply the *Anisminic* principle to coroners' courts ought not to be followed; and again in *Leech*,[21] where John Laws declined[22] to invite

---

[11] 1968–1974.

[12] 1974–1979.

[13] 1979–1984.

[14] 1984–1992.

[15] *Secretary of State for Education and Science v Tameside Metropolitan Borough Council* [1977] AC 1014 (HL).

[16] *Congreve v Home Office* [1976] QB 629 (CA).

[17] *A-G v Jonathan Cape Ltd; A-G v Times Newspapers Ltd* [1976] QB 752 (QBD).

[18] *Laker Airways v Department of Trade* [1977] QB 643 (CA).

[19] *R v Greater Manchester Coroner, ex parte Tal* [1985] QB 67 (DC).

[20] *R v Surrey Coroner, ex parte Campbell* [1982] QB 661 (QBD).

[21] *Leech v Parkhurst Prison Deputy Governor* [1988] AC 533 (HL).

[22] ibid 544F–G, 556H–557C.

the House of Lords to reverse the High Court's landmark decision in *St Germain* that the procedures of prison boards of visitors were justiciable—a reversal that would have won him the case—and instead undertook the sisyphean task of attempting to carve out an exception for adjudications by prison governors. The work of Treasury counsel is now more widely diffused, but it is to be hoped that this culture of candour continues.

For their part the judges continued after 1969 to weave between jurisdictional and non-jurisdictional error.[23] But as time went by they responded to counsel's invitations to build on *Anisminic* rather than to marginalise it. In 1974 (not sooner) Lord Diplock, delivering the de Smith Lecture in Cambridge declared that *Anisminic*

> 'renders obsolete the technical distinction between errors of law which go to "jurisdiction" and errors of law which do not'.[24]

One notes Diplock's dismissive description of the historic distinction as 'technical', which it most certainly was not: although erratically applied, it was a distinction which gave substance to the division of powers between the legislature and the courts. But a collaborative—some might say collusive—process of reconfiguring public law was now under way.

It did not reach fruition until, in the summer of 1980, in *Racal Communications*,[25] Lord Diplock, now seated in the chair of the House of Lords' appellate committee, repeated almost verbatim what he had said in his Cambridge lecture seven years earlier (though this time he declined to dismiss the old distinction as merely 'technical'); and what Diplock said in *Racal* about *Anisminic* has become canonical despite the fact that, since *Racal* concerned the jurisdiction of the higher courts and not of inferior tribunals, it was entirely obiter.

It was nevertheless from this makeshift platform that, two years later, Diplock felt able in *O'Reilly v Mackman*[26] to announce that *Anisminic*

> 'has liberated English public law from the fetters that the courts had theretofore imposed upon themselves ... by drawing esoteric distinctions ...'

[23] See *Pearlman v Harrow School Governors* [1979] QB 56 (CA).
[24] [1974] *CLJ* 233, 243 (the 1974 de Smith Lecture).
[25] *Re Racal Communications Ltd* [1981] AC 374, 383 (HL).
[26] *O'Reilly v Mackman* [1983] 2 AC 237, 278 (HL).

This was the moment at which Diplock, with the assent of the rest of the Judicial Committee, threw open history's door. Years later, in 1996, Lord Cooke of Thorndon, delivering one of his Hamlyn Lectures at All Souls, spoke of Diplock having at that moment

'possibly with a degree of daring and certainly with a *coup de maître*, ... extended *Anisminic* by treating the reasoning there as having abolished ... what he justly called the esoteric distinctions between errors of law going to jurisdiction and errors of law within jurisdiction ...'

The law lords, as every student knows, have since then endorsed as established law the proposition that no tribunal has power to get any material point of law wrong, whether or not the error touches its jurisdiction;[27] and I do not argue that there is anything wrong with this. It has lain at the foundation of the modern recognition that public law is not about ultra vires acts determined by tick-boxes devised in 1948 by Lord Greene, but is about the misuse and abuse of power. What interests me here is how this has come about. It has come about, or so I have suggested, neither by legislation nor by precedent but by an organic process in which the law's practitioners and its exponents have agreed on which way the common law should be travelling and have found a serviceable if not particularly suitable vehicle to transport it.

CRIME AT COMMON LAW

This kind of professional murmuration is not unique. To take another instance, the House of Lords in *DPP v Smith*[28] decided in 1960, in the days of capital punishment, that a defendant charged with murder, whatever his intelligence and state of mind, was presumed to have intended the natural and probable consequences of his actions. Trial courts simply declined to apply the ruling. Judges would ask prosecutors: 'Do you propose to address the jury on the basis of *Smith*?' and, when prosecuting counsel said 'No', would direct their juries as if *Smith* had not been decided. They were right to do so, and Parliament in due course agreed: in 1967 it passed s 8 of the Criminal Justice Act, making intent and foresight once again a matter of evidence and not of presumption. Some years later,

---

[27] *R v Hull University Visitor, ex parte Page* [1993] AC 682 (HL); *Boddington v British Transport Police* [1999] 2 AC 143 (HL).
[28] *DPP v Smith* [1961] AC 290 (HL).

the Privy Council, on conjoint capital appeals from the Isle of Man, held that *Smith* had been wrongly decided in the first place.[29]

Before I am accused of advancing a Panglossian version of legal history in which judicial or legislative dross repeatedly gets spun by the collective wisdom of the profession into jurisprudential gold, let me give a couple of opposite instances.

One is the final abandonment of strict criminal liability for homicide in the course of a joint enterprise.[30] The doctrine that each participant in a joint enterprise—frequently a spontaneous pub brawl—was guilty of murder if it was a foreseeable possibility that another participant would inflict serious or fatal harm, even though the accused had no knowledge or forewarning of it, was devised on an appeal to the Privy Council from Hong Kong in 1984.[31] The courts of England and Wales were not even bound by the doctrine of precedent to follow it, but follow it they did, with the deplorable consequence that people have repeatedly gone to gaol, typically for offences of assault, when they should not have done. You will find one of many examples chronicled (as it happens, from real life) in Ian McEwan's novel *The Children Act*. To describe the eventual reversal of the cruel Hong Kong decision as historic is perhaps to miss the point that it was not in 2016 but 30 years earlier that the law of this country refashioned its own history in the shape of the colonial noose.

Secondly, a quite different example: the abandonment two centuries ago, for ideological reasons, of a set of criminal sanctions designed to protect the poor and to keep civil order without force. The sanctions were the old market crimes of engrossing, regrating and forestalling—creating scarcity and forcing up prices by cornering supplies before or after they reached market. These activities had been criminalised by statute since the reign of Edward VI— a time when, as Keith Thomas notes in *The Ends of Life*,[32] the view that the pursuit of self-interest was both ineluctable and socially beneficial first began to be articulated; and John Baker records prosecutions for regrating and engrossing, evidently at common law, even earlier than this.[33]

---

[29] *Frankland v R, Moore v R* [1987] AC 576 (PC).
[30] *R v Jogee* [2016] UKSC 8; *Ruddock v R* [2016] UKPC 7.
[31] *Chan Wing-Siu v R* [1985] AC 168 (PC).
[32] At p 144.
[33] J Baker, *Oxford History of the Laws of England*, VI, p 272.

Adam Smith, although he was alive to the dangers of monopoly, contended that such market crimes were comparable to 'the popular terrors and suspicions of witchcraft';[34] but when in 1772 Parliament repealed the statutes which created them,[35] the judges held that they were still crimes at common law. In more than one prosecution in the years that followed, Adam Smith's writings were cited to the court as arguments for acquittal. For a time the more conservative judges held out against this. Lord Kenyon CJ, trying a regrater named Rusby at the London Guildhall in 1800,[36] said to his jury:

'A very learned man, a good writer, has said you might as well fear witchcraft. I wish Dr Adam Smith had lived to hear the evidence today. ... If he had been told that cattle and corn were brought to market and then bought by a man whose purse happened to be longer than his neighbour's, so that the poor man who walks the street and earns his daily bread by his daily labour could get none but through his hands, and at the price he chose to demand, ... would he have said that there was no danger from such an offence?'

Kenyon went on to tell his jury:

'It has been said that in one county, I will not name it, a rich man has placed his emissaries to buy all the butter coming to the market: if such a fact does exist, and the poor of that neighbourhood cannot get the necessaries of life, the event of your verdict may be highly useful to the public.'

With Erskine leading Garrow for the prosecution, and encouraged by Kenyon's not entirely dispassionate summing-up, the jury convicted Rusby on the spot.

The unnamed county Kenyon was speaking about in his charge to the Guildhall jury was almost certainly Oxfordshire. When in September 1800 the Vice-Chancellor of Oxford University, acting without consulting the local magistrates, had cavalry sent in to suppress disorder over an engineered inflation of the market price of butter, the town clerk wrote on behalf of the mayor and magistrates to the Secretary of State at War, the Duke of Portland, to assure him that the city was able to control discontent over market abuse by prosecuting speculators. He got a long and pompous answer

---

[34] Adam Smith, *The Wealth of Nations*, Bk IV (1776) Ch 5.
[35] 12 Geo III, c 71. The statutes against engrossing dated from the reign of Edward VI.
[36] *R v Rusby* (1800) Peake Add Cas 189, 170 ER 241: 'though in an evil hour all the statutes ... were at one blow repealed, yet, thank God, the provisions of the common law were not destroyed ...'

criticising the city for failing to prosecute the rioters rather than the speculators and commending a laissez-faire approach to markets. Controlling prices, said the Duke,

'necessarily prevents the Employment of Capital in the Farming Line',[37]

and he wrote to the Vice-Chancellor in support of

'those who instead of being denominated Engrossers are correctly speaking the Purveyors and provident Stewards of the Public'.[38]

By the time of Kenyon's death in 1802, Eldon, who suffered from no such scruples, was Lord Chancellor, and judicial policy was falling into line behind ministerial policy. In 1814 the Statute of Artificers, which enabled magistrates to set minimum wages, was repealed. The following year the legislation enabling the justices to control bread prices in London was also repealed. By the end of the Napoleonic wars grand juries were no longer being asked to indict speculators for market crimes, and judges were no longer inviting petty juries to convict.

The centuries-old market offences look Canute-like today; but the judges who had tried to maintain them at a time when conventional wisdom was shifting steadily in favour of unregulated markets were not ideological or jurisprudential dinosaurs. They were trying to preserve a legal paternalism which formed part of what EP Thompson called the moral economy of the eighteenth-century crowd, a paternalism which sought to maintain living standards and civil order in communities where livelihood was dependent on the integrity of markets, and where the hardship caused by rigged markets was driving rural families into England's proliferating factories and slums. For these people, the alternative to properly invigilated local markets was not, as the Duke of Portland supposed it was, agricultural prosperity. It was the poor-house, enlistment for foreign wars and, when they protested, Peterloo. Both the enforcement and the abandonment of market crimes may today appear to be part of what Alexander Bickel described as 'the sediment of history which is law'[39]—but Bickel's dismissive description overlooks the proactivity of which law is also capable.

---

[37] EP Thompson, 'The moral economy of the English crowd in the 18th century' (1971) 50 *Past and Present* 76, 129–131.
[38] ibid fn 147.
[39] Alexander Bickel, *The Least Dangerous Branch* p 236.

POLITICS AND SLAVERY

It's in the eighteenth century that you find the foundations of two of the grandest of the common law's edifices: the exclusion of political ministers from the administration of criminal justice, and the anathematisation of slavery. The first of these was far from being supported by clear-cut jurisprudence, but Lord Camden's protean judgment in *Entick v Carrington* became accepted—not unlike *Anisminic* in the twentieth century—as solid authority for what its audience wanted to hear. The second, Lord Mansfield's holding in *Somersett's Case* that the state of servitude was unknown to the common law, was the exact opposite: a perfectly clear-cut decision, albeit extempore and brief, which ran into a factitious morass of political, economic and moral self-interest, some of it Mansfield's own.

The raid provoked by issue number 45 of Wilkes' ferociously anti-government paper *The North Briton* in April 1763 spawned a celebrated clutch of lawsuits, principally against the King's Messengers who had executed the Home Secretary's general warrant to search for and arrest the authors, printers and publishers of the paper. These cases established that ministers of the Crown had no judicial powers as conservators of the peace; that the general warrants they had been in the habit of issuing were unlawful; and that they were answerable to the ordinary courts for the consequent trespasses committed by their agents.

It is probable that these decisions would have had a lasting impact without the separate lawsuit brought by John Entick, whose magazine *The Monitor* had been raided late the year before. But Entick bided his time and then brought his own action against the King's Messengers. Since the warrant used against him had not been a general warrant, he limited his claim to trespass to his house and goods; but it turned out to be the opportunity that Chief Justice Pratt (shortly to become Lord Camden) had been waiting for to bring all the issues of ministerial power together in a researched and comprehensive judgment.[40]

Pratt's judgment is a *tour de force* of legal scholarship. In it he rebuts the claim, familiar and more than once successful in the

---

[40] *Entick v Carrington* (1765) 19 St Tr 1029. See further ch 5.

course of the seventeenth century,[41] that the state could commit wrongs under a shield of necessity:

> '[W]ith respect to the argument from state necessity, or a distinction that has been aimed at between state offences and others, the common law does not understand that kind of reasoning, nor do our books take notice of such distinctions.'[42]

This being so, ministers enjoyed no extra-judicial powers of arrest or seizure. But did they possess judicial powers to investigate and suppress sedition, so that both they and their officers enjoyed the same statutory protection as constables whatever the outcome of their warrants? Again Pratt said no.

The problem, as Pratt was compelled to acknowledge, was that there was clear authority to the contrary—the decision of Chief Justice Holt in 1696[43] that the monarch's secretaries of state possessed general powers of committal—that is, arrest—as conservators of the peace. The case had been treated as sound law and followed in at least two subsequent cases.[44] Yet

> 'I ... am satisfied,' said Pratt, 'that the secretary of state hath assumed this power as a transfer, I know not how, of the royal authority to himself; and that the common law of England knows no such magistrate. At the same time I declare, wherein my brothers do all agree with me, that we are bound to adhere to the determination of the Queen against Derby and the King against Earbury; and I have no right to overturn these decisions, even though it should be admitted, that the practice, which has subsisted since the Revolution, has been erroneous in its commencement.'[45]

There is something Denningesque about Pratt's candid acknowledgment of contrary authority and his equally candid refusal to follow it. It might be possible by the use of advanced casuistry to find a thread of consistent jurisprudence in the passage, but history has not bothered with this. It has taken the Court of Common Pleas to have brushed aside the authority of the King's Bench—a court of co-ordinate jurisdiction with the Common Pleas and therefore

---

[41] See S Sedley, *Lions Under the Throne* pp 216–17.

[42] ibid 1073.

[43] *R v Kendal and Rowe* (1696) 1 Ld Raym 65.

[44] *R v Derby*, cited in full at 19 St Tr 1014–1016; *R v Earbury* (1722) 8 Mod 177, (1733) 2 Barnard 293. Holdsworth, whose treatment of the case in his *History of English Law* has acquired canonical status, took Pratt, despite this, to have overruled these authorities by demonstrating the weakness of their premises.

[45] At 1058.

not able formally to bind it—and to have laid down a bright line segregating criminal justice from political governance. It is a line which in recent decades has come under growing stress with the statutory enlargement of ministerial powers of investigation and control. But when in 1993 the Crown in *M v Home Office*[46] argued that, as a minister of the crown, a Home Secretary who had defied an order of the court was not answerable in contempt for his conduct, the rebuff delivered by the law lords was justifiably described by Professor Wade as the most important judicial decision for over 200 years—meaning, as he more than once made clear, since *Entick v Carrington.*

Somersett's Case, decided by Mansfield seven years after Pratt decided *Entick v Carrington*, was in some ways an equal and opposite phenomenon. Mansfield, an experienced politician and a shrewd investor, was not an abolitionist. Not long before, he had told John Dunning, counsel for the West African seaman Thomas Lewis whose employer, Stapylton, had purported to sell him into slavery in England, that the legality of slavery would be best left an open question:

> 'for I would have all masters think them free, and all Negroes think they were not. …'[47]

But Granville Sharp, who had prosecuted Stapylton for kidnapping Lewis and secured a verdict that Lewis had never been Stapylton's property, would not let it rest there. In November 1771 he learned that a West African re-named James Somersett was being held in irons aboard a ship at anchor in the Thames, awaiting transportation to Jamaica where he was to be sold. Within two days Sharp had obtained from Mansfield a writ of habeas corpus calling on the ship's captain to justify Somersett's detention. The widely held belief that Mansfield deliberately delayed a hearing is incorrect: he adjourned it once in the express hope of a settlement, but in June 1772 he sat *in banc* and, with his fellow judges, heard out the arguments. Albeit under pressure of time, Granville Sharp had been able to assemble a formidable team, led by Serjeant Davy and Serjeant Glynn, with a future chief justice of the Common Pleas, James Mansfield, and the scholarly Francis Hargrave as their juniors, all of them appearing without fee; while the slave-owners bankrolling the ship's captain

---

[46] *M v Home Office* [1994] 1 AC 377 (HL).
[47] Oldham, *The Mansfield Papers* p 50.

had briefed Dunning, the former solicitor-general who had appeared on Hargrave's instructions for James Lewis and who in his submissions acknowledged the unpopularity of his cause and took refuge in his duty to his client.

Mansfield's judgment was not quite the rhetorical *tour de force* that legend has made it. The stirring line 'The air of England has long been too pure for a slave, and every man is free who breathes it' was shoehorned in by Lord Campbell when he came in the following century to write his *Life* of Mansfield. But what Mansfield did say, although inelegant, was unequivocal:

> 'The state of slavery ... is so odious that nothing can be suffered to support it but positive law. Whatever inconvenience therefore may follow from a decision, I cannot say this case is allowed or approved by the law of England, and therefore the black must be discharged.'

In other words, the return to the writ had no foundation in English law. As a commercial lawyer Mansfield knew very well what the inconveniences were that would follow from his judgment, which had been given (it should not be forgotten) with the assent of the other three judges of the King's Bench. Not only would the 14,000 black men and women in servitude in England and Wales become instantly free; it was probable that the same had to follow in all Britain's ceded or conquered colonies, where—in contrast to the settled colonies, as Mansfield himself was to hold two years later—the common law had direct force.[48]

That this did not happen, and that instead the judges, with Parliament's acquiescence, continued for decades to endorse or at least tolerate colonial slavery, is an embarrassing example of the law's capacity for moral cowardice in the face of political and economic pressure. Many MPs had interests in slave plantations; slaving voyages, in which many of them had stakes, could return a profit of 2,000 per cent. Mansfield himself in the *Zong* case, some eleven years after *Somersett's Case*, unblinkingly treated jettisoned slaves as insurable cargo.[49] As late as 1827 Lord Stowell held that a slave who had lived in Britain and so had become free could be enslaved again on her return to the West Indies.[50] And as late as 1860 the English courts were prepared to enforce contracts for the sale of

---

[48] *Campbell v Hall* (1774) 1 Cowp 204.
[49] *Gregson v Gilbert* (1783) 3 Doug KB 232.
[50] *The Slave Grace* (1827) 2 St Tr (NS) 273.

slaves in Brazil.[51] Although abolition bills were introduced pretty well every year from 1782, it took Parliament until 1807 to outlaw slave trading and until 1833 to formally abolish colonial slavery[52]— the latter at a monumental price in compensation to the slave-owners, raised by taxes on goods which fell mostly on the domestic working class. Not a penny was paid to the ex-slaves.

Here too the law can be seen making its own history, not in the simplistic sense that as time goes by one decision or statute succeeds another, but in the sense that the judges from time to time, and not necessarily collusively, determine what trajectory the law is to follow. If the trajectory followed by the judges on the issue of slavery was hesitant and unprincipled, it was not, as is frequently suggested, because Mansfield's judgment had been unclear or equivocal. It was the lawmakers both on the bench (Mansfield himself among them) and in Parliament who equivocated.

Their pusillanimity contrasts with what followed elsewhere in the Empire. Here, according to Mansfield's own doctrine in *Campbell v Hall*,[53] the laws of ceded or conquered colonies were required to conform to the fundamental principles of the common law. Each of the American colonies took the opportunity of the War of Independence to legislate either to abolish or to institutionalise slavery within its borders. But the practice of slavery also came in question in Lower Canada, which—unlike the settled American colonies— had become a British possession by conquest. A petition to the Canadian Parliament in 1799 asserted that slaves in Lower Canada had recently

'imbibed a refractory and disobedient spirit under pretext that no slavery exists in the Province'.

The petition went on to recite that the Canadian court of King's Bench, plainly in reliance on *Somersett's Case* and on *Campbell v Hall*, had begun granting writs of habeas corpus to liberate not only two runaway slaves who had been apprehended but, as the chief justice had announced,

'every negro, indented apprentice and servant who should be committed to gaol under the magistrates' warrant in the like cases'.[54]

---

[51] *Santos v Illidge* (1860) 8 CB (NS) 861.

[52] It was succeeded first by a bogus system of 'apprenticeship' and then by the tyrannous system of indentures.

[53] (1774) 1 Cowp 204.

[54] House of Assembly of Lower Canada, minutes 23 March–3 June 1799.

LAW'S WHITEOUT

Let me turn lastly to a quite different way in which legal history is made: by treating inconvenient events as simply not having happened. It is one thing—and not a mere pretence—to hold a measure to be devoid of legal effect; quite another to treat a historical legal fact as never having occurred. Yet that is how my generation (and I suspect others too) were taught legal history: our lecturer at the Inns of Court School of Law stopped at 1649 and moved directly to 1660 because everything that had happened between those years was, he said, a legal nullity.

This was not one teacher's idiosyncrasy. In 1660, on the restoration of the monarchy after 18 years of republicanism, the public hangman was ordered to make a bonfire in Westminster Hall of every copy of a number of republican enactments, and a search was ordered to be made for every copy of 'the traitorous writing called the Instrument of Government'.

The Instrument of Government, enacted in 1653, was Britain's first and only written constitution. Not only did the Protectorate which it created foreshadow the American model of presidential government, with a parliamentary override of any measures promulgated by the Protector; it was palpably the source of a number of provisions of the bill of rights adopted 35 years later by another Parliament which, for all its protestations of legitimacy, had once again unseated a monarch and was setting its own terms of governance. We all know that the Bill of Rights in 1689 declared the regal practice of suspending or dispensing with laws enacted by Parliament, and the raising of revenue without Parliament's authority, to be illegal. How many people know that 35 years earlier the Protectorate's Instrument of Government had provided:

> 'That the laws shall not be altered, suspended, abrogated or repealed, nor any new law made, nor any tax, charge or imposition laid upon the people, but by common consent in Parliament ...'?[55]

We all know that it was the Act of Settlement that in 1701 created the secure tenure of judicial office which still underpins the separation

---

[55] The article continued: 'save only as is expressed in the thirtieth article'. The thirtieth article, echoing the constitutional issue which had led to the Petition of Right in 1628, gave the Protector an emergency power to raise military and naval taxes until Parliament could assemble.

of powers. Who knew that it was in 1642 that the Long Parliament first extracted this principle from Charles I[56] and in 1648 confirmed it by statute?[57] While many of us were taught at school that the Puritans had abolished Christmas,[58] none of us as law students were told that in the years of the Interregnum, Parliament had stopped the use of Latin and French in the courts, had instituted civil marriage, had transferred the criminal, probate and divorce jurisdiction of the ecclesiastical courts to temporal courts, and had stopped the routine gaoling of debtors.

You will not discover any of this from the statute book. If you look at the *Statutes at Large,* they stop short in 1641, just before Parliament, on the eve of the Civil War, began to legislate without royal assent. The next page is dated 1660, 'the twelfth year of the reign of our most gracious sovereign lord Charles the Second'. It was not until 1911 that the *Acts and Ordinances of the Interregnum*—the Civil War, the Commonwealth and the Protectorate—were finally published.[59]

There is more. Who knew that it was under the Protectorate that the origins of a salaried civil service were to be found? Or that it was the criminal courts of the Commonwealth which first recognised the privilege against self-incrimination and stopped the use of paid informers? Or that, as chief justice of Munster in the 1650s, John Cooke, the Commonwealth's former solicitor general, authorised his judges to administer law and equity together, with the result, Cromwell told Edmund Ludlow, that the Munster courts were deciding more cases in a week than Westminster Hall in a year? Or that the law commission set up under Sir Matthew Hale had drafted 16 bills to codify large areas of law and procedure, and by the time it was dissolved in 1653 had on its agenda the regulation of lawyers' fees, a ban on MPs moonlighting as lawyers, the establishment of small claims courts, abolition of the sale of offices and of benefit of clergy, public registries of deeds, the right of accused persons to be defended by counsel, to give evidence and to call witnesses; and (at Cromwell's instigation) modification of the death penalty.

---

[56] SR Gardiner, *History of England 1603–1642,* cited by D Veall, *The Popular Movement for Law Reform 1640–1660* pp 198–99.

[57] CH Firth and RS Rait (eds), *Acts and Ordinances of the Interregnum* i, 1226–27, appointing a number of judges to the bench '*quamdiu se bene gesserint*'. Since 1700, see the Act of Settlement (now the Senior Courts Act 1981, s 11(3)).

[58] See S Sedley, *Lions Under the Throne* pp 88–89.

[59] Firth and Rait.

These might perhaps have been written off as foolish essays in doomed idealism, as irrelevant to the modern legal world as Dicey considered the Witanagemót to be, were it not for the fact that almost every reform of the Interregnum, although annulled at the Restoration, has since been restored. In 1731 English was again made the language of the law. A deeds registry was opened in 1703, and a land registry in 1875. Civil marriage was reinstituted in 1836. The remarriage of law and equity was finally solemnised by the Judicature Acts of 1873–5. Between 1697 and 1898 criminal procedure slowly crept back towards where it had been in the Interregnum. And 313 years after Matthew Hale and his commissioners first set about codifying and reforming the law, England and Wales acquired a standing law commission. Only the refusal of Parliament to stop its elected members taking other employment while collecting their parliamentary salaries has proved unshakable.

HISTORY AND LAW

If there is a moral to these heterogeneous stories, it is, I suppose, that the law, like other subcultures, has its own versions of truth and habitually recasts itself in their image. The late Geoffrey Wilson wrote:

> 'The courts do not operate on the basis of real history, the kind of history that is vulnerable to or determined by historical research. They operate on the basis of an assumed, conventional, one might even say consensual, history in which historical events and institutions often have a symbolic value.'[60]

These versions of history may derive, like the jurisprudence derived from *Anisminic,* from what lawyers perceive as the law's intrinsic logic; though the larger history of the twentieth century, which I have not had space here to explore, suggests deeper reasons of which the lawyers themselves may not have been wholly conscious. They may derive from the opposite: the law's fear, following a decision like *Somersett's Case,* of what it has itself unleashed. Here the judicial casuistry tends to be more visible. They may be dictated more or less overtly by changes in political and economic philosophy, as happened both with the old market crimes and with

---

[60] G Wilson, postscript to M Nolan and S Sedley, *The making and remaking of the British constitution* (the Radcliffe Lectures) (1998) pp 128–29.

the perceived modern need to crack down on gang violence; or more subtly but more radically by the slow growth of a newly autocratic mode of government, like the one which provoked the great show-down between the Hanoverian monarchy's judges and its ministers over state necessity and personal liberty.

Lastly, the law's version of truth may simply be derived from a dominant historiography in which there are good guys (royalists) and bad guys (republicans), and it's not comfortable to accept that history was in many respects on the side of the latter. If so, there may be something after all to be said for reading yesterday through the lens of today. But it would be naive to reverse Leavis's aphorism and to say there's no such thing as law, only legal history. What it *is* possible to say—and I think Tom Bingham would have agreed, though Dicey would not—is that without history there is no law.

2

The History of English Law

This was a review, published in the London Review of Books, *of* The Oxford History of the Laws of England 1820–1914: *Vol XI, English Legal System; Vol XII, Private Law; Vol XIII, Fields of Development (edited by William Cornish et al.)*

DEFYING THE ADVICE of the King of Hearts to the White Rabbit, the *Oxford History of the Laws of England* began in the middle, with the publication in 2003 of its magisterial sixth volume, written by the general editor, John Baker, and covering the years 1483–1558. It then went back to the beginning, with RH Helmholz's opening volume on the early canon law. The rest was silence until in 2010 the final vessels of the series sailed suddenly and magnificently into port without any of the remaining eight early volumes in tow.

The grandeur of this culminating segment, a survey of the near-century from 1820 to 1914, is such that it has needed three stout volumes to contain it. But why bring such a comprehensive history to a close in 1914? The answer, perhaps, is that all history has to end somewhere, and the closer you come to the present the more room there is for idiosyncrasy and the less for perspective. Moreover, it's not that difficult, at least in the law, to bridge those last hundred-odd years. The senior clerk in the chambers where I was a pupil in the 1960s had started work towards 1890 as a boy in the Temple, where he had been trained to write copperplate with the steel-nibbed pen that he would still use to copy out pleadings and opinions for signature when the typist was away. My head of chambers could recall Lord Darling, memorably insulted by the *Birmingham Daily Argus* in 1900, when he lectured the local press on how to report his decisions, as an impudent little man in horsehair who might have made a successful bus conductor, sitting in the 1930s on the judicial committee of the Privy Council and waiting, to the unconcealed annoyance of his colleagues, for an opportunity to make a smart remark.

And here Darling is, now a part of history, contrived wisecracks and all; though the long-held view that Lord Halsbury, the Conservative lord chancellor who put him on the bench, made his choices entirely on the basis of party affiliation has shifted. The *Oxford History*'s judgment is that, despite the expressed belief of the Prime Minister, Lord Salisbury, that appointment to the bench should be a reward for party loyalty, 'the worst choices'—Darling among them— 'seem to have been Halsbury's own.'

Even Holdsworth's massive 16-volume opus was introduced by the indefinite article—*A History of English Law*. Although the present enterprise boasts the definite article, the epithet 'Oxford' no doubt acknowledges that others might have done it differently. So they might; but if the rest of the series matches this final trilogy in breadth, depth, readability and learning, it is unlikely that anyone could have done it much better. Whatever the Oxford brand signifies, it is neither academic nor geographical. The chairs occupied by the authors of the final phase are situated in Cambridge, Otago, Keele, London, Middlesex and Cardiff. The doyen of them, William Cornish, has a distinguished record both as a legal historian—his and Geoffrey Clark's *Law and Society in England 1750–1950* remains an important work—and as an authority on intellectual property, on which he contributes an excellent section linking controversy and change in the law to economic interest and scientific progress.

The 'Manifest' with which the trilogy is introduced (despite the spry nautical metaphor, it opens with an unsettling solecism: 'Any legal history worth salting'—surely not) renounces all ambition to write a social history of the law rather than a history of the law itself. But the siren song that there is no legal history, just law, is faint. The work is rich in social, philosophical, political and economic context. Even the structural categories of the enterprise—institutions, public law and private law—ineluctably leach into one another.

The precision with which a history of the laws of England is able to skirt the laws and legal systems of Scotland and Ireland, both of which throughout its period were constitutionally united with England, is both striking and revealing. Wales had been formally annexed in 1535, and the *Oxford History* records such systemic differences as still existed between the two countries by the nineteenth century. But although Scotland since 1707 and Ireland since 1801 had also formed part of a single political union, their legal systems and to a considerable extent their laws (Ireland's, however, less than Scotland's) remained their own.

FINAL APPEALS

Scotland's principal intrusion into the present trilogy comes in the dismal history of final appeals, which could be brought more or less at will from north of the border, as often in order to delay enforcement as to obtain justice, exacerbating a logjam of English and Irish appeals which was not broken until the jurisdiction of the House of Lords was dismantled and recast in the 1870s. The story of how that happened is well told in Patrick Polden's section on the law courts. Although it was the supreme appellate forum in civil matters (there was no real criminal appeal system), the House of Lords had a chaotic procedure in which the quorum of three could be made up of any peers, legally qualified or not, who happened to be around. Although Blackstone had thought this quite acceptable in view of the 'delicacy of sentiment so peculiar to noble birth', attempts were made in the first part of the century to shift to a voluntary system in which a sitting or former lord chancellor would always preside. But Eldon had held the Great Seal for so much of the period between 1801 and 1827 that ex-lord chancellors were hard to find; and even chief justices were not routinely ennobled, thanks to concerns that they and their male progeny might not be able to live up to the obligations of nobility.

When Lyndhurst, who knew nothing whatever about Scots law, took over the Great Seal in 1827, he persuaded the House to accept two senior judges, one of them a Scot, as deputy speakers who could preside on appeals without being peers. The farsighted and energetic Brougham, who took over in 1830 and had no fear of Scots law, swept up the arrears, organised a peerage for Chief Justice Denman and then, by making sure that the shaky claim of a minor judge, William Courtenay, to the earldom of Devon succeeded, created a just about legally qualified appellate panel. By the time Melbourne's administration fell in 1834, Brougham had set up the Central Criminal Court (a new institution but a chaotic hellhole until the building we all know, in what Polden describes as neo-English baroque, was opened in 1907) and created the judicial committee of the Privy Council. But time was lacking to carry out his plan of diverting all final appeals to the latter. So the old system pottered on, subject to an intermittent and contested convention that lay peers would not sit on appeals. By the mid-1850s the fallings-out of the three ex-lord chancellors who sat as a panel (at least when Brougham, now elderly and querulous, was not doing appeals on his own with a couple of lay peers to make up the numbers) had become so notorious that the solicitor-general said publicly that their conduct 'would disgrace the lowest court of justice in the kingdom'.

It was to meet this reproach that the idea of the life peerage was devised—an injection of red blood which, by being finite, would not dilute the blue. Conservatives, rightly as it turned out, saw judicial life peerages as the thin end of a meritocratic wedge: Prince Albert was believed to see them as a path for scientists and other professionals. But the idea, which had almost died at birth in the 1830s, went lame when it was resurrected in the 1850s, not least because it was uncertain whether the monarch could create life peerages in the exercise of the royal prerogative or whether it required legislation.

It was only in the wake of the Second Reform Act that Bagehot's demand for a supreme court divorced from the legislature began to be taken seriously. Hatherley's initial proposal of a single final court for Great Britain and the empire, including four judicial life peers, was modified by his successor as Lord Chancellor, Selborne, to provide for a new and fully professional Court of Appeal which would be the last stop for all litigation in England and Wales. But before his bill could become law, Gladstone's administration lost office, and Selborne had to watch while his successor, Cairns, was manoeuvred by the right wing of his own party into the unplanned double-appeal structure we still have today. Instead of there being a single imperial Court of Appeal, Selborne's new professional Court of Appeal was to be topped out by a renovated House of Lords, with a committee of lords of appeal 'in ordinary' (ie in regular attendance—a proper job) ennobled for life only: two appellate tiers for not much more than the price of one. It took until 2009 to complete Bagehot's project of divorcing the top appellate tier from the legislature, and even that was in the face of some stiff opposition among the law lords; but not even the most conservative among them can have been overjoyed to see the Supreme Court on a list of dispensable quangos leaked in 2011 to the *Daily Telegraph*.

THE LAW COURTS

The Victorian changeover was marked by the construction of a vast new palace of justice, the law courts in the Strand, behind its handsome façade a chillingly gothic product of wrangling, cheeseparing and bureaucracy, controversially paid for by raiding the Chancery suitors' funds. The architect George Street, whose last major job it was, had to deal with a building firm which, inevitably, had been selected by the Treasury because it was the lowest bidder and which, equally inevitably, went bust after the first phase, leaving subcontractors unpaid and government with a massive bill for rescuing the project. By the time the building opened in 1882, Street was dead and gothic was out of fashion. If you want a glimpse of what might have been, go into the bank[1] on the opposite side of the Strand, designed contemporaneously by Cuthbert and Wimble as a restaurant for the new law courts and still richly ornamented with Doulton tiles and ceramics, the foyer a remarkable harbinger of art nouveau, the interior columns decorated with chrysanthemums, the walnut and sequoia wall panels with scenes from Ben Jonson (who drank in the Palsgrave Tavern which once stood here).

PUBLIC LAW

Alongside the noisy travail of the born-again legal system and its new emporium, novel administrative structures had been quietly growing. These were to transform the state more fundamentally than the reconstitution of the courts. They ranged from railway and canal commissions, headed by a judge and behaving very much like a court, to administrative boards regulating civic amenities and land uses. The courts were not going to be sidelined: they used the old prerogative writs to strike down unfair or unlawful decisions by these bodies and to compel them to act according to law. When Parliament passed hands-off clauses saying that the courts could not interfere with their decisions, the courts held that a decision taken without legal power or due process was no decision at all. By the later nineteenth century there had come into being the lineaments of the judge-made body of public law by which today the legality and fairness of executive action are monitored by the courts.

How this came about is tracked law by law, institution by institution and judgment by judgment in Stuart Anderson's impressive segment of the *Oxford History*. Why it came about is more elusive, but here, too, broad lines emerge. An increasingly complex industrial and mercantile state depended on unfettered enterprise for progress but on regulation for stability. Following the repeal in 1772 of the early statutes that criminalised profiteering in markets by middlemen, Chief Justice Mansfield adopted Burke's view that

---

[1] In 2017 Lloyds TSB closed this branch, leaving the future of the building uncertain.

the corresponding common law offences were 'senseless, barbarous, and, in fact, wicked regulations made against the free-trade in matter of provision'. By the end of the Napoleonic wars and the start of the period covered by this trilogy, the mechanisms of law and custom by which food riots had for centuries been kept under a measure of control by local justices had gone, and social disorder, moving now into machine-breaking, was a major and recurrent threat. Faced with a Parliament that was (in the phrase of the legal historian Douglas Hay) stupendously overrepresentative of the wealthiest, the disenfranchised turned to political reform. It is relevant, therefore, that the period covered by these books opens in the aftermath of Peterloo: political discontent was now being met not with negotiation or compromise but with armed force in the streets and prosecution in the courts.

The institution and spread of civic police forces after 1829 was, however, a good deal more than a new means of repression. The corruption of criminal justice by the venal system of private prosecution, with rewards for informers that set a premium on perjury, called out for reform; and though it was not until later in the century that acceptance of state responsibility for the enforcement of criminal justice brought into being a public prosecutor, local police forces, untrustworthy and inefficient as many were, began to push the private prosecutor out of business.

The nineteenth century thus sees the irregular, unplanned but inexorable and eventually massive growth of new forms of state regulation which Anderson describes in his section on public law—relevantly so, since the growth during that century of the judge-made public law which is a major feature of today's landscape is intelligible largely as a series of responses to the structures of governance that legislation was erecting. Unlike today, however, legislation was not subject to a governmental near-monopoly. Parliament now contained Radical members such as the former Chartist Anthony Mundella, who had a major hand in the 1870 Education Act, the 1871 Factories Act and a series of other progressive measures, culminating in the 1889 act that gave the NSPCC the enforcement powers it still possesses; Conservative members like Russell Gurney, responsible for the Married Women's Property Act of 1870 and for the law, six years later, that opened the medical profession to women; peers like Lord Shaftesbury, with his remarkable record of legislation for the protection of the insane, for workplace safety and for public sanitation, aided by administrators of the calibre of Edwin Chadwick; and, arguably the most heroic of all, Samuel Plimsoll.

THE PLIMSOLL LINE

Plimsoll's story, given its own space in Raymond Cocks's section on social reform, is well told. The carnage of the Victorian merchant shipping trade, prospered in or connived at by MPs, peers and ministers as one overloaded rust-bucket after another put to sea and was lost, enabling the owners to collect insurance moneys from a Lloyds' flush with the prosperity of those vessels that did reach port, still beggars belief. While there was no law against overloading, there was a draconian one to punish seamen who refused to board an unseaworthy vessel. In the early 1870s, Cocks records, more than 1,600 sailors were gaoled for this crime. When the *Peru* sank with all hands, 15 of her crew survived because they were serving prison sentences for having refused to ship aboard her.

Plimsoll, protected principally by the fact that his constituency of Derby was about as far from the sea as it is possible to be in England, faced vilification ('Plimsollism is another word for terrorism') and obstruction on an almost unimaginable scale. A huge philanthropic movement developed in support of him, but a royal commission, swamped by spurious evidence about the difficulty of locating a suitable load-line, reported in 1874 that no universal rule was possible; it must be left to the discretion of the shipowner or, occasionally, to Board of Trade inspectors. The government of India—in this as in other respects a test bed for domestic reforms—had meanwhile introduced a straightforward law that there must be three inches of freeboard for every foot of immersion.

Outside the House, Plimsoll was repeatedly harassed with libel writs. His speeches in Parliament give some idea why. The supine Board of Trade, he asserted, was beset by

> 'shipowners of murderous tendencies outside the House, and who are immediately and amply represented inside the House, and who have frustrated and talked to death every effort to procure a remedy for this state of things ... Every winter, hundreds and hundreds of brave men are sent to death, their wives are made widows and their children are made orphans, in order that a few speculative scoundrels ... may make unhallowed gains.'

Naming three vessels recently lost with all hands and two more abandoned by their crews, he asked 'whether the registered owner of these ships, Edward Bates, is the member for Plymouth, or if it is some other person of the same name'.

Plimsoll's campaign, as Cocks points out, is a vivid illustration of the importance of the immunity of parliamentary speech from the law of defamation. By 1875, Plimsoll had assembled what threatened to become a parliamentary majority. The viability of the mandatory load line temporarily introduced under this pressure allowed Parliament in 1876 to make permanent, albeit still incomplete, provision for what became the Plimsoll line. Few statues are more deserved than the one erected by seamen to Samuel Plimsoll on the Victoria Embankment.

PUBLIC ADMINISTRATION AND CRIME

The state machinery that was needed for such regulation as could be secured in the teeth of vested interests was massive. The Home Office grew in this period from an establishment of 22, supporting a Home Secretary who signed every letter himself, to a department of state controlling inspectorates—some of them highly skilled and employing a surprisingly high number of women—of mines, factories, explosives, prisons, police, reformatory and industrial schools, aliens, anatomy, animal welfare and inebriate retreats. Its personnel, like the personnel of other departments of state, became a professional elite as the reforms advocated by the Northcote-Trevelyan Report took effect, so that by 1914 Britain had a civil service, its luminaries educated at the same schools and universities as the judges, at least as capable of running the country as its transient political masters. Both the development of public law in the nineteenth century to control the hydra-headed state and the long sleep of public law that followed the Great War can best be understood against this backdrop, and it is a pity that it does not form part of the *Oxford History*.[2]

But one has to stop somewhere, and the three volumes, as they stand, are full of matter, elegantly ordered and mostly well written (though someone should have blue-pencilled such clunking coinages as Keith Smith's 'retributivistic'). Every section prompts more thought. Reading Smith's sometimes comical account of the legislative drive against prostitution, gambling and obscenity, I wonder whether the main restraint on the prurient outrage of the good and godly was probably not so much principled libertarianism as the need of respectable male society to have private access to prostitutes, to be able to place bets with its own bookies and to keep its own private libraries. So it was street prostitution, street betting

---

[2] Cf S Sedley, *Lions Under the Throne* Ch 2, 'The dark satanic mills'.

and the public sale of offensive literature that were criminalised by Parliament and energetically prosecuted by the Society for the Suppression of Vice and its avatars.

Then again one wonders why, in an era when property rights were all but sacred, trespass—except in search of game—was never criminalised by either the legislature or the judiciary. The answer, I strongly suspect, is hunting. It was—for that matter it still is—one thing for the hunt to hand out modest compensation to a small-holder who has just had his kitchen garden trashed by a horde of domesticated quadrupeds in pursuit of a feral one. It is another to let the smallholder or the police put the master of foxhounds in the dock and have him fined, eventually giving him more form than the local flasher. Even when Parliament in the twentieth century finally lost patience with squatters and made trespass a crime, it did so only where the trespasser had defied a request to leave: so long as it thundered on, the hunt was still safe.

WOMEN AS PERSONS

One story which pops up in the *Oxford History*'s footnotes but per-haps deserves to be cohesively told is that of the 'persons' cases, the shaming series of decisions in which the judges, licensed by delib-erately feeble parliamentary drafting, repeatedly held that women were not 'persons' for the purpose of exercising the newly enlarged franchise or of accessing professional training. The Reform Act of 1867 used the word 'man' to extend the franchise to all household-ers, but Brougham's Interpretation Act had by then laid down that the male was to include the female unless an opposite intention was plain. When local officials nevertheless struck out the names of hundreds of female householders, proceedings brought by one group of women were shut out by the courts on the grounds that only 'a person aggrieved' could sue, and women were not persons. Another group lost on the grounds that Brougham's act could not operate in the face of the fact that women had never been allowed to vote. In 1873, Sophia Jex-Blake and six other women who had persuaded Edinburgh University to change its regulations so as to admit women to its medical lectures lost their case in the Court of Session when the university reneged on its own recent regulations, claiming that they had been made unlawfully because the historic purpose of the university was to educate young men. And so it went on. When Parliament gave women the right to stand for election,

Lady Sandhurst was unseated from the London County Council by an opponent who claimed that, not being a person, she could not be 'a fit person of full age'. But when a Miss Cobden was elected and waited till the time for challenge was past before taking her seat, she was promptly prosecuted for being a person sitting as councillor when unqualified. She put up the seemingly impregnable defence that if she was not a person for the purpose of being elected she could not be a person for the purpose of sitting when unqualified. Naturally she was convicted.

On both sides of the border, and in the colonies, the judges continued to exclude women from the legal profession. As the period of these volumes ended, the Liberal Lord Chancellor Loreburn, who had not long before instituted a criminal appeal system, delivered himself of the judicial opinion that the legal incapacity of women was so self-evident that it was 'incomprehensible ... that anyone acquainted with our laws ... can think, if indeed anyone does think, there is room for argument'. It was not until 1929 that the Privy Council, in an appeal from Canada about the eligibility of women for appointment as senators, managed to turn the tanker round.

* * *

There are other great tranches of history here: the bitterly contested transition from the outlawing of trade unions as criminal conspiracies to their protection by statute from the hostility of the judges and the eventual protection of their political funds, with consequences for the political system which endure to this day; the policy-driven doctrines by which the judges made employers responsible for their employees' negligence and then excluded fellow employees from this protection (they were deemed, in taking a job, to have accepted the risk that another employee would maim or kill them); the ending of transportation and the segueing of an eclectic and capricious system of capital punishment into the sadistic 'separate and silent' prison regime with hard labour and flogging as optional extras, but from there, as the century ended, into the pioneering policies of the 1895 Gladstone report, articulated in the 1899 prison rules, of encouraging prisoners 'to lead an honest life' and giving them training and employment in their chosen trades.

Among many excellent sections, all of them giving credit to writers who have previously surveyed the terrain, one can perhaps single out Cornish's three-dimensional survey of what is now called family law—three-dimensional because, rather than flatten

the history into a twenty-first-century paradigm, he tracks its dif-
fusion among the common law of property and contract which
gave control to the domestic patriarch, the equitable law of trusts
by which alone wives could be provided for, and the ecclesiastical
courts which, until Parliament finally passed a divorce act in 1857,
possessed such powers as there were (if you put aside the ability
of the wealthy to get divorced by private legislation) to dissolve a
marriage. What then came in was the heavily moralised concept of
matrimonial fault as the ground for divorce, though what ranked
as fault differed critically—hypocritically—between husband and
wife, while those who tried to arrange a civilised end to a failed
marriage could find themselves condemned by reason of collusion
to a marriage without an end. It was not only the slow pressure for
reform but sudden shocks, such as the attempt of the determined
Georgina Weldon to enforce a court order for restitution of her con-
jugal rights (one of the few remedies dispensed by the ecclesiastical
courts) by having her recalcitrant husband committed to prison, that
prompted Parliament to intervene. From England, Cornish glances
north to Calvinist Scotland, where the courts had for a long time
been granting divorces in clear cases on the basis of simple breach
of contract, and ahead to the reforms of the twentieth century which
were to fuse all this, together with the law of child welfare, into a
hardly less intractable but at least more equitable body of family
law. It is a model of how legal history should be written.

3

Human Rights and the Whirligig of Time

This was a lecture given at Edinburgh University in 2015 in memory of the philosopher and human rights worker Ruth Adler.

'And thus,' says Feste in the final scene of *Twelfth Night*, 'the whirligig of time brings in his revenges.'

The revenge I want to talk about is not the political backlash against what the Sun once impartially described as 'the hated law which frees murderers to kill again'—the 1998 Human Rights Act. It is the paradoxically contingent and variable nature, over time and over space, of human notions of incontestable, inalienable and universal rights: the revenge which time is for ever taking on things we imagine to be timeless. How is it that, at least in this country and in much of the western world, sexual relations between persons of the same gender have travelled in little more than a generation from the status of a sin and a crime to a status recognised by the law of marriage and protected by the human right of privacy? How is it that the right to private property has shrunk since the great revolutions of the eighteenth century from a sacred entitlement to a conditioned expectation?

I don't expect to be able to offer more than tentative answers to such questions; but it will not be possible to evade one further question: does it all mean that human rights are little more than thistledown, springing up at random and blowing away as time's whirligig spins?

The human brain processes information through a filter of what it already knows or thinks it knows. We visualise the universal through the prism of the local. It has been called the imperialism of the present. The linguist Guy Deutscher calls it mistaking the familiar for the natural.[1] So when a document describes a proposition

---

[1] G Deutscher, *Through the Language Glass* (William Heinemann, 2010).

as a self-evident truth, that is to say as requiring no extraneous justification, an amber light ought to start flashing. We all know which truths the founders of the French and American republics considered self-evident. In similar mode a century and a half later the composers of the Universal Declaration of Human Rights felt able to state as a self-evident truth: 'The family is the natural and fundamental group unit of society.' Globalisation since then has opened minds to other values, for example non-familial support and kinship; and notions of what constitutes a family have themselves dramatically altered. More negatively, globalism has demanded that other cultures accept dominant ideological and legal norms as part, sometimes almost literally, of a trading relationship. I want to look at both these processes historically.

RIGHTS IN SPACE

First, however, it may be useful to consider human rights not longitudinally—in time—but latitudinally, in space.

In 1998 a conference of Asian states meeting in South Korea adopted an Asian Human Rights Charter. It makes an interesting comparison with the European Convention on Human Rights and the EU's Charter of Rights, in part because it is discursive rather than prescriptive, but mainly because it sees the world and its wrongs differently.

It is set overtly against the background of European colonialism, which has distorted much of Asia's development and left legacies of authoritarianism. It takes account too of contemporary globalisation and the impediment it represents to national autonomy. Unsurprisingly, therefore, the Asian Charter places the right to democracy high on its list; but it places another right higher: the right to live in peace.

Both are preceded by a version of the right to life which differs markedly from its European counterpart. The European Convention, drafted immediately after the Second World War, begins by stipulating that everyone's right to life is to be protected by law. It then qualifies the right by allowing the taking of life not only pursuant to the sentence of a court (it was not until 1983 that a protocol forbade judicial executions) but by way of necessary defence to unlawful violence, in quelling riot or insurrection, or 'in order to effect a lawful arrest or prevent the escape of a person lawfully detained'. How do you effect an arrest by killing the suspect?

And why should the prevention of escape from custody justify homicide? The Universal Declaration, adopted two years earlier, contains no such reservations: 'Everyone has the right to life, liberty and the security of person.'

I mention these anomalies not in order to devalue the European Convention, composed as it was in 1950, but in order to emphasise that it too is a child of time and place. If it were being drafted today, it would without doubt include a right to a wholesome environment. Drafted in 1998, by contrast, the Asian Charter's right to life does not treat life merely as survival hedged by conditions: it expands it to embrace a healthy existence in a clean environment— something which the Indian Supreme Court had by then done by way of interpretation of the right to life recognised by the Indian Constitution.[2]

The approach of the two instruments, European and Asian, to sex and age discrimination differs radically. The illustrative list of forbidden grounds of discrimination in the European Convention, which relates only to the enjoyment of the Convention rights, includes sex and race but does not include infancy or age. To protect children from adult violence Strasbourg has had to resort to the separate prohibition of inhuman or degrading treatment. The Asian Charter starts from somewhere quite different: it acknowledges the presence in most Asian societies of profound historical and cultural gender inequality, and of grave underprivileging and exploitation of children, and it calls upon member states to work towards the eventual elimination of these injustices.

The difference of provision flags up a historic gulf between east and west. Where the Council of Europe has been able from the start to require member states to place men and women on the same plane and to keep them there, Asian states are looking at entrenched patterns of oppression and discrimination which it may well take generations to redress.

Still outside the west, Islam has its own take on human rights. Although there is no human rights treaty between Islamic states mirroring the European one, more than one endeavour was made during the 1980s and 90s to draw up a code which would match the secular codes of the west. In 1981, to mark the beginning of the 15th Islamic century, a Universal Islamic Declaration of Human Rights was promulgated by the Islamic Councils in London and Paris,

---

[2] *Kumar v State of Bihar* (1991) AIR 420, SCR (1) 5.

'based on the Qur'an and the Sunnah': another amber light. Islamic texts on human rights have been prey to the Sunni–Shi'a divide, on the face of it a doctrinal dispute about the correct textual sources to supplement the Qur'an, in modern reality a cause of, or more realistically an excuse for, tribal and national bloodshed. Even so, the Paris declaration appears laudably unequivocal in its prescription of equal treatment of the sexes and freedom of religion within the law. The equivocation comes in its glossary, which defines the word 'law' as meaning the Shari'a, a system which does not treat women and men equally and which makes Muslim apostasy a capital offence.

The 1981 declaration is generally regarded as less approachable than the Cairo Declaration drawn up in 1990 by the Islamic Conference Organisation and formally adopted by a number of Islamic states. But the Cairo Declaration too is explicitly based on and subject to the Shari'a. Accordingly it too fails to protect all religious belief equally, heresy included, or to insulate apostasy from reprisal. It has been criticised not only for these and other internal flaws but as a calculated attempt to undermine the broad guarantees of the Universal Declaration, to which many Islamic states are party and which in any event now forms part of international law.

The Universal Declaration includes a right to freedom of thought, conscience and religion which explicitly includes freedom to change one's religion or beliefs. The Islamic codes deny Muslims this right. The main reason why Saudi Arabia abstained from endorsing the Universal Declaration in 1948 was that it included the right to change one's religion. But religious exceptionalism is not confined to the Islamic world. Ever since the churches in the UK demanded exemption from the requirements of the Human Rights Bill there have been insistent claims that aspects of Christian belief and practice should be ringfenced from the general requirement to respect the human rights of others—claims to which the United States Supreme Court has recently been showing itself sympathetic.

A BRITISH BILL OF RIGHTS?

You might have expected the proposed British bill of rights to feature in this latitudinal survey. But the repeated political promises to replace the Human Rights Act by a domestic bill or charter of rights turn out—so far at least—to have little to do with its substantive content.

The proponents of a British bill of rights argue, first of all, that our courts need to be liberated from adherence to Strasbourg's case-law. This has crystallised around a series of issues on which decisions of the European court have provoked political hostility, most vocally in recent times on the issue of prisoners' voting rights. The first thing that needs to be observed about this critique is that, even if it is accepted, it does not require a domestic bill of rights, because it has nothing to do with the textual content of the Convention—here, for example, with whether voting should be a primary entitlement and unreasonable discrimination in its exercise be barred. It has to do with how a judicial majority in Strasbourg considered that our domestic legislation measured up to these principles. Given that, although all British prisoners are forbidden by law to vote, those serving up to 12 months are allowed by law to stand for election to Parliament,[3] it's not entirely surprising that the Strasbourg judges found our law less than coherent.

The rhetoric is accordingly about making it clear that our courts do not have to follow Strasbourg's jurisprudence if they consider it wrong. This is a perfectly defensible objective, but it doesn't require replacement of the Human Rights Act by a domestic bill of rights. All that is necessary is that politicians take the trouble to read section 2 of the Human Rights Act, which requires material decisions of the Strasbourg court to be taken into account but not necessarily followed by our courts—a prescription which has led on more than one occasion to a salutary divergence of view and to a change of mind in Strasbourg.[4] Moreover, it is not always our courts which are required to take notice of Strasbourg's decisions. Where, as with prisoners' votes, the issue is the compatibility not of judicial decisions but of domestic legislation with the Convention, the answer sits in the hands of ministers and of Parliament, not of the judges.

One piece of history will illustrate these points. When the Court of Human Rights in 1996 handed down its unfortunate decision in the case brought by Ernest Saunders, the former chairman of Guinness plc, against the United Kingdom, and forbade the use before a jury of evidence of criminality extracted from the accused by an official investigation, it was ministers who dutifully asked Parliament, and Parliament which dutifully agreed, to gut eleven

---

[3] Representation of the People Act 1981, s 1.
[4] See Ch 10.

separate pieces of crime-fighting legislation, as well as several subsequent bills, by barring the use of investigatory findings to support criminal prosecutions. The effect of this parliamentary capitulation on the fight against corporate crime has been catastrophic, but somehow it has passed the political class by. By contrast, when the *Saunders* decision was founded on in this country's courts in order to frustrate the prosecution of a drunk driver based on an admission made by her in answer to a police officer's enquiry, the UK judges refused to follow Strasbourg.[5] A few years after that, Strasbourg acknowledged that it had gone wrong and reversed itself.[6]

Slavish adherence of the UK's courts to Strasbourg's rulings, in other words, is a fiction. There is a powerful case nevertheless for not departing arbitrarily from Strasbourg's jurisprudence. No court, and certainly not as large and heterogeneous a court as the European Court of Human Rights, is going to get everything right. But if you are serious about the universality of human rights, the Convention cannot mean one thing in Britain and another thing, on indistinguishable facts, in Denmark or Russia. The answer has to lie not in national exceptionalism but in a better resourced and led international court: for example one in which oral hearings are the rule and not, as they have been for many years, the exception; and whose judgments, or better still summaries of whose judgments, are issued in the languages of all the member states and not, as at present, only in English or French. How else are the judiciaries of non-anglophone and non-francophone member countries expected to give effect to them?[7]

So it's worth being aware of what is not, as well as what is, a genuine difference about the nature and content of human rights. The argument about a British bill of rights is not such a difference. Its agenda, not very far below the surface, concerns major issues of national sovereignty; but to Lord Bingham's question—which of the Human Rights Act's critics would prefer to live in a country where these rights do not exist?—the response remains a very audible silence.

---

[5] *Brown v Stott (procurator fiscal, Dunfermline)* [2003] 1 AC 681 (PC).
[6] *O'Halloran v United Kingdom* (2007) 46 EHRR 397.
[7] See Ch 11.

RIGHTS IN TIME

Let me turn from human rights in space to human rights in time. It's possible, at least from the vantage point of the twenty-first century, to discern three historical phases in the development of human rights.

The first can be called the declaratory phase. As early as 1569 the court of Star Chamber, denying a man named Cartwright the right to beat a slave he had bought in Russia, proclaimed that the air of England was too pure for a slave to breathe.[8] Decisions of the Scottish and English courts over the course of the eighteenth century reiterated that the state of slavery was not countenanced by the common law. But the financial power of the slave trading interests was too great for the principle to be allowed to acquire legal effect, and when in 1772 Lord Mansfield ordered the discharge of James Somersett from the vessel in which he was about to be transported as a slave to the West Indies, he did so reluctantly, recognising what he called the 'inconvenience' of his decision. By then, however, the tide of sentiment against slavery was becoming too strong to resist.[9]

The modern analogue of this process can be seen in the period following the Second World War, when the great international human rights instruments were composed and adopted, starting in 1948 with the Universal Declaration. These did not come out of the blue. The proclamation of incontestable truths about fundamental human entitlements went back at least as far as the American and French revolutions (and arguably much further[10]), and much had been written during the war years about the future entrenchment of human rights. Strikingly, too, the United Kingdom did not hide behind the provision of the European Convention which stipulated that the tabulated rights applied only to those overseas territories which member states expressly chose to include: in 1953 it extended the Convention to almost the whole of its empire, including five countries (Kenya, Uganda, Malaya, Singapore and British Guiana) where a state of emergency was in operation. The discrepancy that is now plainly visible between the Convention rights and the often brutal governance of Britain's colonies was simply not visible then

---

[8] Lilburne 'A true relation of Lt. Col. Lilburne's sufferings' (1645).
[9] See Ch 32.
[10] See Ch 28.

in Whitehall, which went on to include exemplary bills of rights in the constitutions which it composed for Britain's colonies on the grant of independence. This was very much a declaratory phase for European human rights.

The second phase can be called the propagandist phase, forming a bridge between proclamation and enforcement. It was there in the humanitarian and evangelical movements which played a major part in pushing Lord Mansfield into accommodating the denunciation of slavery, and which by 1833 had secured its abolition throughout the Empire. In the modern international human rights movement you find it in the change of gear which followed the Helsinki accords of 1975.

It's worth pausing for a moment to look at this sometimes over-looked chapter of modern history. In 1972 Finland convened a Conference for Security and Cooperation in Europe, designed to de-escalate the tensions of the Cold War by securing mutual recognition of the major powers' existing spheres of influence. The Final Act of the Conference, signed in 1975, did this, but it also set up a procedure for monitoring the observance or violation of human rights by states signatories. One almost immediate response was the setting up within the Soviet Union of the Helsinki Group of dissidents. A second was the adoption by Jimmy Carter, the new Democrat president, of a rhetoric of human rights as the US tried to come to terms with Vietnam, Watergate, Chile, and the exposure by Senator Church's committee of state lawlessness in the Cold War. But this was not a phase of penitence. With growing effectiveness US foreign policy turned the rhetoric of human rights against the USSR. In 1977, the year Amnesty International was given the Nobel Peace Prize, Carter, evidently forgetting the biblical injunction about motes and beams, made worldwide human rights the centre-piece of his inaugural address. There is today little doubt that the post-Helsinki process made a significant contribution to the eventual demise of the Soviet Union.

The third phase can be called the institutional phase. It was not until 1833 that Parliament finally abolished slavery in Britain's colonies, but from that point the change was decisive: slaving ships became pirate vessels and slavers who were captured were hanged. In modern Britain the long haul started by Lord Scarman in his 1974 Hamlyn Lectures finally bore fruit in the Labour Party's 1996 consultation paper *Bringing Rights Home* and in the Blair government's enactment in 1998 not only of the Human Rights Act but of the Scotland Act, giving Scotland its own human rights regime, and in the Good Friday Agreement which brought the makings of peace to Northern Ireland.

Since the 1990s, first NGOs and then legislators have worked to make a legal and practical reality of the rhetoric of rights; and in the United Kingdom at least the going has proved unexpectedly rough. It may be because the parliamentary adoption of a European rights instrument administered by a supra-national court has proved repugnant, but I doubt this. If, as I suspect, what has generated the hostility of a significant tranche of the media and the political class to human rights is the quantum leap from lofty declarations of principle to enforceable obligations towards the querulous, the disaffected and the unrespectable, the future, like the present, is going to be heavy going.[11]

WHY HUMAN RIGHTS?

Let me go back, then, to what it is that makes human rights special. The idea that there exist rights, whether unconditional or qualified, to which all human beings are entitled is neither obvious nor longstanding. Aristotle's articulation of the idea of natural law—law which human beings do not make for themselves but which lies in the nature of things—flowed into Cicero's contention that the law of nations is external to mankind. But these perceptions had to be self-sustaining: they possessed, and today still possess, no visible means of external support.

The need to justify the idea that there exist certain universal rights, rights which either cannot be taken away by states or which can be diminished by them only on strictly controlled conditions, leads ineluctably to a search for a unitary explanation or foundational principle. But what principle is it to be? In fact why should there be one?

The Kantian idea of universal dignity is frequently advanced as an answer—the axiom that every human being has an unquantifiable but equal share of entitlement to respect. Kant's proposition was revolutionary at a time when conventional wisdom allocated dignity differentially according to birth, status and economic power. To invest every human being with an undifferentiated claim to be

---

[11] The vocal political assault on the UK's human rights régime ceased overnight with the 2016 Brexit referendum result, confirming the suspicion that the assault had been largely an oblique attempt to make the UK's membership of the EU untenable.

treated with respect was a step which has taken two hundred years to become our conventional wisdom. But is it any more verifiable, any better founded, than the rights which are built on it? In what sense does the fraudster who cheats a pensioner of her savings, or the joyrider who kills a passer-by, enjoy a dignity comparable with that of his victim? Is it more intelligible, and more defensible, to abandon the rhetoric of dignity and simply accept, and expect others to accept, that there are some things a civilised society can't do to anyone—for instance condemn them without a trial or inflict a disproportionately savage punishment on them? Whatever principle you choose to derive fundamental rights from, both the rights themselves and their foundational axioms depend in the end not upon some external principle but upon consensus; and consensus shifts both with time and with place.

Thus a fair trial is now universally taken to be a human right. In fact the only human right which a sceptic like Roger Scruton considers to be universally accepted is the right to due process before an independent judge.[12] What then makes a trial fair? For a good four centuries the common sense of the common law has been that no trial is fair unless it takes place in public and each party knows the case it has to meet and has a realistic opportunity to answer it. It took much longer to make this part of criminal procedure than of civil procedure, but by the beginning of the twentieth century most of the world's legal systems understood it to be axiomatic. In particular, if the state did not want or feel able to disclose all it knew, it had to choose between proceeding without it and throwing its hand in; it could not give its evidence behind the back of the accused. Yet by 2009 Justice was able to count 14 British statutes passed since 1997 authorising the use of secret evidence in tribunals dealing with issues, some of them as remote as employment and planning, in which security considerations might arise.[13]

The retreat from due process is not arbitrary: it results from a symbiosis of undoubted terrorist activity with the desire of the security establishment to manage the administration of justice in its own interests. Its success in doing this can itself be accounted for in the vocabulary of human rights: freedom from fear (one of Roosevelt's four freedoms) and from harm, balanced against the odium (as Churchill called it) of detention without charge and the right

---

[12] R Scruton, *A Dictionary of Political Thought*, 2nd edn (Macmillan, 1996), *cap* Human rights.
[13] *Secret Evidence* (Justice, 2009).

to due process of law. What cannot be accounted for by this arithmetic is the abandonment of even the trappings of due process by successive US administrations in Guantánamo and the black sites associated with it. The reversion to the Dark Ages in the officially sanctioned use of torture and incarceration without trial has forfeited any American claim to leadership—indeed of membership—of the international movement for human rights.

HOW EVIDENT IS SELF-EVIDENT?

How heavily conditioned even natural law is by time and place is apparent from another of Aristotle's propositions. He takes it be self-evident that human beings may not be hunted for food or sacrifice; but he also takes it to be obvious that this does not prevent their enslavement if they are natural slaves. The grand sweep of self-evident truths begins to look time-warped and self-serving.

Jeremy Bentham certainly thought so. In his *Anarchical Fallacies*, published in 1843, belatedly debunking the ideology of the French Revolution, he argued that nature accorded individuals no identifiable rights, much less rights which were absolute:

'Natural rights is simple nonsense: natural and imprescriptible rights, rhetorical nonsense—nonsense on stilts.'

Yet, almost as famously, in his *Introduction to the Principles of Morals and Legislation*, published in the year of the French Revolution, Bentham had advanced his own self-evident truths:

'Nature has placed mankind under the governance of two sovereign masters, pain and pleasure. It is for them alone to point out what we ought to do, as well as to determine what we shall do.'

It was from these putatively natural premises that Bentham derived his principle of utility as the path towards what he took to be the self-evident goal of human felicity. If Kant in the previous generation had advanced human dignity as the bedrock value, or John Rawls in the following century was to make justice the ultimate value, who was—who is—to say which, if any, was right?

And what of the slave trade, which made the felicity of some dependent on the misery of others? Bentham's answer was to resort to natural rights, though in a characteristically oblique way:

'The day has been, I grieve to say in many places it is not yet past, in which the greater part of the species, under the denomination of slaves, have been treated by the law exactly upon the same footing as, in

England for example, the inferior races of animals still are. ... The question is not: can they reason? nor: can they talk? but: can they suffer?'

Bentham, in other words, addresses racial oppression through animal rights, charging mankind with a duty of compassion towards all its fellow creatures, human or not. But a duty of compassion for animals requires not one but two leaps of faith: first the inclusion of non-human creatures within the moral compass of human society, and then the enlargement of the concept of rights to include an entitlement to compassion. Both propositions may be acceptable to us, but neither is self-evident.

For centuries the colossal profitability of the slave trade and of slave economies had fuelled an elliptical debate about whether Africans or native Americans ranked as human beings or—putting the same issue theologically—possessed immortal souls. If they did not, then human rights were not for them. What swung the debate round was not a change in the philosophy of human rights but a slowly growing moral and political recognition among Europeans and their colonial offspring that slaves were human beings.

To reach this point, it became necessary first to move beyond the Aristotelian notion of natural slaves. The Dominican friar Bartolomeo de las Casas did this in his *Defence of the Indians* by propounding a single test of humanity, the capacity to reason. But by doing so he became drawn into factual disputes: if native Americans practised cannibalism or human sacrifice, could they be rational beings? The debate sank into pragmatism. Ignobly, Las Casas argued for the importation of African slaves in substitution for native Americans, and in lieu of arguments about whether Africans possessed reason Jean Gerson, the chancellor of the University of Paris, developed a free-market justification: an African who was enslaved had putatively sold himself. John Locke, who famously denounced slavery as 'vile and miserable ... and ... directly opposite to the generous temper and spirit of our nation', managed at the same time to argue, as a stockholder in the Royal Africa Company, that the slave trade was saving Africans from an even worse fate in Africa.

The capacity to reason has continued to bedevil human rights theory and practice. It has run far wider than assumptions about skin colour or race. Lynn Hunt says of the first generation of human rights:

'Children and the insane lacked the necessary capacity to reason ... Like children, slaves, servants, the propertyless, and women lacked the required independence of status to be fully autonomous.'

Hunt was writing in the past tense; but modern human rights instruments continue to treat children as extensions of their parents in relation, for example, to religion. Rather than protecting the right of the child, as an incipiently rational being, to learn about every viewpoint and belief and make up its own mind, both the Universal Convention and the European Convention, replicating the Islamic conventions in this regard, treat it as axiomatic that a child is to be brought up in its parent's religion. The impact of this in allowing state-funded schools in Britain to discriminate in the admission and rejection of children on the basis of their parents' religious beliefs—something that would be unconstitutional in France or the US—is an issue for another day.

ENGINES OF CHANGE

What was it that, over three centuries and more, changed the consciousness and the conscience of the metropolitan population first in relation to the acceptability of slavery as a domestic institution (about a tenth of the population recorded in the Domesday Book were slaves) and then in relation to the enslavement of Africans abroad? In *The Ends of Life* Keith Thomas tracks the growth in early modern England of the concept of human individuality, supplanting the mediaeval mentality in which, as Jacob Burckhardt described it,

> 'man was conscious of himself only as a member of a race, people, party, family or corporation—only through some general category'.

You have only to consider whether John Aubrey's *Brief Lives*, chronicling his idiosyncratic contemporaries, could conceivably have been written earlier than the seventeenth century to realise how profound the change was.

> 'The great motor behind the sense of individual identity,' says Thomas, 'was the growth of a market economy, in which land, goods and labour were freely bought and sold. New economic opportunities ... widened the scope for personal choice ... and they made acquisitive and ego-centred behaviour increasingly common.'

If, nevertheless, that very market economy was prospering by treating one class of human beings as chattels and other classes as inferior races undeserving of equal treatment, modern ideas of human rights were going to have—as they did have—a painful and protracted birth. In the course of the nineteenth century both humanism and evangelism played a part in shaming metropolitan populations into a slow retreat from the racial and national supremacism by which they justified their conduct and laws. So did the possession or acquisition by subject peoples of some of the metropolitan attributes of dignity: literacy, education, monotheistic religion, artistic skills, business acumen, property. Metropolitan populations in their turn began to value indigenous skills and art-forms. Missionaries stopped destroying native artefacts as pagan symbols and began sending them to museums.

You have only to look at present-day racism to see how contested and imperfect the process has been; but a watershed was without doubt reached in the United Kingdom in the 1960s and 1970s when, first tentatively and then more firmly, racial discrimination was forbidden by law.[14]

Arguably the most important struggles of the last hundred or more years have been those by which human rights have been not conferred or granted but claimed and won—by women, by racial minorities, by gay men and lesbian women. All of these have made their way against heavy opposition into the arena of equality, and in doing so have changed the common sense of what is acceptable. The governing echelons of society, when this happens, tend to claim the credit for themselves. Women, we are told, would have obtained the vote, and perhaps obtained it sooner, without unseemly agitation. It was Parliament's race relations legislation which—it is said—made racial discrimination unacceptable in the United Kingdom, much as it is often said to have been *Brown v Topeka Board of Education* in the US Supreme Court which in 1954 turned the tide and ten years later prompted the passage of the Civil Rights Act.[15]

I don't argue that legislation is irrelevant to the shifts in our collective perception of fundamental rights and wrongs. Arguably the most profound effect of the Race Relations and Sex Discrimination Acts of the mid-1970s has been not the successful lawsuits brought under them but the change they have helped to bring about in the public sense of what conduct is acceptable and tolerable. That was a change, however, which had to be fought for by the people who were most affected by discrimination. In parallel, the desegregation decision of the US Supreme Court in *Brown*, far from being, as Alexander Bickel called it, 'the beginning ... of substantive changes

---

[14] Race Relations Acts 1966, 1968 and 1976.
[15] *Brown v Board of Education* 347 US 483 (1954).

in the American social structure', was a response to changes which organisations like the NAACP and activists like Rosa Parkes had been working to bring about since the 1930s and even earlier.

LAWFUL VIOLATIONS

You would think at least that the human right not to be enslaved was as secure today as a right can be. If so, you would be wrong. Nobody—almost nobody—tries to defend slavery as an institution, though it is little more than 30 years since it was finally outlawed in Mauritania. But it is estimated that today enforced prostitution both female and male, child labour, the conscription of child soldiers, debt bondage and the use of indentured and forced labour mean that some 30 million individuals worldwide are held in conditions practically indistinguishable from slavery.

My concern here is not with the extent or gravity of these violations of human rights (that is something which makes the rights more, not less, important) but with the fact that much of the violation is lawful. Indentured labour and some other forms of contractual employment may legally rob the worker of autonomy to a point indistinguishable from servitude. In other instances the state itself may be the offender, for example in the use of prisoners as a source of forced and unpaid labour, or in compulsory military service.

Once again, perception dominates. We draw a mental line between the right not to be enslaved and the power of states or corporations to dictate their own terms for the use of labour. In effect, it is only chattel slavery—the power to buy and sell other human beings—which is perceived as a violation of human rights. But when the Confederates in the American civil war claimed that many slaves were better housed and fed than impoverished workers in the northern cities, they had a point. The denial of dignity and autonomy to the millions of people trapped in the relationships and setups I have listed escapes condemnation except by campaigners.

RELATIVISM AND ABSOLUTISM

The point I am interested in here is not the obvious one that human rights are widely violated. It is that what is perceived as a human right is itself determined, in large part, by a historical contest between self-interest and compassion; that historically all human rights claims and entitlements have been culturally loaded; that, although it is not easy for us to escape the grip of reflexivity, the same is perceptibly true today; and that there is no reason to believe that there exists some plateau of objectivity or universality which may one day be reached. Human rights will continue to be whatever a segment or (very occasionally) the whole of mankind for the time being agrees that they are.

Does this matter?

The conventional riposte to the kind of relativism I have been describing is one version or another of absolutism: an insistence that there is in reality a single standard by which human rights are to be measured. A good deal of modern human rights philosophy, much of it—perhaps significantly—emanating from the US, adopts or supports this position.

Take two opposite examples. Female genital mutilation is practised in significant parts of the Muslim world. It is defended as a cultural norm and a religious requirement; but I doubt whether there is anybody who would be prepared to modify the human right to bodily integrity to accommodate FGM, or to accept that it should enjoy the human rights protection accorded to religious practice. On this issue we are all absolutists. However, male genital mutilation, or circumcision, is almost universally tolerated as a religious norm. Like FGM, the practice is indisputably an invasion of the bodily integrity of a child far too young to consent; in most cases it has no medical justification. But it is not believed, barring accidents, to do lasting harm, and to ban it would cause widespread protest within developed societies. Is it worth it? Here, I suspect, we are more or less embarrassed relativists.

It's at the very end of *Twelfth Night* that Feste makes his parting speech. Some are born great, he says; some achieve greatness, and some have greatness thrown upon them. It's then, having disclosed the plot to make a fool of Malvolio, that he remarks: 'And thus the whirligig of time brings in his revenges.' Malvolio's response is laden with rage: 'I'll be revenged on the whole pack of you.'

The concern which I've been trying to address, and which I believe is widely felt, is that unless they can be given a self-evident and therefore impregnable foundation, human rights can become, and sooner or later will become, victims of time and tide. The argument which I've put forward is that, greatly as such a foundation might be desired, it does not exist and cannot exist. What does exist in every society in any epoch is a collective sense of what is tolerable in the conduct of states, organisations and individuals. It is a sense which lies deeper than ordinary laws; indeed it conditions what laws can acceptably be enacted. The signal achievement of the later part of the twentieth century has been to articulate and codify this collective sense of right and wrong in texts which are simple and catholic and through forums which speak for the greater part of humanity. Yet although in many places they have been given the force of law, the realisation of the rights vouchsafed by these texts to every human being is in large part a story of failure: they are regularly ignored or defied.

The consequent dilemma is typically posed as a choice between absolutism and relativism: either we stick to our version of human rights as the only acceptable one and denounce all the others as legally inadequate or morally inept, or we shrug and accept that one version is as valid as the next: we prefer not to cut off the hands of thieves but if others think it's okay, then for them it's okay. I want to suggest that this is a false dichotomy and a bogus choice; but if so, what is to replace it?

The philosopher Steven Lukes contends that there is a non-sequitur at the heart of moral relativism, since the inevitability of moral diversity and plural values does not require abstention from mutual criticism and judgment. This is no doubt true, but by itself it offers no prospect of legally enforceable standards. To that problem the American political scientist Jack Donnelly advances this solution:

> 'Faced with … perverse "unilateral universalism", even some well-meaning critics have been seduced by misguided arguments for the essential relativity of human rights. This, however, in effect accepts the American confusion of human rights with US foreign policy. The proper remedy for "false" universalism is defensible, relative universalism.'

I agree with the premise, but I doubt the conclusion. Is 'relative universalism' more than a semantic attempt to reconcile two philosophical opposites? And is it actually a good description of what Donnelly goes on to argue for, which is 'functional, overlapping consensus' and 'international legal universality'? Are these not precisely the artefacts of time and place which, as I have argued, make up the shifting pattern of human rights? If so, there is a simpler and more realistic answer than relative universalism: it is that human societies, and more particularly individuals and minorities within those societies, need and seek consensual ground rules on which legal and ethical structures can be built. Either on its own or—increasingly—in agreement with other societies, our society has moved over centuries towards an articulated consensus on what these rules or principles are. But because neither society nor history stands still, the consensus retreats like a mirage as societies approach it. It changes with time and varies with place, and it always will.

To understand this is to be neither relativist nor universalist nor, may I add, defeatist. It is to recognise that principles exist not in a vacuum or in some moral ether but in real time and real space. The long haul of history which the Asian Charter of 1998 recognised as lying ahead of any worthwhile human rights regime for the East lies equally ahead of, as well as behind, the universalist systems of the West.

History furnishes a final reflection. There is a striking and perhaps significant contrast between, on the one hand, the centuries which it took to make the transition from largely self-serving ideas and ideologies which underpinned slavery and race discrimination to the modern unacceptability of both, and on the other hand, the brief span of years from the Stonewall raids and riots of 1969 to the decriminalisation of homosexual acts and the legal recognition of same-sex marriages. Whether simple economism can explain the contrast—slavery and racial exploitation are highly profitable; homophobia in general is not—is a debate for another day. The only thing that can be treated as certain is that human rights will not stay where they now are. The whirligig of time will see to that. Whether they will advance or retreat, and what will cause them to do so, we cannot say; but one has to hope in the present political climate that it is not Caliban, rather than Malvolio, who is about to be revenged upon the whole pack of us.

* * *

SOURCES

Jack Donnelly, *Universal Human Rights in Theory and Practice*, 3rd edn (Cornell, 2013)

Anthony Lester and Geoffrey Bindman, *Race and Law* (Penguin, 1972)

Lynn Hunt, *Inventing Human Rights: a History* (Norton, 2008)

Steven Lukes, *Moral Relativism* (Profile, 2008)

Samuel Moyn, *The Last Utopia: Human Rights in History* (Harvard University Press, 2012)

AW Brian Simpson, *Human Rights and the End of Empire: Britain and the Genesis of the European Convention* (Oxford University Press, 2001)

Keith Thomas, *The Ends of Life* (Oxford University Press, 2009)

Christian Tomuschat, *Human Rights—Between Idealism and Realism*, 3rd edn (Oxford University Press, 2014)

Geraldine van Bueren, *Child Rights in Europe* (Council of Europe, 2007)

Bernard Williams, *Essays and Reviews 1959–2002* (Princeton University Press, 2014)

4

A Glorious Revolution?

A review of The Glorious Revolution and the Continuity of Law *by Richard Kay.*

IN 1944, RICHARD Kay records, an optimistic litigant challenged the validity of a Victorian statute under which he was being sued, on the ground that Queen Victoria, like all her predecessors since 1689, had had no title to the throne. The argument, which would have wiped the statute book almost clean, was dismissed without much ceremony; but in 1688 and 1689 it occupied the centre of the political and constitutional stage. Could a hereditary monarch, either by violating the constitutional laws of his own realm or by physically abandoning his throne and his country, forfeit the Crown? If he could, did the throne pass to his heir? If not, who had power to appoint his replacement? If it was Parliament, could it also set conditions of tenure?

When Charles II died in 1685 without legitimate offspring, the throne passed to his brother James, Duke of York, who had been brought up in exile in France as a Catholic and who now began publicly attending mass. Within a few months the Duke of Monmouth's abortive rebellion and Baron Jeffreys's judicial revenge, the Bloody Assize, spread fear that a new Catholic reign of terror was on the way, a fear enhanced by James's use of his powers as ex officio head of the Church of England to romanise the liturgy. The following year he packed the high court bench to ensure a favourable decision in a collusive lawsuit, *Godden v Hales*, designed to validate his repeated waiver of the statutory requirement that all MPs, peers and public officials must formally abjure Catholic doctrine. James then asked Parliament for funds to create a standing army, commanded by men whose oath of allegiance he had waived. Parliament offered a compromise, but James prorogued and then dissolved it, creating a void in political authority which was to bedevil the tricky business of replacing him.

Before that point was reached, James had issued two Declarations of Indulgence, authorising public worship by both Protestant and Catholic dissenters. Seven bishops who petitioned for the withdrawal of the second declaration were prosecuted for seditious libel. Their acquittal by a jury in June 1688 coincided with the birth of a male heir to the throne, James Edward Stuart. To the Protestant establishment this was the last straw. While gossip ran around that the child was not the royal couple's and had been smuggled into the palace in a warming pan, ambitious politicians were converting to Catholicism.

The Vicar of Bray, too, had his finger in the wind:

> When royal James possessed the crown
>
> And Popery grew in fashion
>
> The penal laws I hooted down
>
> And read the Declaration.
>
> The Church of Rome I found would fit
>
> Full well my constitution
>
> And I had been a Jesuit
>
> But for the Revolution.

The Dutch ambassador in London had been in contact with leading English politicians, a group of whom, on the day the bishops were acquitted, invited William of Orange, the king's Protestant son-in-law, to invade. James panicked and tried to reverse some of his reforms; but William, concerned at the possibility that Louis XIV of France would soon have a militant ally in Britain, crossed to Torbay in November 1688 with a force of 4,000 horse and 11,000 foot and marched on London—the last successful invasion of England. James, deserted by his generals at Salisbury, fled the country.

Pretty much as had happened in 1660 before the reinstatement of Charles II, a parliament convened without a royal summons—though William purported to convene it—and asserted its own authority to govern. The difference was that, while the 1660 Convention took itself to be simply restoring the legitimate succession, the 1689 Convention was tacking between hereditary entitlement and powerful political and religious imperatives. Could a legally non-existent parliament clothe itself with the authority to break the genetic line of succession and enthrone a monarch of its own choosing? The short answer is that, lawfully or not, that is what happened. The Convention declared itself a parliament and resolved 'That King James the Second ... by breaking the original contract between king and people, and ... having withdrawn himself out of this kingdom, hath abdicated the government, and that the throne is thereby vacant.' It offered the vacant throne to William and Mary.

What if James returned? Isaac Newton consulted Robert Sawyer, the distinguished lawyer who, with him, represented Cambridge University in the Convention, and received the reassuring advice that to oppose a de facto king, even if on behalf of a lawful king, was treason. But James's attempt to regain his throne by invading England through Ireland met its bloody end at the Battle of the Boyne.

The fact that the incoming king, William III, was a foreigner played little part in the debates: the Stuarts, as Scots, had also been foreigners. In any case William was of Stuart descent and his wife, Mary, was a Stuart. The overarching problem was that a Protestant succession to the throne was assumed—how else could effect be given to the English monarch's status as head of the established church?—but not demanded by positive law. Kay also argues (though I'm not sure he's right) that the judgment James II secured in *Godden v Hales*, upholding the royal power of dispensation, was perfectly orthodox: as the chief justice had put it, 'there is no law whatsoever but may be dispensed with by the supreme lawgiver', and the laws were constitutionally the king's laws. Although the Convention Parliament's Declaration of Rights denounced the dispensing power as unlawful, the real objection was to the use James had made of it. As Kay notes, the Bill of Rights which was extracted from the Declaration of Rights purported to set out only pre-existing rights, not the numerous new rights that the Declaration also contained. Its outlawing of the regal dispensing power was accordingly presented as a restoration of legality—a revolution in the seventeenth-century sense of a return to a starting point—rather than as the corralling of the Crown which in reality it was.

Although the events of 1688–89 are often characterised as a coup d'état, Kay intelligibly contends that they amounted, as many of the protagonists claimed they did, to a revolution in its modern sense—an oversetting of the political and legal order. The epithet 'Glorious' is not a later historian's conceit. It appears to have been coined by the Whig MP John Hampden, grandson of the hero of resistance to Charles I's ship money, in testimony to a committee of the House of Lords in the autumn of 1689. Hampden was exulting that, in contrast to the Cromwellian revolution of the 1640s and 1650s which his ancestor had helped to bring about but which had culminated ingloriously in regicide, the ousting of James II and the enthronement of William and Mary had been a noble, a glorious, revolution. It was in nobody's interests to admit that there had been usurpation by military conquest abetted by a fifth column powerful enough to call most of the subsequent shots.

For all its meticulous scholarship, there are two principal puzzles about Kay's book. One is the thesis, reflected in its title, that the continuity of law was preserved, when the very reason the events of 1688–89 were revolutionary was that they involved a rupture of legality. The other is his concern to dissociate the Glorious Revolution from the Cromwellian revolution, rather than to appraise the long-term continuities of which both revolutions formed a part. There were undoubted parallels between 1649 and 1689: in each case an unpopular monarch was militarily ousted and the space filled by a self-authorised parliament. But, unlike the court that in 1649 had sentenced James's father to death for treason against his own people, the politicians of 1689 were nervous about regarding their acts as lawful simply because it was they who were now in charge. It was still possible that James would regain the throne, and it had not been forgotten that only a generation before the protagonists of a republican revolution had been hunted down by a returning monarchy.

Kay's central subject is the consequent resort to legal reasoning either to justify or to oppose the transfer of sovereign power in England, Wales and Ireland from one monarch to another. Noting the legal flaws in the mooted justifications, he tracks and analyses the arguments. Could a king be lawfully deposed by a parliament? Was there a higher law forbidding a Catholic to wear the Crown? Was there a contract between king and people? If so, what constituted a breach sufficiently grave to terminate it? Had there been an abandonment of the throne amounting to abdication? Could either a breach of contract or an abdication be acted on by a parliament that had not been duly summoned? If so, could that parliament alter the line of succession and lay down terms of tenure of the throne?

None of these was capable of being resolved in terms of existing law. A social contract between king and people was at best political theory. A constructive abdication might well pass the throne to the male heir. Parliament, even if lawfully convened, had no known power to depose a king or set conditions for his successor. A new legal order was needed to authorise and consolidate the transfer of sovereignty from monarch to parliament.

In the background stood the longstanding assumption that no English monarch, as head of the Church of England, would be, or could be, a Roman Catholic. But no statute spelled it out. In consequence the single most potent factor in the events of 1688–89, the perceived threat to the nation's safety and religion presented by a Catholic monarch, played little part in the legal arguments; but the institutionalising of a Protestant succession, first in the new coronation oath and then in the 1701 Act of Settlement, was one of the revolution's most fundamental achievements. The undertaking to defend 'the Holy Church' was replaced by the (still requisite) promise to maintain 'the Protestant reformed religion established by law'. And, confirming the surrender of autocratic power, the ancient formula that the incoming king or queen would 'confirm to the people of England the laws and customs to them granted' by their predecessors was replaced by an oath to govern 'according to the statutes in parliament agreed on, and the laws and customs of the same'.

It is a feature of constitutions, and not only unwritten ones, that facts can become law: witness the US presidential practice of suspending congressional legislation, which is nowhere permitted by the constitution but which the Supreme Court has more than once legitimated. In 1688 the factual and constitutional reality was that the throne was vacant and an acceptable and co-operative candidate, a monarch whose wife was the ex-king's daughter, was willing that the two of them should assume the throne. The consequent offer to William and Mary of the Crown on terms set out by the Convention Parliament was a defining moment in Britain's constitutional history because it placed the authority of the Crown in the gift of Parliament and thereby decisively shifted the location of sovereign power from monarchy to legislature. Even abdication was no longer to lie in the monarch's own hands. When Edward VIII gave up the Crown in 1936, both his declaration of abdication and the succession to the Crown were given effect by an act of Parliament which also barred him and any of his progeny from resuming the throne. The throne was now in Parliament's unquestioned gift, and the debates of 1688–89 were in every sense history.

What then of the English republic? Although he is content to characterise it as revolutionary, Kay elects to treat the Commonwealth and Protectorate of 1649–60 as a legal non-event, with the result, or so he contends, that there was no true interregnum until James II vacated the throne in 1688:

> The [Glorious] Revolution created a true interregnum for the first time in
> English legal history. The period from the execution of Charles I to the

Restoration of Charles II was a more obvious practical interruption in the political life of the kingdom. But in retrospect and as a matter of legal theory, it was not an interregnum. Charles II was king from the moment of his father's death.

This doesn't add up. If the absence of a monarch created an interregnum between November 1688 and February 1689, how can there not also have been one starting from 1642, when the Long Parliament began to legislate without royal assent, or at the latest from 1649, when the king was executed for treason, the House of Lords abolished as 'dangerous and useless', and state sovereignty became vested, in practice and in law, in the Commons? Kay's answer is to adopt the blank refusal of conservative historiography to acknowledge that sovereignty in the British Isles was exercised without royal authority for almost two decades, and for more than a decade of that time resided in a republican government. 'If in time as in place there were degrees of high and low,' Hobbes wrote, 'I verily believe the highest of time would be that which passed betwixt 1640 and 1660.' Kay, however, adopts Macaulay's calumny that for the Civil War radicals 'it was necessary that they should first break in pieces every part of the machinery of government; and this necessity was rather agreeable than painful to them'. The reality, carefully traced in GE Aylmer's *The State's Servants: The Civil Service of the English Republic 1649–60* (1973), was pretty much the reverse.

Kay's expressed purpose in locating the sole genuine interregnum between November 1688, when James II fled, and February 1689, when William and Mary accepted the throne, is to suggest that 'recognition of a period in which there was no king or queen was built into the revolution settlement'. But if constitutional legitimacy depended on heredity in 1649, the same had to be true of the succession in 1688: as Jacobites have always contended, the succession passed, either on James II's abdication or on his death, to James Edward Stuart, the Old Pretender, making William and Mary usurpers and leaving no space between reigns.

The argument about what constitutes an interregnum would be unimportant if it did not form part of a much larger issue. The official whiteout of the English republic can be seen in the *Statutes at Large*, which to this day break off in 1641 and continue on the next page with the first act of the Restoration Convention Parliament in 1660, 'the twelfth year of the reign of our most gracious sovereign lord Charles the Second'. It was not until 1911 that the *Acts and Ordinances of the Interregnum* were published, relying in part on copies which survived the bonfire of republican legislation lit in

Westminster Hall at the Restoration by order of the Convention Parliament. Edited by two good scholars, CH Firth and RS Rait, they make interesting reading. The republican Parliament abolished the use of law French and Latin in the courts, instituted civil marriage, stopped the use of prison for debt, set up a national postal service, and reformed jury trial in the interests of the accused. It continued the security of tenure which, subject to proper conduct, the Long Parliament (anticipating the Act of Settlement) had granted judges, but stopped them pocketing court fees and put them on fixed salaries. It tried, but failed, to abolish the corrupt Court of Chancery. And it established, under Sir Matthew Hale, the first ever law commission, which set about systematising and codifying large areas of the law and planning a legal system in which lawyers' fees were regulated, poor litigants were given access to justice, MPs were forbidden to moonlight as lawyers and criminal procedure was improved.

Beyond this, the interregnum saw the enactment, in 1653, of Britain's first and only written constitution, the Instrument of Government. If he were not treating it as a nullity, Kay would have found much in the Instrument of Government that anticipated (and may possibly have been a template for) the Bill of Rights. The Instrument vested sovereignty in a single person, the Lord Protector, but made all his acts subject to the will of Parliament. It then provided 'That the laws shall not be altered, suspended, abrogated or repealed, nor any tax, charge or imposition laid upon the people, but by common consent in Parliament.' Whether or not the framers of the Bill of Rights 35 years later were drawing directly on this, the parallelism is striking: 'The pretended power of suspending of laws ... without consent of Parliament is illegall,' the Bill of Rights said, going on to say the same of 'the pretended power of dispensing with laws or the execution of laws by regal authority as it hath been assumed and exercised of late' and of 'levying money for or to the use of the Crown ... without grant of Parliament'. Both statutes unblinkingly barred Catholics from public office, but the Protectorate's model of a presidential republic can be discerned in, for example, the United States constitution.

In spite of the restored regime's (and Kay's) corresponding treatment of all laws made from 1642 to 1660 as void, the reforms of the republican years returned like a slow tide. At the Restoration the postal service had to be re-established and the civil marriages and judgments of the Interregnum validated. In 1701—not earlier—judicial independence was again secured by law. In 1731 English finally became the language of the law. Civil marriage was reintroduced in 1836. The predatory Six Clerks of Chancery were finally got rid of in 1842. A national land register was set up in 1875, though it did not become public until 1990. And 313 years after the setting up of the Hale commission, the modern standing law commission was established.

These are significant historical continuities in the law. The Glorious Revolution, provoked by a monarch who had apparently learned nothing from his father's obduracy, consolidated the transfer of power to Parliament which had been first achieved and then forfeited between 1642 and 1660. Both events necessarily involved a series of ruptures, making it all the odder that Kay should say of the Cromwellian republic that 'the rhetorical resources available to that earlier generation … were insufficient to maintain the pretence of uninterrupted law'. The court that in 1649 tried the king and the Parliament that abolished the monarchy and the House of Lords made no attempt to pretend there was no interruption of the law. It was the revolutionaries of 1689 who, as Kay himself shows, were trying, and failing, to maintain such a pretence. But the negotiated offer of the Crown by a sitting parliament on the basis that ultimate state power was to vest in itself, not the monarch, were fundamental innovations. In these respects the story is not the continuity but the discontinuity of Britain's constitutional law. It is in the long march of political events which produced these sudden shocks that continuities are to be found.

A fitful history was to follow the Glorious Revolution: both monarchs and ministers went on purporting to suspend legislation; kings and queens interfered in government; parliament remained unrepresentative and corrupt; ministers abused their powers in order to silence opposition; and unchecked prerogative powers survive to this day. But the corner that was turned in 1689 was one the polity had been negotiating throughout the seventeenth century: the supplanting of the authority of a hereditary autocracy by that of an at least partly representative legislature. If it was finally achieved under the flag of monarchist legitimacy, that would not have worried Don Fabrizio, who, contemplating the advance of Garibaldi's republicanism, reflects in Lampedusa's *The Leopard*: 'If we want things to stay as they are, things will have to change.'

5

Judges and Ministers

A review of a volume of essays, edited by Adam Tomkins and Paul Scott, marking the 250th anniversary of the case of Entick v Carrington.

WHEN THE EARL of Bute resigned as Prime Minister in April 1763 it looked as if the *North Briton*, a paper whose vituperative attacks had dogged his administration, had achieved its ambition and would now cease publication. But a week later George III opened the new Parliament with a speech from the throne which, by its support for the peace terms being negotiated with France, reignited the wrath of the *North Briton's* flamboyant co-editor John Wilkes and his backers in the City, prompting the publication of another withering issue, number 45. The new Prime Minister, George Grenville, and his secretary of state, Lord Halifax, decided it was time to put a stop to this constant assault on government policy. Advised by the Treasury Solicitor that number 45 constituted a seditious libel, Halifax signed a warrant authorising the King's Messengers to arrest—without naming anyone—the 'authors, printers and publishers' of the paper. The messengers made more than 40 arrests and ransacked a series of offices and homes, helping themselves liberally to private papers.

Searches for unlicensed and seditious publications had been authorised by the 1662 Licensing Act, with a concomitant power of arrest for possessing them; but despite Parliament's refusal in 1695 to renew the act, ministers had not only continued to issue warrants authorising officials to trawl for evidence but were now authorising the arrest of individuals for interrogation. In more than one case, the courts had upheld the entitlement of the Crown's ministers, as conservators of the peace, to issue search and arrest warrants for crimes against the state. For these purposes, general warrants, which didn't identify suspects, had proved too useful to be abandoned in spite of long-standing suggestions that they were illegal. So the *North Briton* raids looked very much like business as usual, and the government and its lawyers were taken by surprise when the raids provoked an avalanche of successful lawsuits, brought not only by the authors and publishers but by the jobbing printers whom the warrants were in large part designed to intimidate.

By July 1763 (litigation in those days could be brisk), 14 printers whose shops had been raided had been awarded almost £3,000 by juries in damages for trespass, assault and false imprisonment. The government's attempt to challenge an award of £300 to the printer William Huckle gave the Court of Common Pleas an opportunity to point out that treating him with beefsteaks and beer had not diminished the gravity of the state's 'exercising arbitrary power, violating Magna Carta, and attempting to destroy the liberty of the subject'. The judges, manifestly, were not siding with the government any more than jurors were. In December 1763, Wilkes himself was awarded £1,000 against the undersecretary of state, Robert Wood, for trespass to his house and papers. Much later, in 1769, he secured judgment for four times that sum against Lord Halifax personally for trespass and false imprisonment. In neither case did the defendant's counsel try to argue that office as a minister of the Crown carried any immunity from civil liability. The chief justice, Lord Wilmot, told the jury: 'The law makes no difference between great and petty officers. Thank God, they are all amenable to justice, and the law will reach them if they step over the boundaries which the law has prescribed.'

When the government's lawyers took the question of general warrants to the King's Bench, where Lord Mansfield, a former Attorney-General, was expected to be more helpful than Camden, they were again rebuffed. 'It is not fit,' Mansfield ruled, 'that the receiving or judging of the information should be left to the discretion of the officer. The magistrate ought to judge.' None of this saved Wilkes and two of his printers from conviction in Mansfield's court for publishing a seditious libel. What the judges had become concerned about was not the suppression of dissent but its investigation by methods of such arbitrariness that no one was safe.

John Entick was one of the editors of the *Monitor*, another outspoken opposition paper, which had been raided in November 1762, before the more sensational raids on the *North Briton*. The warrants named him and his co-editor, the lawyer Arthur Beardmore, and so did not fall foul of the objection to general warrants, but they had been issued, like the *North Briton* warrant, by a minister and not a magistrate, and they authorised the seizure not only of any incriminating material but of all the suspects' books and papers. Entick and his printers bided their time; then, as the *North Briton* ninepins started to go down, they issued writs against the messengers and Halifax for trespass. The jury decided, among other things, that one element of the state's trespass was its invasion of Entick's privacy by searching his house and 'reading over and examining several of his papers'. The other legal issues arising from their verdict came to trial in 1765 in the Court of Common Pleas before Lord Camden, who had decided to bring the multiple questions of state power together in a comprehensive judgment. It was its 250th anniversary that prompted the conference out of which this book comes.

Entick v Carrington (Nathan Carrington was one of the messengers who carried out the raid), allied with the other cases, established or confirmed at least four things of lasting importance. One was that ministers of the Crown had no authority to issue search or arrest warrants: with the possible exception of high treason, the prosecution of crime was a judicial and not an executive function. A second was that general warrants were illegal: warrants had to specify who was to be arrested and the subject and object of the search, enabling the lawfulness of searches and arrests to be judicially determined. A third was that ministers were answerable to the courts for the legality of their acts: there was no refuge in high office. A fourth was that the common law does not recognise state necessity as a defence to wrongdoing. A knock-on effect, arguably the most radical if the least direct, was to inhibit the use of political power to suppress dissent—a message taken up in 1789 by the US Bill of Rights (and thereafter repeatedly honoured in the breach) and in 1948 by the Universal Declaration of Human Rights.

The most challenging essay in the book is Tom Hickman's interrogation of Lord Camden's reasoning, especially on the claimed power of ministers to issue arrest and search warrants. The problem, as Camden himself recognised, was that there was solid authority— four false imprisonment cases decided by the King's Bench between 1696 and 1733—either holding or assuming that secretaries of state, as privy counsellors, were conservators of the king's peace and so possessed powers that included search and arrest. Holdsworth, in his *History of English Law*, argued that Camden had exposed the shaky foundations of these decisions and had made a solid case for not following them. Hickman is not convinced. He quotes the judgment:

> 'There has been not only a clear practice [of issuing ministerial warrants], at least since the Revolution, confirmed by a variety of precedents; but

the authority has been recognised and confirmed by two cases in the very point since that period; and therefore we have not a power to unsettle or contradict it now, even though we are persuaded that the commencement of it was erroneous.'

Taking this at face value, he suggests that Camden's own contrary views were obiter dicta—that is to say, remarks unnecessary to his decision and so of no legal force—because there was actually no claim in Entick's case for false imprisonment. The problem with this is that Camden manifestly thought otherwise, for the heart of his judgment is his scholarly demonstration that since 1689 the monarch's ministers had 'assumed' a power of arrest—'I know not how'—as part of the royal authority with which their offices invested them. Camden manifestly was not prepared to follow what he regarded as illiberal and dangerous precedents founded on this historically unsupported assumption.

Camden's refusal to follow precedent was not simple judicial bloody-mindedness. The court was sitting, as it generally did, in banc, meaning that Camden had to carry the three other judges with him: hence, very probably, his genuflexion to the earlier cases. But in the mid-eighteenth century the doctrine of precedent was still developing. The axiom that like cases should be decided alike bound lower courts to follow appellate courts, as it still does; but the two principal first-instance courts of common law, the Common Pleas, where Camden presided, and the King's Bench, where Mansfield presided, were courts of co-ordinate jurisdiction. Even today, judges of first instance are not bound to follow one another's decisions if they are satisfied that these are wrong. In the nineteenth century, as Carleton Allen wrote in *Law in the Making*, 'the pattern was far more confused ... and it was by no means easy to say that decisions were "binding" solely by reason of the source from which they emanated'. Camden's court might be 'bound by' the earlier cases in the sense that it could not overrule them, but if they were based on false constitutional premises he was not obliged to follow them.

In this, Camden has been vindicated by history. During the two centuries that followed, the principle that ministerial power is distinct from judicial power and must be exercised in conformity with law, although it came periodically under pressure, faced few direct challenges. Probably the most notorious was the wartime case of *Liversidge v Anderson*, when all but one of the law lords abandoned any pretence of supervising executive action and held that 'reasonable cause' to suspect an individual of enemy associations meant

any cause that seemed reasonable to the home secretary.[1] The failure of the antique dealer James Malone in 1979 to obtain redress
in the English courts for the police's tapping of his phone without
legal authority was held in Strasbourg to be incompatible with the
European Convention on Human Rights. It was not until the 1990s
that a frontal challenge to the principle of legality was offered.
Kenneth Baker, the home secretary, in breach of an undertaking
given to the High Court, deported a Zairean asylum seeker and then
ignored a court order to bring him back. On appeal to the House of
Lords, an application on the asylum seeker's behalf to have Baker
penalised for contempt of court succeeded. Rejecting the argument
of counsel for the Crown that the courts had no power to make or
enforce orders against the monarch's ministers, Lord Templeman
said: 'The proposition that the executive obey the law as a matter
of grace and not as a matter of necessity ... would reverse the result
of the Civil War'.[2] The judgment was hailed by the doyen of public lawyers, Sir William Wade, as the most important decision of
our courts for more than two hundred years—that is since *Entick
v Carrington*. Yet *Entick v Carrington* is not mentioned in the House
of Lords' judgment. Nor is it much mentioned in the body of Scots
law that Tom Mullen's chapter in this volume surveys. Nor do you
find more than a fleeting mention of it, as Adam Tomkins points
out in his chapter, in Dicey's revered work on the rule of law. It is
only in modern commentaries (and even then not in Tom Bingham's
now classic writings) that the case has come to enjoy a foundational
status as the source of what is sometimes known as the principle of
legality.

It was with the publication in 1938 of the volume of Holdsworth's
History covering the eighteenth century that the near-silence about
Entick v Carrington was broken. Where Plucknett's *Concise History
of the Common Law* and Denning's celebrated edition of *Smith's
Leading Cases*, both published in 1929, ignored the case, Holdsworth
a decade later gave it pride of place. He quoted Lord Camden: 'With
respect to the argument from state necessity ... the common law does
not understand that kind of reasoning, nor do our books take notice
of such distinctions.' This statement, he commented, 'embodies the
traditional attitude of the common law to the executive'. Traditional

---

[1] *Liversidge v Anderson* [1942] AC 206 (HL).
[2] *M v Home Office* [1994] 1 AC 377 (HL).

it may have been, but by Holdsworth's day the judges had fallen into a complaisant doze in relation to the state's powers, repeatedly deferring to a civil service now led by a mandarin class drawn largely from the same schools, universities and clubs as the judges themselves. The elevation of *Entick v Carrington* to iconic status—Holdsworth put it on a par with the abolition of Star Chamber and the institutionalisation of habeas corpus — can be seen as one of the first stirrings of resistance to this torpor. Such are the ways in which law manufactures its own history.

But the making of history passes largely out of courts' hands when Parliament steps in. The lacuna in authority to tap Malone's phone was rapidly filled by the 1985 Interception of Communications Act, and ministers are now authorised by much wider-ranging legislation to issue interception and surveillance warrants for national security, crime prevention and economic purposes. Lord Halifax would no longer have any concerns on this score; he might even welcome the current proposal to co-opt the judiciary by giving them oversight of ministerial anti-terrorism warrants. But he would still have no power to authorise arrests or bring charges, and neither his status nor a plea of state necessity would shield him from proceedings for wrongs committed in office. To this extent, at least, we are still living in the age of *Entick v Carrington*, even if we are also grimly contemplating Lord Camden's parting observation: 'Tyranny is better than anarchy, and the worst government better than none at all.'

6

Obscenity and the Margin of Appreciation

This essay was written for a 2012 festschrift marking the centenary— yes, the centenary—of the British Board of Film Classification, which the British Board of Film Censors had by then become.

BESIDE ME AS I write this are two small books, each one adapted from a Danish text and published in the United Kingdom in 1971. One is *The Little Red Schoolbook*; the other is *The Little White Book*. Both are written for children and young adults with the aim of helping them to get their bearings in the adult world.

The Little Red Schoolbook says this about masturbation:

'Some girls, and a very few boys, don't masturbate. This is quite normal. It's also normal to do it. Some do it several times a day, some several times a week, some more rarely. Grown-ups do it too. If anybody tells you it's harmful to masturbate, they're lying. If anybody tells you you mustn't do it too much, they're lying too, because you can't do it too much. Ask them how often you ought to do it. They'll usually shut up then.'

The Little White Book says this about it:

'It is only in the last few years that this subject, which is of a very personal nature, has been given great prominence. All this publicity provokes curiosity and perhaps experimentation which might never have otherwise arisen.

This being the situation, we feel we must say a few words here.

You live in a sex-mad world, and we know this makes it difficult for you. We only want to help you not to become a slave to this habit.

God created you not to be dominated by your passions, but to rule over them. It is worth remembering that sex as God gave it is for sharing between male and female in a life-long partnership.

There is only one way in which you can emerge through this sexual propaganda which is raging against you day and night—by continually following Jesus Christ.'

Evangelists were handing out free copies of *The Little White Book* outside the Inner London Quarter Sessions—now the Inner London Crown Court—in the autumn of 1971 as, inside the building, John Mortimer QC argued the appeal of Richard Handyside, the publisher of *The Little Red Schoolbook*, against his conviction by a stipendiary magistrate for obscenity. The prosecution had been brought largely at the instigation of the promoters of *The Little White Book*. Handyside could not believe that his conviction would be upheld; but it was.

My own memory of the appeal, as John Mortimer's junior, is of something resembling a mumming play, as a parade of vicars, bishops, public moralists, doctors, headteachers and psychologists passed through the witness box either denouncing or defending the book, while a wigged judge and two magistrates listened solemnly. The unscripted part was when Mortimer's clerk slipped in to tell him that his wife Penny, who had just given birth to their first child, was haemorrhaging. John, who was cross-examining a bishop, turned to me, said 'Carry on' and shot out of court. He returned two hours later to find me still grappling with the bishop.

The case went on to the European Court of Human Rights in Strasbourg,[1] which sat in plenary session to hear it. Here, surely, a stand would finally be made for the right of free expression guaranteed by Article 10 of the Convention. And a reader of the eventual judgment of the Grand Chamber would have been justified in feeling optimistic as he or she read the court's stirring vindication of the importance of free speech and the need for tolerance in a democratic society. Article 10, you will recall, starts by saying:

> 'Everyone has the right to freedom of expression. This right shall include freedom to hold opinions and to receive and impart information and ideas without interference by public authority and regardless of frontiers.'

By the time the case reached Strasbourg *The Little Red Schoolbook* had been published without reprisal not only in Denmark but in Belgium, Finland, France, Germany, Greece, Iceland, Italy, the Netherlands, Norway, Sweden and Switzerland, to name only states subscribing to the European Convention. It was circulating freely elsewhere within the member states of the Council of Europe, including the part of the UK north of the Border, where a Glasgow bookseller who stocked it had been acquitted by the sheriff court of selling an obscene publication.

[1] *Handyside v United Kingdom* (1976) 1 EHRR 737.

Article 10 of the Convention goes on to permit restrictions and penalties on the exercise of the primary freedom if these are prescribed by law and necessary in a democratic society in the interests of—among other things—the protection of morals. This, said the Court, 'leaves to the Contracting States a margin of appreciation', a margin which is enjoyed both by the national legislature and by the courts which apply the legislation. It was also by then well established, however, that what was 'necessary' was not a matter of local judgment: it required the member state to establish the objective existence of a pressing social need.

The English phrase 'margin of appreciation' has no discernible meaning. It is a literal translation of the French phrase (French being the Strasbourg court's only other official language) *marge d'appréciation*, meaning scope for judgment, which is more or less how the expression has come to be understood since it first appeared in an early judgment of the Court. It signifies a grey area in which states may legitimately differ as to what interference with a fundamental but conditional human right is necessary in a democratic society. But it is subject, the court stressed, to 'European supervision'.

So stated, the doctrine appears unobjectionable; and, as I shall suggest later, it is capable of taking on a valuable role as a basis of dialogue between the courts of member states and the Court of Human Rights itself. But in the *Handyside* case and other relatively early cases of obscenity and blasphemy, the margin of appreciation was used more frequently as a means of ducking difficult questions of free speech.

Handyside v United Kingdom illustrates the paradox. The judgment resonantly limits what it calls 'the power of appreciation' by recalling that 'freedom of expression constitutes one of the essential foundations' of a democratic society, and that no such society can exist without pluralism, tolerance and broadmindedness. To these qualities, said the Court, its supervisory functions required it to pay 'the utmost attention'.

The Court's reason for stepping back, having noted the conditions to which the primary right was subject, was put in this way:

'[I]t is not possible to find in the domestic law of the various Contracting States a uniform European conception of morals. The view taken by their respective laws of the requirements of morals varies from time to time and from place to place, especially in our era which is characterised by a rapid and far-reaching evolution of opinions on the subject. By reason of their direct and continuous contact with the vital forces of their countries, State authorities are in principle in a better position than the international judge to give an opinion on the exact content of these requirements as well as on the "necessity" of a "restriction" or "penalty" intended to meet them.'

This passage overlooks one crucial variable: as well as differing from state to state and from time to time, moral standards differ from individual to individual. And it is to the protection of the individual's right to speak according to his or her own lights that Article 10 is principally directed. The article goes on to allow a societal restriction where this is objectively necessary 'for the protection of morals'. But whose morals? Both the Convention and the Court assume, without apparently recognising the paradox inherent in it, that the morals requiring protection are a consensual, or at least a majoritarian, set of values of which the domestic courts are the best judges. To assume this is arguably to exclude the very thing that Article 10 exists to protect: the right, even shockingly, to contest conventional wisdom.

Close behind the moral excoriation of *The Little Red Schoolbook* there may have lurked a political agenda. The book had taken its name from the booklet in which the Thoughts of Chairman Mao were being circulated worldwide. But although *The Little Red Schoolbook* presented itself as a parallel gesture of defiance, its content was a great deal less abstract than Mao's. It encouraged children to stand up for themselves against adults but took great trouble to explain the difficulties under which adults themselves—teachers for example, and parents—functioned. It gave sane and accurate advice about drugs, sex and contraception. It counselled honesty in relationships. It explained that homosexuality was not abnormal but that homosexuals 'in our Christian culture ... are considered sick, abnormal or even criminal'—an assertion which, if proof were needed, could be readily confirmed from the pages of *The Little White Book*:

> 'The danger for you is that practising homosexuals are very aggressive, not only in order to get equal rights, but also in order to satisfy sexual desire by seducing people into this way of life who were not born homosexual. ... Jesus Christ can deliver the homosexual. Instead of excusing his tendencies the homosexual must turn away from his sin.'

And a page later:

> 'It is questionable whether it is not abnormal and artificial for young people to feel compelled to take sides about the situations in Vietnam, South Africa, Pakistan, Czechoslovakia, or the Middle East.'

The *Handyside* case continues to prompt concern that the book's real offence was to encourage young people to think unofficial thoughts, to defy conventional wisdom and to take responsibility for themselves. It seems inconceivable that it could be successfully prosecuted in England today. But there remains a corresponding worry that the Strasbourg court, in deferring to the judgment of the Inner London Quarter Sessions, failed to stand up for the right to contest accepted moral standards.

Handyside was followed during the 1990s by two comparably problematical cases. One[2] arose out of the seizure by the Austrian authorities of a satirical film on a charge of disparaging religious doctrines. The other,[3] not long afterwards, arose out of the refusal by the BBFC of a classification certificate for a video, *Visions of Ecstasy*, which from a Christian standpoint was blasphemous. Both bans were found by the Strasbourg court to involve no violation of the Convention, in each instance by reason of the state's margin of appreciation.

The Otto Preminger Institut had scheduled a showing of a satirical film, *Das Liebeskonzil,* to persons 17 years of age or over. Proceedings were brought under a section of the Austrian penal code which criminalised disparagement or insult directed at objects of veneration or belief and 'likely to arouse justified indignation'. According to the regional court which ordered forfeiture of the film, in it 'God the Father is presented ... as a senile, impotent idiot, Christ as a cretin and Mary Mother of God as a wanton lady ...'. But the Austrian basic law guaranteed 'freedom of artistic creation', and the Institut contended that the forfeiture violated Article 10 of the Convention. The government contended that it was aimed at protecting the rights of others and the prevention of disorder.

The Court this time acknowledged that, as to the significance of religion, 'even within a single country ... conceptions may vary'.

> 'For that reason it is not possible to arrive at a comprehensive definition of what constitutes a permissible interference with the exercise of the right to freedom of expression where such expression is directed against the religious feelings of others. A certain margin of appreciation is therefore to be left to the national authorities. ...'

The Court went on to reiterate that the margin was not unrestricted: 'The necessity for any restriction must be convincingly

---

[2] *Otto-Preminger Institut v Austria* (1995) 19 EHRR 34.
[3] *Wingrove v United Kingdom* (1997) 24 EHRR 1.

established'—as it was by the fact that 87 per cent of the local population was Catholic and by the need to 'ensure religious peace' and prevent the giving of religious offence. The fact that nobody was obliged to watch the film seems to have been overlooked.

The second case, *Wingrove v United Kingdom*, by contrast involved a permissible assumption that the video, if released, would be watched. It was an 18 minute sequence reimagining the ecstasy of St Teresa of Avila in terms which, while not wholly different in kind from much Catholic martyrology, were overtly erotic in presentation. The British Board of Film Classification, in the exercise of its statutory powers, refused the video a classification certificate and thereby prevented it from being distributed. It considered the video to be blasphemous according to the common law definition which effectively limited hostile publications about Christianity to 'decent and temperate' criticism.

In Strasbourg this view was held to sit within the UK's margin of appreciation and so to have caused no breach of Article 10. Whereas, the Court said, the scope for restricting political speech was very limited, 'a wider margin of appreciation is generally available to Contracting States when regulating freedom of expression in relation to matters liable to offend intimate personal convictions within the sphere of morals or, especially, religion.' This, moreover, would vary significantly from time to time and from place to place. But in UK law 'the high degree of profanation that must be attained constitutes in itself a safeguard against arbitrariness'.

So it was that a visual commentary on what some quite rational people consider to be the sado-eroticism of much Catholic martyrology was denied an airing.

STRASBOURG AND EUROPE

What the margin of appreciation has arguably enabled the Court to do in these cases, touching as they do raw nerves of embarrassment and credence, is to uphold intolerant and populist decisions without the responsibility of forming its own judgment on what are *par excellence* Convention questions. That, at least, is one view. The other is that the Court has been doing in these cases something it ought to have been doing much more widely—leaving member states, and especially the older democracies, to do things their way unless a clear and inexcusable departure from the Convention has been established.

The second of these models of Convention adjudication has received increasingly vocal support, first from the UK's right-wing press and politicians, but more recently from one of the engineers of the Human Rights Act, Tony Blair's first Lord Chancellor, Lord Irvine. Derry Irvine in December 2011 came out of retirement to argue that the United Kingdom's courts had been slavishly following Strasbourg jurisprudence instead of having no more than a decent regard to it (as mandated by the Human Rights Act) in the course of developing their own human rights jurisprudence.

Among a number of criticisms to which Irvine's thesis is open is the fact that there has in reality been no consistent history of slavish adherence to Strasbourg. It was evident to the UK judges, for example, that the Court had made a serious mistake in the *Saunders* case[4] on the admissibility of self-incriminating evidence obtained in the course of a statutory inquiry, a mistake which had led to the gutting of a large number of crime-fighting statutes. So when, following Scottish devolution, the Privy Council had to deal with the case of a visibly drunk woman in a Dunfermline supermarket who had told police officers, as she was legally obliged to do, that it was she who had driven her car there, it refused to follow the *Saunders* decision and held that the woman had been lawfully convicted of drunk driving on her own admission.[5]

In fact the abscess was lanced the day after Irvine's speech by a groundbreaking decision of the Strasbourg court in *Al-Khawaja and Tahery v United Kingdom*.[6] The British president of the Court, Sir Nicolas Bratza, had already trailed the change of position in a published article.[7] He now led the Court in establishing a fresh paradigm: not the top-down supervision of national decisions by an international tribunal—albeit leaving a margin of local judgment in certain cases—but a 'judicial dialogue between national courts and the European court on the application of the Convention'.

The metaphor of dialogue is not new: it has been used for many years to describe the relationship (or at least the hoped-for

---

[4] *Saunders v United Kingdom* (1997) 23 EHRR 313; reversed *sub silentio* in *O'Halloran v UK* (2008) 46 EHRR 21.

[5] *Brown v Stott* [2000] UKPC D3.

[6] *Al-Khawaja and Tahery v United Kingdom* (Application Nos 26766/05 and 22228/06) [2012] Crim LR 375. The Court on 7 February 2012 confirmed its policy in an important decision, *Von Hannover v Germany (No 2)*, which spelt out a mechanism for invigilating national courts without second-guessing them. See further Ch 10.

[7] 'The relationship between the UK courts and Strasbourg' [2011] *EHRLR* 505.

relationship) between the courts and the legislatures of Canada in implementing the 1983 Charter of Rights and Freedoms. But its application in the *Al-Khawaja* case to the relationship between the supranational court and the national ones is a radical departure. For many years the Court had held that a criminal trial was not fair if it produced a conviction based solely or decisively on hearsay testimony. In a Europe with widely divergent criminal processes one size was not going to fit all, and in no case more so than that of the United Kingdom, with a system of jury trial unlike any other in Europe. The Supreme Court had said as much in *R v Horncastle*,[8] declining to follow Strasbourg's jurisprudence on the issue, not only because it is often impossible to know whether a particular piece of evidence has been decisive in the jury's thinking, but also because decisiveness is itself an elusive concept.

> 'I share the view of the majority,' said the President, 'that to apply the [Court's] rule inflexibly, ignoring the specificities of the particular legal system concerned, would run counter to the traditional way in which the Court has, in other contexts, approached the issue of the overall fairness of criminal proceedings.'

It was not entirely helpful that this change of position was taking place under the shadow of xenophobic and nationalistic attacks on the competence of a court which those who know it consider to be of generally high calibre. But it is sufficient for the present to observe that the latitude which member states can now expect is not the old margin of appreciation. It was one thing to defer to a local judgment as to whether a book or a film breached an accepted legal standard which incorporated an indeterminate moral standard. It is another to recognise that, while due process is an unyielding requirement of the Convention and its fairness a matter of objective judgment for the Court, it has in practice to accommodate widely differing legal systems, none of which can be classed as inherently unfair.

This is a very different thing, not least because it means the margin is now located not in the member state but in Strasbourg. In other words, rather than merely allowing each member state to do things despite the fact that they impinge on human rights, the Court has now undertaken the task of differentiating between national legal systems and coming to its own conclusions about them.

---

[8] *R v Horncastle* [2009] UKSC 14.

7

Does the Separation of Powers Still Work?

These reflections on the use of parliamentary privilege to circumvent court injunctions were published in the London Review of Books *in June 2011.*[1]

FOR MORE THAN 300 years the UK's constitution has functioned remarkably well on the basis of the historic compromise reached in the course of the seventeenth century. The 1689 Bill of Rights forbade the impeachment or questioning of parliamentary debates and proceedings 'in any court or place out of Parlyament'. Parliament in return has made it a rule, enforced until now by the Speakers of both Houses, that it will not interfere with the decisions of the courts, whether by anticipating their judgments or by attacking them. If Parliament does not like what the courts do, it changes the law. The sovereignty of Parliament as the final source of law and the sovereignty of the courts in interpreting and enforcing the law are the twin pillars on which democracy and the rule of law in the UK rest. It was the courts themselves which, in the nineteenth century, extended the privilege of Parliament to cover any fair and full report of what was said there even if it was libellous.

When a member of either House, protected by the privilege which prevents his being prosecuted for it, consciously breaks a High Court injunction by naming an individual who has been anonymised by court order, it suggests two possibilities. One is that he does not understand the constitution; the other is that he does and has set out to transgress it. In spite of protests from members of both Houses who understand very well what is at stake, neither Speaker has taken any steps against the offenders.

---

[1] Concerns about the separation of powers are developed in Chapter 8 under the subheading 'Impartiality and independence'.

This is the seriousness of the naming of Fred Goodwin in the House of Lords and Ryan Giggs in the House of Commons as claimants who had obtained injunctions forbidding their identification. It does not have to do with limiting free speech in Parliament: it has to do with the misuse of that undoubted historic freedom. It does not even depend on the fact that Giggs's name was initially disclosed by the *Sunday Herald* in Scotland, and not in England where the injunction was issued (cross-border jurisdiction is hideously complex). Nor is it, as the media keep saying it is, a situation of chaos or confusion. It is a simple breach of a simple constitutional principle. What is chaotic and confused is much of the media coverage of the law of privacy and injunctions, both of them repeatedly described as 'judge-made'.

The courts had long ago developed limited remedies to prevent breaches of confidentiality, but these failed in 1990 to protect the actor Gorden Kaye from a shameful invasion of his hospital room by journalists, and it was Parliament that brought the individual's right to respect for his or her private life into UK law when it enacted the Human Rights Act in 1998. It is this right that the courts have a constitutional obligation to make effective. What the tabloids do not like about it is that the law now recognises that celebrities too have aspects of their lives that are private.

Over many years the courts have also developed, with Parliament's tacit approval, a range of sanctions to make their orders effective. These necessarily include a power to punish anyone who knowingly defies a court order. For a long time the media respected court orders, making it possible simply to forbid any repetition of the contested allegations so that they could be fairly tried in court. What then started to happen was that some newspapers would name the claimant and hint unmistakably at what was being alleged. When the courts in consequence began to suppress the name of the claimant, the papers would instead spell out the anonymised allegations and sometimes run adjacent stories or pictures which made it not too hard to guess who the claimant was. Hence the super-injunction forbidding both. This is anathema not only to the press but to any system of open justice, but it was forced on the courts by the repeated undermining of their orders. Hence too the fact that very few have been granted, since by definition they have been obtained by people who can afford to litigate and are famous enough to have attracted the tabloids' eye.

When the European Convention on Human Rights was written and adopted in the early 1950s, few doubted that the chief threat to private life was the state—the informer, the watcher, the secret policeman. Today there is widespread agreement that segments of the press and television pose a different but still real threat to private life, and the jurisprudence of the Convention has shifted to keep pace with the change. In Strasbourg the UK was initially found to lack any proper law to protect privacy (which goes much wider than confidentiality). When the early human rights claim brought by Michael Douglas and Catherine Zeta-Jones over the intrusion into their wedding reception of a pirate photographer who sold his pictures to *Hello!* magazine came before the Court of Appeal, I suggested that the common law governing confidentiality had matured to a point at which the courts could recognise privacy as a protected value rather than relying on a fictitious duty of confidentiality owed by *Hello!* to the Douglases. This was rejected by the House of Lords, bringing down on our head the Strasbourg court's decision that the UK had failed to give effect to the Article 8 privacy right in its domestic law. Hence Naomi Campbell's subsequent, even though pyrrhic, victory in relation to the exposure of her treatment for drug addiction.[2] The German courts were then found to have given insufficient protection to Princess Caroline of Monaco, swarmed about by paparazzi wherever she went; while the French courts were found to have given excessive protection, under Article 9 of the civil code, to news of Mitterrand's cancer, a subject of legitimate public concern. None of this suggests either unworldliness or excessive interventionism on the part of the European Court of Human Rights: rather the striking of a balance between the entitlement of the public to know about things that matter and the right of individuals (including famous ones—why else would anyone care?) to some space of their own. The huffy official reaction in Germany to the Princess Caroline decision, and the accompanying threat that the case would be taken to the Grand Chamber, subsided as it dawned on politicians that Strasbourg had done them something of a personal favour.

Observers with a sense of history have noted that the tabloids' self-justification, advanced in the name of press freedom, mirrors that of the authoritarian state. The *Sun* columnist Jane Moore admonishes errant public figures: 'If you don't want your private life splashed all over the papers, then behave yourselves.' Or, as it was once put, if you have nothing to hide you have nothing to fear—for there is only

---

[2] For a fuller account of the rapid shifts in UK privacy law, see S Sedley, *Lions Under the Throne* pp 202–205.

one way the state or the *Sun* can know whether you are behaving yourself.

This is why the issues are large. It can be credibly said that the fourth estate is close to being a state within the state, unregulated except to the modest extent that it chooses to regulate itself and alternately feared and pandered to by public figures. Its merchandising of voyourism might be worth debating if that were the way it was promoted; but the eye at the keyhole is presented as that of the public moralist: because stars are role models, it is argued with a straight face, the exposure of their promiscuous sex lives will appropriately deflate the young's perception of them. The near certainty that the exciting prospect of being able to have sex with anyone you choose will add to the glamour of being a professional footballer does not appear to enter the mind of the tabloid moralist, for whom double standards are what somebody else has.

The Goodwin-Giggs debacle has not come out of the blue. More than one minister in the Major and Blair governments broke convention by publicly attacking not only decisions they found objectionable but the judges who had given them. But ministers speak as the heads of executive departments, and the executive is not party to the dual sovereignty of Parliament and the courts: despite its great power, it answers politically to the one and legally to the other. The current crisis was prefigured when David Cameron in Parliament spoke damagingly about the Supreme Court's decision that some sex offenders ought to be able in the course of time to ask to be removed from the register, calling it 'completely offensive' and contrary to common sense; an attack taken up by the Home Secretary, who thought it appropriate to question the sanity of the decision.

But the naming of Goodwin and Giggs is on a different plane from ministerial briefings against judges, inappropriate as these are, because it disrupts the historic equilibrium between the judiciary and the legislature. The media may present themselves as amused or bemused spectators, but it is they who have provoked and exploited the breakdown of a component of the democracy they themselves inhabit.

Law and Rights

8

The Role of the Judge

Part of a paper given to the New Zealand judiciary in March 2014—
perhaps slightly more unbuttoned than an article for a public journal
would have been.

INDEPENDENCE AND DICEY

EVERYBODY BELIEVES IN the rule of law, but few people could tell you what it means; and for everyone who could tell you, there would be two others to say they were wrong. But we at least know, or think we know, that the concept originated with Albert Venn Dicey's *Introduction to the Study of the Law of the Constitution*, first published in 1885.

Dicey's book was divided into three parts. The first was 'The sovereignty of Parliament', something which Dicey took to be fundamental, total and beyond challenge. As Brian Simpson wrote:[1] 'Dicey announced that it was the law that Parliament was omnicompetent,[2] explained what this meant, and never devoted so much as a line to fulfilling the promise he made to demonstrate that this was so.' Moreover, when some three decades later Irish home rule came on to Parliament's agenda, Dicey changed his mind about its omnipotence, lamenting in his final edition in 1915 that parliamentary sovereignty had fallen prey to the party system—something repeatedly pointed out by political scientists before him.[3]

Dicey's second section was 'The rule of law'. His third dealt, much more briefly, with constitutional conventions. He listed the components of what he took to be the rule of law as follows: first, that there could be no punishment or penalty save for a proven breach

---

[1] 'The Common Law and Legal Theory' in AWB Simpson, *Legal Theory and Legal History* (1987) p 378.

[2] In fact Dicey's word was 'omnipotent'. Even he recognised that Parliament had to devolve many of its functions because of its limited competence.

[3] Eg Walter Bagheot.

of the law; secondly that the same law applied to everyone and was administered in the ordinary courts; and thirdly that it was from decisions of the courts, and not from any fixed constitution that these principles sprang. Even though Dicey continues to be credited with having both identified and articulated the concept of the rule of law, no modern account of it comes anywhere near adopting these as its defining components. For example, although Dicey forgot to mention it, trial before independent and impartial courts is one of the most fundamental requirements of anything worth calling the rule of law.

One striking characteristic of Dicey's thesis, so apparent that it is commonly overlooked, is that it is not couched in theoretical or normative terms at all: it is a Panglossian account (and an incomplete and inaccurate one) of the English legal system at the height of its Victorian self-assurance, as disparaging of foreign systems as it is boastful about our own, reading more like a pamphlet than a textbook. But where Mr Podsnap considered that our constitution had been 'Bestowed Upon Us By Providence', Dicey dismissed as 'absurd' the proposition that the British constitution 'has not been made but has grown'; on the contrary, Dicey said, it was 'a judge-made constitution'—an assertion of comparable absurdity. He was seemingly unable to comprehend the complex mass of historical forces—political, legislative and prerogative, as well as judicial—which had gone into the making of a constitution which contained far more than his account of it allowed. Dicey has now been debunked many times,[4] but he is still taught in the law schools because the rule of law continues, for good reason, to have a totemic importance. Yet it is hard to dispute Ferdinand Mount's appraisal: 'It seems extraordinary that such an erratic and violent thinker could ever have achieved such monumental status as a constitutional authority.'[5]

THE SEPARATION OF POWERS

There continues to be a consensus that, whatever else the rule of law demands, it requires a significant measure of separation between the legislative, the judicial and the executive powers of the

---

[4] Starting with WA Robson, *Justice and Administrative Law* (Macmillan, 1928); see also HW Arthurs, *Without the Law* (University of Toronto Press, 1985) and 'Rethinking administrative law: a slightly Dicey business' (1979) 17 *Osgoode Hall LJ* 1.

[5] Ferdinand Mount, *The British Constitution Now* (Mandarin, 1992) p 56.

state. But it is increasingly doubtful whether this tripartite division, derived from Locke at the end of England's century of revolution and enshrined by Montesquieu in the twilight French autocracy and Madison in the dawn of American republicanism, is any longer adequate. Even in the eighteenth and nineteenth centuries the established church in England and the Catholic church in France were arguably discrete powers within the state. (There was nothing comparable in the USA because the constitution deliberately excluded it.) In many modern democracies it can be argued that the security services have acquired a degree of autonomy and of influence over the other limbs of the state which ranks them as a separate power. And while Burke's characterisation of the press as the fourth estate of the realm was probably intended as a compliment, it also represents a serious truth: that the media are today able to influence, even dictate, tranches of public policy, basing their claim to democratic legitimacy on a popular mandate which they themselves have constructed. I will come in a moment to the implications of this for judicial independence.

Before I do so, I want to focus a little more sharply on the judicial component of the state's powers. Madison was very clear, in the *Federalist*, that Montesquieu had been right to characterise the judiciary as the weakest of the state's three branches, so that 'all possible care is requisite to enable it to defend itself' against attack by the other two. By the end of the nineteenth century Dicey, by contrast, felt able to claim that the English constitution (he always excluded the Scots) was in all its essentials judge-made. He was as wrong about this as about most other things, but he would have gone along with Madison, were it not for his xenophobic refusal to say anything good about the French, in adopting Montesquieu's adage: 'There is no liberty, if the power of judging be not separated from the legislative and executive powers.'[6]

A significant measure of interdependence between legislature and executive, albeit it has come close in our era to symbiosis, has always been recognised as unavoidable. The same is not the case with the judicial power. While the judiciary, following the historic compromise at the end of the seventeenth century, accords Parliament the last word on what the law is to be, it is the function of the courts alone to determine what the law is, and to apply it.

---

[6] *The Federalist*, LXXVIII; Montesquieu, *L'esprit des lois*, I.181.

IMPARTIALITY AND INDEPENDENCE

To say independent, however, is to beg some large questions. Independent of what and of whom? The judicial oath, to do justice according to law without fear or favour, affection or ill-will, says most of what needs to be said; but it needs unpacking. First of all, justice according to law is something of a paradox. Not all law produces justice, and not all justice accords with the law. We struggle with this conflict almost daily, and valuable things have been written about it;[7] but it is not my topic now.

Affection and ill-will are the enemies of impartiality—a state of mind. They have to do, of course, with more than the obligation to declare an interest and to recuse oneself.[8] They are palpable in the mental struggle that Crewe CJ described in his judgment in the *Oxford Peerage* case in 1625: 'I have laboured to make a covenant with myself, that affection may not press upon judgment.'[9] For Crewe on that occasion judgment and affection turned out to run in the same channel. But it isn't always the case. All judges know both the satisfaction of reaching a conclusion that feels just, and the dissatisfaction of being driven to a conclusion we would rather not reach. What few of us can do is put it in prose like Crewe's.[10]

I said a moment ago that impartiality is a state of mind. Independence, by contrast, is a state of being, and fear and favour are its enemies. It is easy enough to get public agreement that judges should not have to fear for their jobs every time they give an unpopular judgment, and easy also to get judicial agreement that judges who are no longer fit to sit should stand down. It's in the vast hinterland of these twin peaks that the difficulties arise.

ACCOUNTABILITY

Take, first, the constant use of the adjective 'unaccountable' to describe the judiciary. Of the two distinct things the word signifies, one is false and the other is destructive. The false suggestion is that judges do not explain what they are doing, when the fact is that they

---

[7] Among New Zealand judicial scholars, see EW Thomas, *The Judicial Process* (2005).

[8] See Grant Hammond, *Judicial Recusal* (Bloomsbury, 2009).

[9] *Oxford (Earldom) Petitions*, sub nom *Willoughby of Eresby and Oxford (Earl) Case* (1626) Rolle 173; 82 ER 50.

[10] See the epigraph to this book. But the successful claimant himself died without issue, and the peerage became defunct.

account publicly and in detail for every single thing they decide; and for all but the most elevated of us the account has to bear scrutiny by a superior court. But the commentators who wave the word about don't mean this: they mean that we cannot be unseated and so are beyond democratic control. The fact that making judges removable by some kind of journalistic anathema or fatwa is antithetical both to independence and to the rule of law is eclipsed by the alluring prospect of editors and proprietors being able to campaign for the removal of judges whose decisions they dislike, and—just as useful—to put the fear of God into the rest.

It's perfectly true that there are elected judiciaries in states which respect the rule of law. But anyone who has read John Grisham's *The Appeal*, which knowingly or unwittingly tracked an actual case,[11] will appreciate how candidates for the state bench can be bought by powerful litigants. I recall a conversation with a chief justice of Texas, who had to run periodically for office ('You run as a Republican—you don't get elected any other way in Texas'), his campaign bankrolled by law firms who appeared regularly in his court. Was that embarrassing in any way? 'Not a problem,' he said.

But the federal judiciary is appointed for life—and for judges in the US, as for many prisoners, life means life—albeit through a heavily politicised process. Once appointed, federal judges can be removed only for misconduct. The same is true of the English judiciary under the 1701 Act of Settlement;[12] but no bad English judge in three centuries and more ever faced impeachment for unfitness or misconduct.[13]

JUDGES AND THE MEDIA

Accountability aside, media pressure is a present and growing problem for judges at all levels. Reaction to it can take two extreme forms. At one end, there is the occasional judge who has an uncontrollable urge to ingratiate himself or herself with the media. In England the worst modern example has probably been James Pickles, the circuit judge who boasted publicly about his dubious judicial talents and ended up, briefly, as a chat show host and a columnist for the *Sun* newspaper. At the other is the judge who is so publicity-shy that

[11] See Ch 14.
[12] Now the Senior Courts Act 1981, s 11.
[13] Constitutional Reform Act 2005, ss 108, 109. See further Ch 14.

he will not have a drink in a pub for fear of being photographed there—in parodic form, the Most-Feared Judge in Theo Mathew's *Forensic Fables* who, at the end of a day spent bullying counsel and terrorising witnesses, would return to the digs he had lived in since he was a student and cry himself to sleep with a children's book.

Most of us try to position ourselves somewhere between these two poles. But we are not sophisticated in media relations, and a number of judges have been caught off guard by a polite and deferential approach that has resulted in toxic publicity. The old journalistic trick of politely asking for an interview too often works: the judge, in the course of declining to be interviewed, explains at length why he or she has nothing of interest to say (sometimes disastrously including the words 'We're just good friends'), and realises too late that the request for an interview was a red herring: the journalist by now has everything necessary for a story.

Media training, which the UK judiciary have at times been offered, tends to compound the problems. PR consultants advise you to turn up in the studio with three points which you propose to make regardless of the questions. This is bad enough when politicians do it, as they regularly do. If a judge does it, it suggests evasiveness and arrogance. But even if you deal candidly with the questions, you cannot stop the broadcaster editing, misreporting or sensationalising what you have said.

In the UK this has not meant total radio silence. A series of sound broadcasts called 'Unreliable evidence', made for the BBC using judges and practising lawyers to discuss serious issues for a full hour and going out with only minimal editing, has set a high standard for public service broadcasting about the law. But the big problem is not what judges say to the media. It is what the media say to and about the judges. In the UK, and it would be surprising if it were only the UK, both the tabloid and increasingly the broadsheet press no longer have any fear of denouncing and on occasion traducing judges whose decisions they do not like. The era when Lord Hewart was able to announce 'His Majesty's judges are satisfied with the almost universal admiration in which they are held',[14] and in which a Lord Mayor could tell the judiciary that they had 'a greater understanding of human nature than any other body of men in the world',[15] is mercifully gone. So are the days when murmuring

[14] Hewart's speech at the Lord Mayor's dinner, 1936.
[15] The Lord Mayor at the 1953 dinner.

judges, as contempt of the judiciary was called in Scotland, could be visited with fines or imprisonment. To take free speech about ourselves seriously we need broad backs, for a bench which sits as judge in its own cause is bad news for the rule of law. But that does not mean that the law of libel should not protect judicial reputations, or that judges should not use whatever extra-judicial mechanisms exist for correcting falsehoods in the media.

None of this, however, addresses what I believe to be the most radical effect of the media on the judicial function: the probability that a particular decision in the case before you will provoke media outrage, whether real or simulated. The pressure is increased by the knowledge that some papers—the *Daily Mail* most prominently in the UK—specialise in personalising issues on their editorial agenda.[16] It is in such cases that the constitutional obligation to decide without fear or favour comes under the greatest stress. I don't imagine any of us has consciously given in to it; yet its effects are everywhere. When I became a judge in 1992, the going rate for a daytime burglary of an unoccupied house was 18 months. It is now three years, and the prisons are bulging. The main thing that has changed in that time has been the amplification of the media chorus denouncing judges as soft on crime. The fact that government research has shown that most jurors, asked afterwards, would have given lighter sentences than the judge[17] is not a fact which sells newspapers. The dominant canon of journalistic faith is that judges are out of touch with what the press considers itself entitled to characterise as public opinion, since it is the press itself which generates it.

Possibly the central paradox in the judicial role is that judges are simultaneously intensely private and intensely public individuals: public because everything they do as judges is open to scrutiny and criticism, not least from their own colleagues; private because they must avoid situations which may compromise their independence or appear to do so. Yet it is the refrain that we are out of touch that drives the critique. The fact that judges learn more than most others, including journalists, about the detail and the downsides of other people's lives passes the critics by.

---

[16] The lowest point so far is probably the *Daily Mail*'s 2017 denunciation, with prominent photographs and personal details, of the three judges who had ruled against the government on the power to give notice of departure from the EU, as 'Enemies of the people'.
[17] JM Hough and JV Roberts, *Attitudes to Punishment* (Home Office Research Study #179, 1998).

JUDICIAL IMMUNITY

There is one genuinely problematical dimension of accountability which I have not yet touched on: judicial immunity from suit. Every other professional person is today liable in damages for losses directly caused by professional misconduct on their part. Why not judges?

The immunity of judges from tort claims arising out of their conduct of proceedings or their judgments is of long standing. Tom Bingham in *The Rule of Law* traces it to statutory provisions long antedating the Act of Settlement 1701, though manifestly postdating the impeachment by the Long Parliament of the judges who upheld the imposition of the Ship Money. But as articulated since then it has been an artefact of the common law.

Even viewed in isolation, the judiciary creating law for its own protection is not an attractive sight. But the language in which it has been done has on occasion been truly embarrassing: 'The public are deeply interested in this rule, which indeed exists for their benefit and was established to secure the independence of the judges' said a judge in 1863. 'There is something so monstrous in the contrary doctrine,' a judge had said half a century earlier, 'that it would poison the very source of justice and introduce a system of servility'.

It really is not helpful to conflate two quite different things in this way. There can be no question about the need for protection from the threat of reprisal by way of a negligence claim for an unwelcome decision or for the way a case has been conducted— for example by believing a witness whose veracity or reliability is contested. Without protection from such claims, judicial independence is devoid of meaning. But does it follow that a judge who can be proved to have acted maliciously or corruptly should share the immunity?

I have argued in the past, and still think, that if there is one topic on which it is Parliament and not the judges who should have the last word, it is the breadth of judicial immunity from suit. When Trinidad achieved independence, the constitution it was given by the Crown included fair trial rights enforceable against the state. When a young Trinidadian barrister, Ramesh Maharaj, was improperly gaoled for contempt by a judge to whom he had stood up, the Privy Council upheld his claim for damages against the state. For if it is the state which guarantees a fair trial and the state which provides the judge to conduct it, it is not illogical that it is the state which should pay if the judicial oath is violated by ill-will.

Lawsuits aside, there is also the possibility of limited tenure. Dr Johnson regretted the demise of the old custom by which all judicial offices became vacant on the death of the monarch, enabling the Crown not to reappoint those who had come to the end of their shelf-life. It's a system which would certainly produce a degree of fervour as the judges, joining in the national anthem at the service in Westminster Abbey marking the start of the legal year, reach the line 'Long may she reign'. But such a system would allow the executive to pay off old scores and the press to campaign for lapsing judges they disliked.

An alternative is what Kenya has set up under its new constitution: an independent board including judges from other countries, charged with vetting the entire judiciary one by one for corruption or unfitness for office. In its first report the board advised the removal from office of four members of the Court of Appeal whose behaviour in court had, in its judgment, habitually been so bad as to deny parties a fair trial. Notwithstanding the board's elegantly crafted report,[18] such intervention comes perilously close to a breach of the principle of secure tenure of office; but in a country where public confidence in the judiciary had hit the floor, there was reason for it.

Elsewhere the reason has been less good. Eastern European states with no tradition of judicial independence continue to regard the dismissal and replacement of their senior judges as a natural perquisite of political office. Advice given to the Serbian judges, to which I was party, after the fall of Milosevich was to follow the South African philosophy and accept that leaving appointees of the old regime in office until retirement was a wiser course, however painful, than purging the bench and placing the judiciary from then on in permanent fear of dismissal. The advice was not taken, and the rule of law has been the sufferer.

---

[18] Kenya Judges and Magistrates Vetting Board, *Determinations*, 2012–13 ff.

9

Anonymity and the Right to Lie

This was a London Review of Books *article (published here in slightly fuller form) on a book by Eric Barendt,* Anonymous Speech: Literature, Law and Politics *(2016), which raised a series of important issues about the concealment of identity.*

THE ITALIAN PAPER *Il Sole 24 Ore* recently took it on itself to identify the pseudonymous author of the Neapolitan novels, Elena Ferrante, as the translator Anita Raja. Assuming that the journalist responsible for the exposure has got it right (there is some evidence pointing to Raja's husband, the writer Domenico Starnone, as the true author), has the press—or anyone else come to that—any moral right to do this? Is an author's identity an aspect of her personal privacy, to be disclosed or withheld as she chooses? Or is it information which belongs as much in the public domain as the books she writes?

Anonymous and pseudonymous publication has a long history, painstakingly documented in Halkett and Laing's *Dictionary of the Anonymous and Pseudonymous Literature of Great Britain*, first published in 1883. John Mullan, in *Anonymity: a Secret History of English Literature* (2007), proposed a broad taxonomy of the reasons authors have had for concealing their identity: diffidence (especially in relation to first novels); fear of consequences (the Marprelate tracts); mischief-making (Swift and Pope *ad lib*); disguising the author's gender (Jane Austen, George Eliot, the Brontë sisters); and more besides.

For some writers the mask becomes the face. George Eliot is one instance; George Orwell another. Why, though, did Eric Blair choose as his pen-name a modest river in Suffolk? The question has exercised critics, biographers and commentators, Eric Barendt among them. Louis Marks, the last of the Fleet Street booksellers who bought surplus review copies from newspapers' literary editors at one third of cover price and resold them at two thirds, once told me that he had asked Blair, on one of his visits to Marks's shop with

Tribune's unwanted review copies, why he had chosen the pen-name George Orwell. Blair said that it was to ensure that his books were near the centre of Marks' alphabetical arrangement of authors. He was probably pulling Marks's leg; but has anyone considered the alternative likelihood that he had self-deprecatingly adopted, as a suitable pen-name for a polemicist, a homophone for 'jaw-jaw well'?

In literary and specialist journalism anonymity may now be the exception, but at the start of the nineteenth century it was pretty much the rule, to the extent that France in 1850 legislated to forbid the publication of unsigned articles on philosophical, political and religious issues. Barendt traces the contemporaneous voluntary abandonment of anonymity in England and the often pompous arguments that accompanied it. The fact was that journals' recruitment of well-known writers—Thackeray, Dickens—was starting to put a premium on names. So when the *Fortnightly Review* started up in 1865, it announced that all its articles would be signed and free of editorial pressure. By contrast, from its foundation in 1913 the *New Statesman* anonymised its contributors, though the editor, having explained that this was necessary in order to establish a common style and tone, couldn't resist announcing that Sidney Webb and Bernard Shaw would be writing for it. In 1925 the *Spectator*, after not quite a hundred years of unsigned articles, abandoned anonymity, and the *New Statesman* followed not long afterwards. Articles in the *Times Literary Supplement* remained anonymous until 1974, and obituaries in *The Times* and *Telegraph* are unsigned to this day. So are the entirety of the *Economist* and the bulk of *Private Eye*.

As an academic lawyer Barendt, while acknowledging his debt to Mullan's work, is interested in who benefits, who profits and who loses by anonymity. Important among the first of these are whistle-blowers, journalists' sources and internet trolls; among the second, government and the media; among the third, trolls' victims.

TROLLING

Take trolls, whom the shield of anonymity enables to disseminate insult and calumny which they would not have the nerve to transmit if it was known who they were. Psychologists have baptised it the online disinhibition effect. Not only where it involves threats to kill, as it frequently does, but also where it is obscene, menacing or racist, as it frequently is, it constitutes a criminal offence. It also does widespread, often lasting and sometimes lethal harm. Not every target of trolling has Mary Beard's or Caroline Criado-Perez's fortitude. But human rights law still does not tell us whether the right of free expression includes a right to withhold the writer's or speaker's identity. And behind this silence lurks a larger one which free speech theory has trouble in even addressing: is there a right to lie?

LYING

There are many kinds of lying which the law already catches: lying to defraud people of money or property; lying about someone's character; lying to obtain a job. In Germany and a number of other states Holocaust denial is a statutory lie and a crime. But, such offences aside, human rights law has found itself unable to draw a line between freedom to speak your mind and freedom to fabricate, falsify or mislead. The reason is not hard to see: a court called upon to adjudicate on, for instance, some of the tall stories propagated in the course of the EU referendum campaign would have had to assume the role of a ministry of truth. At the same time, free speech advocacy needs to face up to the full magnitude of what it advocates; for nobody today can seriously believe that there exists some utopian forum, a marketplace of ideas, where the true drives out the false. If anything, the converse is true. Timothy Garton Ash, acknowledging in his book *Free Speech* the ubiquity of lies in American political argument, responds: 'Yet at least in most democratic countries there are two (or more) competing false narratives, and having two is more than twice as good as having only one'. Are lies really self-cancelling, or is the candid answer that freedom to lie is part of the price paid for freedom to speak?

ANONYMITY

Anonymity compounds the conundrum. To expose or refute falsehood can be hard, but it can be far harder when you don't know who the falsehood is coming from. Internet providers, who know who their users are, claim to be as fully justified in protecting their identity as Elena Ferrante's publisher in protecting hers. Does the law have anything useful to say about such claims?

The Court of Appeal has declined to accept that the right of free expression in Article 10 of the European Convention on Human

Rights accords a source any right to the preservation of his or her anonymity. In consequence, and also because it was being relied on to conceal criminal conduct, it afforded no protection to a prison officer who had sold a journalist information about some notorious prisoners. The journalist was acquitted on grounds of public interest; the prison officer went to jail for misconduct in public office.

In 2009 a serving police officer whose blog, written under the alias Night Jack, had just won the Orwell Prize for citizen journalism, tried to stop *The Times* revealing his identity. His case was based both on his entitlement to privacy and on his right to freedom of expression. He lost. The High Court held that he had no reasonable expectation of privacy since blogging was an essentially public activity, and that in any event the public interest in knowing that it was a policeman who was excoriating politicians and the police service outweighed any privacy interest Night Jack might lay claim to.

So far so liberal, you might say. But there is an unwholesome contrast between the judicial vindication of journalists' right to name names and the protection afforded by the law to the identity of journalists' own sources. If, as Barendt points out, Night Jack, instead of running his own blog, had taken his criticisms and revelations to *The Times* and *The Times* had published them, any attempt by the police to force the paper to identify him would in all probability have failed. Since 1981 contempt of court legislation has restricted the courts' power to compel the disclosure of journalists' sources to cases where to do so is necessary for national security or for the ends of justice, law and order; and the Strasbourg court has adopted a parallel approach to the privacy and free expression rights in the European Convention. This works well enough where sources are honest and dependable; but when the source is plausible but malicious, or the story, though almost certainly invented, is irresistibly sensational, justification of the protection begins to look dubious. Yet how can you judge whether information is contaminated by malice without knowing who the source is—assuming, what is not always the case, that the publisher itself knows?

SOURCES

It is not widely appreciated that the largest beneficiary of journalistic source protection in Britain is central government. Whitehall's regular off-the record briefings, feeding friendly journalists unattributable departmental versions of events and policies, make

it unsurprising that legislation delivered in Westminster but con-
ceived in Whitehall has taken good care to shield the identity of
journalists' sources; though here, at least, freedom of information
legislation offers diligent journalists some chance of checking on
what they are told, and some journalistic codes—for instance that
of the *Financial Times*—require two separate sources for stories
that are to go unattributed. But add to the gentlemanly Whitehall
briefings the pseudonymous armies deployed by governments from
China to Israel, Turkey to Russia, to post purportedly disinterested
commentaries in their favour, and the notion of the internet as a
forum of information begins to wilt.

LEGAL CONTROLS

How fundamental in any event is the right to remain unidentified?
The US Supreme Court in 1972 decided that the First Amendment
prohibition on laws abridging the freedom of speech or of the press
did not make the preservation of sources' anonymity a constitutional right capable of defeating a grand jury subpoena. But they left
it open to states to enact legislation protecting journalists' sources,
and at least 40 states have since done this. In other words, anonymity in US law is not a fundamental right but one instrument in the
toolbox for balancing privacy and publicity. The Canadian Supreme
Court has taken a similar line. It is a line which had the dramatic
consequence of landing the *New York Times*' international reporter
Judith Miller in jail for nearly three months in 2005 for refusing to
disclose to a grand jury her source for a story linked to the malicious
outing of Valerie Plame as a CIA operative by Bush administration
officials.

Barendt is correspondingly sceptical of fundamentalist arguments
for source anonymity. Knowing the originator of a press story, he
suggests, will among other things make it easier for the public to
gauge its reliability. Maybe; though when other publications then
set out to discredit the originator, the public is likelier to find itself
in a hall of mirrors than in the light of day. But these and other
nuances are now all but eclipsed by the unprecedented fact that
internet trolling has turned anonymity from a shield for the concerned and the opinionated into a bludgeon for liars and bullies.

There is no decent excuse for social media providers' continuing refusal to expose trolls. There is neither moral justification for
refusing nor technological difficulty in doing it, and some providers

(for example Facebook and Google+) as a matter of principle do it. The greater number of providers who shield their users' identity at least pay a penalty in their inability to sell advertisers access to their customers; but the shield they provide for malice and worse is difficult to defend. Security services, for their part, have relatively little trouble in identifying the authors of transmissions, at least unencrypted ones. And there's the rub: in many parts of the world, anonymity is all that stands between the purveyor of unofficial views or information and prison or torture. It is why the UN's special rapporteur on freedom of expression, David Kaye, has defended the right to communicate anonymously on the internet, and why Germany has actually legislated to protect anonymity and pseudonymity on social media.

Barendt advances two particular arguments against the protection of anonymity. One is the general absence of any responsible intermediary, such as there is in the print media, capable of filtering out mendacious or defamatory messages and posts. The second is the added fear experienced by victims of trolls and cyber-mobs, who cannot be sure how close they are physically to the source of the threats they are receiving. The first of these has an air of unreality in relation to agenda-driven media to which factuality and balance are all but strangers. The second is real and important and deserves serious police resources to deal with it. Under the Communications Act 2003, which criminalises the senders of grossly offensive or menacing messages, jail sentences were handed out in 2014 to two individuals who had directed violent online abuse at Caroline Criado-Perez and her supporter Stella Creasy MP over the not exactly revolutionary suggestion that it might be time to commemorate a woman on English banknotes. (The moronic hair-triggers which seem to set trolls off are another curiosity of the anonymity business.) Barendt is right to suggest that social media platforms could do a lot more to block trolling, to ban known trolls and to call in the police where appropriate.

Libellous posts, as opposed to threatening or purely abusive ones, are more of a problem. One of the arguments against compelling internet service providers to identify the authors of defamatory posts is that because they are anonymous nobody takes them seriously. Barendt is rightly sceptical of this: the internet, he points out, can destroy a reputation worldwide in a few seconds, and there are not a few instances of journalists making uncritical use of such material. He endorses the view of the Australian judge Michael Kirby that libel law needs to be 'technology-neutral', in other words to be the same whatever the medium; but that approach has not stopped courts on both sides of the Atlantic treating what the California appeal court has called 'a looser, more relaxed communication style' as a modifier of the meaning that a damaging post might otherwise have borne. The 2013 Defamation Act supplies a trade-off here. A website operator which is sued for disseminating anonymous defamatory matter may be able to escape liability if it assists the claimant to identify the author. The US courts, more chary of chilling free speech, will rarely order such unmasking where the defamatory material, however extreme, is political, but they will readily order it where the libel is personal.

SECRET BALLOTS

Given that the 1948 Universal Declaration spells out the right to vote in elections by secret ballot as a fundamental human right, it is useful to be reminded that this paradigmatic form of anonymous speech is not that old and is still contentious. Its introduction by the 1872 Ballot Act, ending centuries of intimidation by local landowners and employers and bribery by candidates, was heavily contested. Conservative politicians contended that secret ballots were contrary to our traditions of honesty and openness. The argument, disingenuous and self-interested as it may have been, was in reality not dissimilar to the contemporaneous argument, today no longer contentious, for signed literary reviews.

Ominously, the late Justice Scalia pointed out in 2010 that the US Supreme Court had never upheld a right to vote anonymously. Unlimited campaign funding, discriminatory voter identification, restricted polling hours ... may anonymous voting be the next target for the Republican wrecking ball? Or does it no longer matter?

10

Dealing with Strasbourg

By 2012 the European Court of Human Rights was under vocal attack for allegedly trying to micro-manage member states' legal systems. In the UK the attack had an oblique objective: to get the UK abandon the Convention and thereby make it ineligible for continued membership of the EU. With the 2016 referendum this goal was independently achieved (in principle at least) and the xenophobic critiques of Strasbourg faded. This article, published in April 2013, looks at the complex interplay between national legal systems and Strasbourg's supervisory jurisdiction.

THE STATES COMPOSING the Council of Europe, now 47 of them, have their own supreme court, the European Court of Human Rights, which—not unlike its US counterpart—has come under increasing fire for interfering unduly in member states' affairs and trying to make one size of human rights compliance fit all. At a theoretical level there seems something wrong with this critique: one size *should* fit all, for the meaning and effect of fundamental rights cannot logically vary from one country to another. But at a practical level it addresses a real problem: decisions about legal processes framed at a level of generality large enough to embrace all member states may well be unworkable in some of them.

The first of these difficulties has historically been tackled by the use of the margin of appreciation, a literal rendering, meaningless in English, of the French *marge d'appréciation*, which means margin of judgment. It has proved handy in obscenity and blasphemy cases, allowing the court not to interfere with intolerant decisions made by national courts (the UK's included) on the ground that the latter have a better sense of local conditions and feelings—the very thing that intolerance thrives on and that the European Convention on Human Rights is there to guard against.[1]

The margin of appreciation has furnished an occasional bolthole, but it's hard to call it a legal principle. It is in any case not an

---

[1] See Ch 6.

expedient which by itself can resolve the second difficulty, the step down from the general to the particular. The reason for this is well illustrated by what has happened in relation to the use of hearsay evidence in criminal trials. In contrast to the unequivocal requirement of the US constitution that the accused must be able to confront the witnesses against him or her, the European Convention guarantees a more protean right to a fair trial. In an attempt to reconcile the confrontation principle with the need to protect frightened witnesses or to introduce the testimony of now dead ones, the European court has in the past held that the use of written statements will render a trial unfair if, but only if, their evidence is 'decisive' or 'potentially decisive'.

The logic of this is arguably self-defeating. If a piece of evidence is not capable of contributing to the decision (and therefore potentially decisive), it ought not to be admitted at all. In any event, where the trial is by jury and the verdict consists of one word, it is often impossible to know what evidence was decisive. There is also a problem of principle: fairness embraces more interests than those of the accused. A trial needs to be fair to victims, to witnesses and to the public. To accept this, however, is to exchange any unitary notion of a fair trial for the least unfair way of adjusting competing claims to fairness. It may be unrealistic to inject into such a complex process a formulaic solvent like 'decisiveness'.

Recognising the dilemma, English criminal procedure has in recent years become readier, subject to safeguards, to admit hearsay evidence. Parliament made statutory provision for it in 2003, but insisted—conformably with the human rights convention—that it was not to happen at the expense of fairness. When, in 2009, the UK Supreme Court was faced in the *Horncastle* case with convictions based on what was probably decisive hearsay evidence, it declined to follow the Strasbourg jurisprudence, concluded that the trials had been fair notwithstanding the admission of hearsay, and upheld the convictions. In the pair of cases decided by the Supreme Court in *Horncastle*,[2] two of the defendants had been charged with intentionally inflicting grievous bodily harm on a victim who had died (from alcoholism) by the time the trial took place, and the victim's statement, which was read at trial, was almost certainly decisive in securing convictions. The other defendants were charged with kidnapping a young woman, who was so frightened of giving

---

[2] *R v Horncastle; R v Marquis* [2009] EWCA Crim 964.

evidence that she ran away. The Supreme Court's carefully reasoned judgment came at a time when political pressure was building to reduce the European court's interventions in the UK's legal system.

How then was Strasbourg going to react to something approaching defiance of its rulings by a national judiciary? A showdown seemed imminent because at the time of the Supreme Court's decision two other cases, in each of which a chamber of the human rights court had found the UK to have denied a fair trial by admitting hearsay evidence, were waiting to be heard in the Grand Chamber. These cases raised the same issue in very different situations. One concerned a doctor charged with indecently assaulting two patients, one of whom killed herself before the trial took place. Her statement was read to the jury. In the other, the victim had been stabbed in the back. The accused had been identified as his assailant by a witness who absented himself from the trial, pleading fear. His statement too was read to the jury. Both men were convicted.[3]

It was while the Strasbourg court was waiting to decide how to respond to the Supreme Court's challenge to its approach that the president of the court, the UK's judge, Sir Nicolas Bratza, delivered a measured paper defending the court's record but arguing for a fuller and more constructive dialogue between the supranational court and national ones on issues such as this. The two Grand Chamber decisions, when they came out in December 2011, exemplified his approach. The court stood up for its own jurisprudence on fair trials and unseen witnesses, but accepted that the test of decisiveness could not be universally used. It held that, in the specific circumstances of each case and notwithstanding the admission in both of potentially decisive hearsay evidence, the trial of the doctor for indecent assault had been a fair one but the unlawful wounding trial had not.

These two Grand Chamber judgments were delivered the day after Lord Irvine, who as Lord Chancellor had been one of the main architects of the Human Rights Act, delivered a fiercely critical lecture on the way British courts had interpreted the act's requirement that they 'take into account' what the Strasbourg court has decided. He denounced what he saw as slavish adherence in some cases and commended the Supreme Court's independent stance in the *Horncastle* case, going so far as to say that the obligation placed

---

[3] *Al-Khawaja and Tahery v UK* (2009) 49 EHRR 1.

by Parliament on the courts was to depart from Strasbourg's rulings where our courts considered them mistaken.

Irvine's critique will have played well with the lobby which, for reasons that in some cases have little to do with the promotion of human rights, was aiming to use the Council of Europe's High Level Conference on the future of the Strasbourg court, held in Brighton in April 2012, to bring the court to heel. But the insularity of his argument constrains its logic. If it is acceptable for the UK to dismiss a Strasbourg judgment as insufficiently sensitive to the UK's legal culture, why is it not acceptable for, say, Russia or Moldova to do the same in relation to some of the unsavoury practices of their own systems? The adjustment that was called for was not of the kind Irvine was advocating but of the kind Bratza was adumbrating; and it was the latter which was endorsed by the Brighton Declaration: 'The conference ... welcomes the development by the court in its case law of principles such as subsidiarity and the margin of appreciation.'

I started by suggesting that the margin of appreciation hardly qualifies as a legal principle; but the same is not true of subsidiarity. Subsidiarity is—or should be—a principled approach which recognises that the primary obligation for compliance with the convention rests on the member state, and that the way the state goes about complying may legitimately vary from one legal system to the next. This is not the same thing as holding, as Strasbourg has done in the past, that the suppression of free speech can be justified by calibrating free expression to local prejudice.

Then, importantly, some eight weeks after its twin judgments on the fairness of the UK trials, the Strasbourg court handed down two more judgments which, perhaps because they related to Germany, passed almost unnoticed in the British press. In both cases, the media had been allowed to intervene in the argument through representative organisations.

The first concerned the personal privacy of Princess Caroline of Monaco, whose marriage to a German aristocrat had provoked years of unsought publicity, frequently involving personal harassment, in the German press. In 2004 she won a landmark case against Germany for failing to protect her privacy through its courts. The decision provoked outrage in the German press ('Europas Richter hebeln die Pressefreiheit aus'—'European judges throw out press freedom'—the *Frankfurter Allgemeine* said, replicating the British view that Europe is always somewhere else); but German politicians rapidly realised that it was an unsolicited donation to their own personal privacy rights and assured the Council of Ministers that the ruling was being respected.

Princess Caroline then brought fresh proceedings for further invasions of her privacy. Since these had taken the form of unctuous *Hello!*-style coverage of her family's affairs, the refusal of the German courts to give redress against them might simply have been endorsed by Strasbourg. But the Grand Chamber took a more radical course: it held that Germany had adjusted its jurisprudence to accord proper respect to private life, so that strong reasons—which were not present here—were now needed if the European court was to upset a national court's judgment about it.[4] Still more interestingly, the Grand Chamber on the same day handed down a judgment in favour of the Axel Springer press empire, which had been forbidden by injunction to report the arrest on a minor drugs charge of an actor known for his role as a TV police inspector. The case, which was decided under Article 10 (the freedom of expression provision), set out a checklist of relevant factors and concluded that, despite the contrary view of the national courts, they did not here add up to a proportionate interference with free expression.[5]

One listened for the sound of trumpets in the British media, but there was none. So it goes.

---

[4] *Von Hannover v Germany* (2012) 55 EHRR 6.
[5] *Axel Springer AG v Germany* (2012) 55 EHRR 6.

11

Speaking in Tongues

While the European Court of Justice enjoys translation and interpretation into every member state's language, the European Court of Human Rights uses only two languages—French and English—limiting the authorship and readership of its judgments to judges, citizens and lawyers with a command of these. This proposal for rectifying the anomaly was a contribution to a festschrift in honour of the French judge and former president of the ECtHR, Jean-Paul Costa.

A PROBLEM

It seems an elementary principle of justice that those to whom a judgment is addressed should be able to understand it.

The judgments of the European Court of Human Rights are addressed not only to the petitioner and his or her state but to every citizen and member state of the Council of Europe. So it was unfortunate even in the Court's early years that it was only a bilingual institution. French was still—literally—the *lingua franca* of diplomacy; English had become the dominant world language of commerce and science. But from the start the Council of Europe contained more than francophone and anglophone nations.

Yet nothing systematic was done then or has been done since to cope with its expansion to include judges from states with some 37 principal languages, each bound by treaty, and frequently too by its laws or its constitution, to abide by the Convention. The contrast with the Court of Justice of the European Union could not be more stark. At the last count, the 27 member states of the EU had between them 21 languages, excluding (for the time being) Irish Gaelic and Maltese.[1] In the CJEU, as in the EU's other organs, all these languages are of equal status. For practical reasons a single language, French, is used

---

[1] The enlargement of the EU in 2004 by itself brought in nine new languages, each with its own translating and interpreting facilities.

as the working language in which all judgments are drafted and into which all pleadings must be translated. But from it radiate hearings and final judgments in all the EU's languages, each with its own interpreting booth and translation unit.

Much of this can no doubt be legitimately regarded as a luxury, especially in days of economic stringency within member states. But as a model it illustrates the poverty of the Strasbourg arrangements, for its purpose is in no way luxurious: it is to ensure that the court's proceedings and decisions can be read and understood throughout its jurisdiction. This arguably should be a fundamental purpose of any system of justice; and as a principle it has been readily recognised by the Committee of Ministers.[2] It is reality which lags behind.

Given, then, that Strasbourg has no arrangements for the dissemination of its judgments in any language other than French or English, what is being done in the member states themselves to repair the deficiency? A random and unscientific survey (all that I have been able to conduct) suggests that progress is little and uneven.

Some states—Germany, Slovenia and Sweden for example—depend on national legal journals or bulletins to identify and summarise major Strasbourg decisions relating to other countries as well as their own. Others—Denmark and Italy among them, as well as Germany—produce periodical volumes of major ECtHR cases in the national language. Italy also has such a service, though again selective, online. Yet others, notably the Netherlands, the Scandinavian countries and Greece, count on their national familiarity with English to bridge the gap—a reliance which cannot extend to judgments written in French. And the higher courts of some states, such as Poland and Estonia, are assisted by bulletins circulated by their diplomatic services as well as by national or in-house researchers.

So far as one can discern a pattern of selection, it suggests a focus in each member state on decisions concerning the member state itself, with more peripheral attention, usually in legal journals rather than official bulletins, given to cases brought against other states.

All of this stands in unhappy contrast to the ease with which a British judge can not only take down from the shelf and read volumes containing verbatim Strasbourg judgments but can do online research in English to bring the case-law up to date. The judgments of the

---

[2] See for instance the 2002 recommendation of the Committee of Ministers to member states in relation to the dissemination of judgments.

United Kingdom's courts, from the Supreme Court to the local magistrates' or county court, reflect this ease of access. You may find in them extensive citation and analysis of ECtHR jurisprudence, downloaded, cut and pasted in the writer's and reader's own language. Can a Russian judge, who is equally expected to respect Strasbourg's jurisprudence, do the same?

A SOLUTION

What can be done?

The ongoing enterprise of making the HUDOC database more ecumenical and user-friendly is welcome, but it is dependent on collating extant translations. A replication of the Luxembourg system is clearly out of the question. Moreover, with over 1,000 human rights judgments a year, selection is inevitable. But it will be increasingly difficult, as the Court continues to focus its admissibility criteria on issues of general principle, to treat any judgment as marginal or inconsequential, whichever state is the respondent. Any process of selection, then, needs to concentrate on the substance and content of the Court's judgments. And here there may be room for development.

The judgments of the Court, departing from the laconic French style, have come to resemble the British narrative judgment, with a detailed recital of the history of the case, a recapitulation of the *acquis* of relevant law, and an application of the law to the issues before the court. All of this—and not only to Anglo-Saxon eyes— is helpful: it means that a judgment is self-sufficient and self-explanatory. But much of it is unnecessary to understanding what principle the case has established.

The *acquis*, for example, represents a process of recalling (to use the Court's favoured verb) the precedents now established in a forum which once proclaimed itself precedent-free but which has inexorably had to follow its own decisions in the interests of legal certainty. The recital of facts, for its part, frequently contains far more information than is needed to understand the decision. All these elements are thus capable, in most cases, of condensation and even elimination. The indispensable element at the heart of most Strasbourg judgments consists typically of two or three key paragraphs which set out the application or the adaptation of the relevant principles to the established facts. It is these which need reproduction, translation and dissemination.

Is it too much to hope that a system can be devised by which, either within or outside the Registry, every full-length judgment is accompanied by a condensed version spelling out the key facts and reproducing the paragraphs which contain the reasons of principle for the Court's conclusions. Two pages should generally suffice. That would be stage one.

Stage two would be the translation of the case summary (with a caveat that it is not a substitute for the full judgment) into the language of every member state. There is no need for this to be done in Strasbourg, and every reason for it to be done locally. In many countries a university law department ought to be able, with a modest subsidy, to undertake the task. In others it may be that the diplomatic service has the necessary facilities. But it is to the Council of Europe that the obligation should undoubtedly fall to assure the funding and oversee the functioning of the system.

Stage three ought, in the twenty-first century, to be simple and almost cost-free: putting the translated summaries on a dedicated website for judicial, professional and public access, with links to the full French or English text for those who wish and are able to read the original judgment.

It is both surprising and sad that something so simple and so necessary has not yet happened. Before the Committee of Ministers shrugs its shoulders, it might wish to recall Article 46 of the Convention, which places upon it the obligation to secure the execution of the Court's judgments. If the individuals whose rights depend on it and the states and courts whose obligations flow from it cannot gain access in a language they understand to the jurisprudence which gives the Convention life, much of the work of the Court will continue to be less effective than it ought to be.

12

The Public Interest

In 2014, when this article was written, the Lord Chancellor and Secretary of State for justice, Chris Grayling, a politician without legal qualifications, was renewing an attempt first mooted by Margaret Thatcher to eliminate or restrict judicial review of government action. His attempts at justification showed little comprehension of the legal meaning of the public interest.

T HE PREPAREDNESS OF the High Court to consider whether the state has abused its powers, and to do so at the instance of an applicant who has nothing personally to gain, is one of the modern cornerstones of the rule of law.[1] It is not an open door: for every individual or NGO that secures permission to apply for judicial review in the public interest, a good many are turned away. Some are considered to be busybodies, like the Anglican vicar who wanted to stop the ordination of women in Wales. Others are genuinely disinterested but lack a strong enough case. But where, as also happens, an NGO or a concerned individual calls attention to what appears to be a real and serious abuse of government power, albeit one that does not directly affect them, the courts may call on the executive to explain itself and may intervene if the explanation does not stand up.

In all such cases the court has to determine whether the particular claimant has what the law calls a 'sufficient interest' in the subject matter of the claim. The phrase itself is deliberately elastic, calling on occasion for a complex judgment. It recognises the fact that the public importance of an issue may sometimes be sufficient to compensate for the absence of a personal motive for litigating it, and that it is for the judges to work out, issue by issue, who is entitled to be heard.

---

[1] For a striking example, which involved the justiciability of the royal prerogative, see *R v Speyer* [1916] 1 KB 595 (DC).

In September 2013, in the wake of a consultation paper which proposed among other things to choke off judicial review by reducing the availability of legal aid for it, Chris Grayling as Secretary of State for Justice and Lord Chancellor (two distinct offices now merged, in Gilbertian mode, in one person) published a further consultation paper dealing specifically with the judicial review process. The paper proposed to restrict the meaning of a sufficient interest to a 'direct and tangible interest' in the outcome: in other words, to wipe out two or more centuries' jurisprudence, in the course of which the courts have adjusted the gateway of judicial review to meet the needs of the rule of law (which Grayling's oath of office commits him to respect) by according standing not always to those acting for private advantage but occasionally to individuals acting in the public interest.[2]

The blinkered attitude to public interest litigation was visible in the paper's treatment of the 1995 Pergau Dam case. The facts of the case were startling. The foreign secretary, Douglas Hurd, was proposing, for overtly political reasons, to go ahead with a subvention of £316 million to Malaysia for a hydroelectric project which the government's Overseas Development Administration had advised would be uneconomic, an abuse of the overseas aid programme and 'a very bad buy'. The High Court held that the rule of law, the importance of the issue, the probable absence of challenge from any other source, the nature of the breach of legality and the prominent and responsible character of the World Development Movement combined to give it a sufficient interest in the challenge. On the substantive issue, the court held that the statutory power to provide assistance for the purpose of promoting development did not include promoting unsound development, which this incontrovertibly was. They struck down the decision. There was no appeal. It later became known that the foreign secretary had not sought the advice of his own lawyers, which would have been that the proposed funding was illegal.

Could it be seriously contended that it would have been better had the World Development Movement not been allowed to bring the issue before a court, leaving more than £300 million of public money to be squandered? It seems it could be. Grayling's consultation paper cited the Pergau Dam decision as a prime example of

---

[2] See *R v Kemp* (1789) 1 East 46, noted in *R v Clarke* (1800) 1 East 38, per Kenyon CJ: 'a stranger ... ought to come to the court with a very fair case in his hands'.

challenges which ought not to happen, especially (I am not making this up) since such challenges are 'relatively successful compared to other judicial review cases'. The paper displayed no awareness at all that this aspect of the law of standing has a long history and a principled purpose, not to supplant or embarrass ministers, but to ensure, first, that government functions within the law and, second and no less important, that within the law government retains freedom of action.

Instead Grayling's paper fudged the two distinct meanings of 'public interest'. It proclaimed the principle 'that Parliament and the elected government are best placed to determine what is in the public interest' with the evident purpose of suggesting that judges have been usurping this function. But the paper failed to cite a single case (and I know of none) in which a court has substituted its view of the public interest for that of a minister. The reason is that public interest litigation does not mean litigation about what is in the public interest: it means litigation brought in the interest of the public in seeing the law upheld. The fallacy that public law can be limited to the vindication of private rights and interests was exposed in the consultation paper's own recognition that the Aarhus Convention, to which the UK is a party, requires the preservation of public interest access to the courts on environmental issues; but the paper was blind to the fact that there are numerous other kinds of issue to which the same logic applies.

The history of such litigation includes the interventions of the Child Poverty Action Group;[3] Greenpeace;[4] the actors and scholars who tried to save the remains of the Globe Theatre from destruction;[5] the GPs who saved a local hospital in Hillingdon from closure;[6] the National Federation of Self-Employed and Small Businesses seeking to enforce the taxation of casual print-workers;[7] and a considerable number of private individuals concerned with the legality of official action or inaction. The power of the courts to intervene where an arguable misuse of power affects the public as a whole is, as more than one judge has pointed out, an aspect of their function

---

[3] *R v Secretary of State for Social Services, ex parte Child Poverty Action Group* [1990] 2 QB 540 (CA).

[4] *R v HM Inspectorate of Pollution, ex parte Greenpeace Ltd (No 2)* [1994] 4 All ER 329, 350.

[5] *R v Secretary of State for the Environment, ex parte Rose Theatre Trust* [1990] 1 QB 504 (QBD); criticised in S Sedley, *Lions Under the Throne* pp 235–36.

[6] *R v Hillingdon Health Authority* [1984] ICR 800 (QBD).

[7] *R v IRC, ex p National Federation of the Self-Employed Ltd* [1982] AC 617 (HL).

(and, one might add, the Lord Chancellor's) of protecting the rule of law. Departments of state have on occasion welcomed public interest challenges as a means of clarifying the law. In 1990, for instance, a consortium consisting of the Child Poverty Action Group, two London borough councils and the National Association of Citizens' Advice Bureaux challenged the way social security legislation was being interpreted and administered by the department and the independent adjudicators.[8] The department did not contest their standing; the ruling helped everyone.

Following a barrage of criticism, including a sharp response from the judiciary, the proposal to restrict standing was dropped. Thanks apparently to a sudden conversion, Grayling's response to the consultation began: 'I believe in protecting judicial review as a check on unlawful executive action …'. Whether the abolition of public interest standing was actually a serious proposal or an example of the distraction technique now used in the drafting of controversial bills[9] we may never know.

RELATOR ACTIONS

One possibility thrown up by the threatened advance of the constitutional bulldozer was a revival of relator actions: proceedings authorised by the Attorney-General in the public interest so as to cure the claimant's lack of standing. The use of this power has become rare as public interest standing has developed, but it is a judge-made instrument (not a prerogative power) for securing justice.

The problem is that the Attorney-General, like the justice secretary, is something of a pantomime horse: both custodian of the public interest in the observance of the law (and in that regard the government's legal adviser) and a government minister with political obligations of collective responsibility. In 2007 the Commons' Constitutional Affairs Committee, in a well-reasoned report, concluded that the Attorney's dual role was constitutionally unsustainable: 'Real and perceived political independence has to be combined with a role of an intrinsically party political nature in one office holder.' The committee advised that the Attorney-General's functions should be split between a non-political legal adviser and a government minister. Nothing has been done to act on the advice.

---

[8] See n 3 above.
[9] See Sedley, *Ashes and Sparks* Ch 10, pp 128–29.

In 1977 John Gouriet and his Freedom Association tried to obtain an injunction to stop the Union of Post Office Workers boycotting mail destined for South Africa.[10] Gouriet's lawyers recognised that he had no personal standing and therefore needed the Attorney-General's authority to sue. The Attorney-General, Sam Silkin, refused his consent and turned up in person to submit that his decision was final and beyond judicial review. He found himself before an incandescent Court of Appeal which included Lord Denning and Lord Justice Lawton. In a judgment memorable not only for its rhetoric but for the spoof law report it generated,[11] Denning held that if the Attorney-General improperly refused his consent the Court could proceed without it.

Denning's premise, at least, is not fanciful. A refusal of the Attorney's consent on the ground that it is not in the public interest for well-founded proceedings to be brought is entirely possible— indeed it was Silkin's ground for refusing to authorise Gouriet to sue in his name. It is here, however, that the two meanings of public interest collide. For the intending claimant the public interest lies in maintaining the rule of law; for the Attorney-General it will lie in an amalgam of legal and political considerations dominated by the interests of the government of which he or she is a member. The consequence is that the Attorney-General, if asked to authorise a claim such as the Pergau Dam claim, may recognise, as the government's legal adviser, that the claim is entirely sound but decide, as a member of the government, that it is not in the public interest for it to be litigated.

This is among the reasons why the courts have developed their own principles of standing, and why Parliament, recognising that it is for the courts to decide whom they will hear, has not—or not so far—attempted to restrict or define what amounts to a sufficient interest for a judicial review claim. Grayling's proposal was thus rather more than an attempt to adjust court procedures: it was part of a renewed assault on the constitutional separation of powers.

Denning's conclusion that if necessary the courts could proceed without the Attorney's consent is, however, problematical. A legislative roadblock on public interest claims may mean that the court cannot simply decide to entertain such proceedings in the absence

---

[10] *Gouriet v Union of Postal Workers* [1977] 1 All ER 696 (CA); *Gouriet v A-G* [1978] AC 435 (HL).

[11] Marcel Berlins, *Grenouille v National Union of Seamen (Not Yet The Times)* quoted in S Sedley, *Ashes and Sparks* pp 203–204.

of the Attorney-General's fiat. But it does not mean that the court cannot require the Attorney-General to reach a decision about authorising the proceedings without regard to political considerations and with exclusive regard to the maintenance of the rule of law. Such a course would at least have the virtue of disaggregating the Attorney's inconsistent roles; it would also give the concept of public interest a single and intelligible meaning dovetailing with the rule of law.

But reliance on the Attorney-General's support would not work in the most critical class of case, where the decision under challenge is one for which the Attorney is responsible. In 2006 the director of the Serious Fraud Office decided that it was in the public interest to discontinue the SFO's investigation into possible corruption affecting British Aerospace's arms dealings with Saudi Arabia, because Saudi Arabia had threatened to withhold its cooperation in combating terrorism within the UK if the investigation was pursued. The SFO's director had acted throughout in consultation with the Attorney-General, to whom he was answerable, and the Attorney-General in turn had consulted his ministerial colleagues. A group of NGOs, led by Corner House Research, challenged the director's decision as an unlawful abdication of his duty to investigate serious crime, and in the High Court, before a panel of two lord justices of appeal, they succeeded.[12] The House of Lords, not long before its transmutation into the Supreme Court, reversed the decision, holding that the choice made by the director of the SFO, with the Attorney-General's authority, was a legitimate choice between two competing public interests: the prosecution of crime and the safety of British citizens.[13]

The lawsuit itself crystallised two things. One was the complex of factors going to make up a government decision about where the public interest in relation to the investigation lay. The other was that, unless disinterested groups like Corner House Research were able to bring as serious an issue as this before the courts, the public interest in the maintenance of the rule of law would be rendered impotent—for who, other than British Aerospace and the Saudi government, would have had a 'direct and tangible interest' in the issue?

---

[12] *R (on the application of Corner House Research) v Director of the Serious Fraud Office* [2008] EWHC 714 (Admin).
[13] *R (on the application of Corner House Research) v Director of the Serious Fraud Office* [2008] UKHL 60.

13

Judicial Misconduct

This was an occasional piece published in the London Review of Books *in December 2015.*

NOT FOR THE first time, Mr Justice Peter Smith, a judge of the Chancery Division of the High Court, got his personal life and his judicial work entangled. This time it concerned his luggage, which had gone missing on a BA flight from Florence. While the luggage was still missing, BA appeared in his court as a litigant and the judge demanded to know what had happened to it; he stood down only after an unseemly wrangle with BA's counsel. The same judge in 2007 had tried a case[1] involving a firm of solicitors with whom his private negotiations to leave the bench had not long before broken down in rancour. On that occasion he refused to recuse himself and went on to display such hostility to the firm that the Court of Appeal set aside his judgment. A complaint to the newly set up Office of Judicial Complaints resulted in a public reprimand from the Lord Chancellor and the then Lord Chief Justice The latter stated that a firm line had now been drawn under the issue and that the judge enjoyed his full confidence.

Whether Mr Justice Peter Smith continues to enjoy the full confidence of the present chief justice we do not know. What we do know is that there is very little beyond a reprimand that can be done. Judges of the higher courts have for three centuries been able to be dismissed from office only by parliamentary resolution. This is now laid down by the Senior Courts Act 1981, which provides that a judge of the higher courts 'shall hold that office during good behaviour, subject to a power of removal by Her Majesty on an address presented to Her by both Houses of Parliament'. The formula, which comes from the Act of Settlement 1701, was intended to prevent any recurrence of the Stuart practice of dismissing judges at will.

---

[1] *Howell v Lees Millais* [2007] EWCA Civ 720.

The 1701 act provided that 'judges' commissions be made *quamdiu se bene gesserint* [during good conduct] ... but upon the address of both Houses of Parliament it may be lawful to remove them'.[2] It is generally accepted, despite the ambiguous phrasing, that the two limbs form a single condition—that a senior judge may be removed only for misconduct, and then only by Parliament. But is the procedure workable? And should the last word on judicial tenure be in the hands of politicians?

There is no prescribed procedure, and no self-evident format, for trying a judge at the bar of either House. The only judge ever to have been dismissed on parliamentary motion was an Irish Admiralty judge, Sir Jonah Barrington, who in 1830 was found guilty of misappropriating litigants' funds. The case against him, having been accepted by the Commons, was argued at the bar of the House of Lords by the Attorney-General, a member of the government as well as its legal adviser. More than one attempt has been made since then to get Parliament to vote for the dismissal of a senior judge. In 1924 the MP George Lansbury put down (but eventually withdrew) a motion for the dismissal of Mr Justice McCardie, who had told a libel jury that General Dyer had acted rightly in firing on an unarmed crowd in Amritsar. More menacingly, over 180 Labour MPs signed a motion in 1973 for the dismissal of Sir John Donaldson. Donaldson, then a High Court judge and president of the National Industrial Relations Court, later Master of the Rolls, had sequestrated £100,000 held in the political fund of the Amalgamated Engineering Union as a penalty for contempt of court. The motion accused him of 'political prejudice and partiality'. The Lord Chancellor, Lord Hailsham, publicly attacked the signatory MPs for abusing parliamentary privilege, provoking a motion of censure on Hailsham himself for violating the privileges of Parliament. The motion for Donaldson's dismissal fell for the least democratic of reasons: the whips refused to allocate parliamentary time to it.

Something like this could happen again, and the government of the day might this time support the motion. Far from guaranteeing the independence of the higher judiciary, the Act of Settlement in such a situation would be its undoing. It's not inconceivable that the Attorney-General (who in spite of repeated calls to end his dual status continues to be both the government's legal adviser and a

---

[2] The Latin qualification was taken without acknowledgment from the ordinance by which the Long Parliament in 1648 had begun making judicial appointments.

political minister) could again appear as counsel seeking to persuade the Lords to endorse a Commons motion for dismissal. A spat
over a judge's missing luggage may therefore be an opportunity to
consider the wisdom of the process without passion. Are there more
appropriate ways of dealing with allegations of misconduct in the
higher judiciary?

Since the abolition of the Lord Chancellor's role as head of the
judiciary by the 2005 Constitutional Reform Act, there has been an
Office for Judicial Complaints which investigates allegations against
judges and can make recommendations for disciplinary action to
the Lord Chief Justice and the Secretary of State.[3] For judges of the
lower courts, these can include dismissal. Allegations of professional misconduct on the part of judges of the senior courts also
come within its remit, but in these cases dismissal is not an option.
There seems no strong reason why a decision-making panel of
appropriate status should not have power in serious cases to recommend dismissal (New Zealand has already legislated for this), and
the Chief Justice be empowered to act on it. Correspondingly, there
may be good reason (going beyond the New Zealand system, which
still leaves the decision to Parliament) for taking the power of dismissal out of the hands of two political assemblies before the habit
(inaugurated by Michael Howard as home secretary in the 1990s
and adopted by some of his Labour successors) of publicly attacking
judges whose decisions upset the government moves towards a replication of the Donaldson episode—or, just as unacceptably, before
a serious adverse finding by the Office for Judicial Complaints is
ignored by a government or sidelined by a parliamentary majority
which for political reasons favours the judge.

Kenya, whose judiciary had for years been plagued with allegations of corruption, grasped this nettle under its 2010 constitution
by setting up a vetting board, including three non-national judges, to
review the suitability for office of the entire judiciary. It found four of
the nine judges of the Court of Appeal unfit to continue in office, not
for corruption but for repeated unjudicial behaviour on the bench.
But vetting, as opposed to adjudication on specific allegations of
misconduct, has its own dangers. Where South Africa in 1994 took
the difficult decision to leave all judges appointed by the apartheid
regime in office as a lesser evil than a political purge, a number of
states in eastern Europe have since 1989 politically cleansed their

---

[3] Constitutional Reform Act 2005, ss 108, 109.

courts, some (for example, East Germany and the Czech Republic) by examining judges' political pasts, others (Bosnia-Herzegovina) by making the entire judiciary apply for reappointment. In some states (Albania) the opportunity for incoming governments to repopulate the bench with their own supporters has proved irresistible. But individual judicial misconduct is another story.

14

Recusal: When Should a Judge Not Be a Judge?

This article on judicial recusal was published in January 2011.[1]

F EW PEOPLE IN the United Kingdom, I would guess, reading this headnote to the official report of a recent decision of the US Supreme Court, would regard it as a difficult case:

'After a West Virginia jury found respondents, a coal company and its affiliates (hereinafter Massey), liable for fraudulent misrepresentation, concealment, and tortious interference with existing contractual relations and awarded petitioners (hereinafter Caperton) $50 million in damages, West Virginia held its 2004 judicial elections. Knowing the State Supreme Court of Appeals would consider the appeal, Don Blankenship, Massey's chairman and principal officer, supported Brent Benjamin rather than the incumbent justice seeking re-election. His $3 million in contributions exceeded the total amount spent by all other Benjamin supporters and by Benjamin's own committee. Benjamin won by fewer than 50,000 votes. Before Massey filed its appeal, Caperton moved to disqualify now Justice Benjamin under the Due Process Clause and the State's Code of Judicial Conduct, based on the conflict caused by Blankenship's campaign involvement. Justice Benjamin denied the motion, indicating that he found nothing showing bias for or against any litigant. The court then reversed the $50 million verdict.'

To all appearances, a key member of the appeal court which absolved the appellant company of liability had owed a debt of gratitude to that company. He should not have sat, and the decision in which he participated should be regarded as a nullity. What not everyone in this country will know is that in the 39 states of the US where judges are elected, it is routine for candidates' campaigns to

---

[1] To recuse means to take objection to an office-holder, such as a judge: it thus shares with 'recusant' a connotation of rejection of authority. Used reflexively ('to recuse oneself') it signifies a judge standing down.

be sponsored by the law firms, and sometimes by the litigants, who will be appearing before them. Recusal in such states is going to require more than the occasional dollar in the judicial collecting tin.

Would it matter if the same judge had in other cases found against a company that had sponsored his campaign? The risk of bias is not limited to favouritism. There is an equal and opposite risk that a judge, in endeavouring not to show favour, will bend over backwards and lose his balance that way. The only safe route is the exit.

The West Virginia court of appeals was by no means insensitive to the issue of apparent bias. When the petitioners applied for a rehearing of the appeal, there were motions for disqualification of three of the five original justices. Photos had been produced of one of them, Justice Maynard, vacationing with Don Blankenship on the French Riviera while the case was pending; Maynard correctly stood down. Justice Starcher too agreed to stand down because he had said publicly that 'Blankenship's bestowal of his personal wealth, political tactics and "friendship" have created a cancer in the affairs of this court.' That his remark might have been entirely justified made no difference. But Justice Benjamin, now in the role of acting chief justice, refused to stand down.

What Europeans may find remarkable is not only that it was by a single vote that the US Supreme Court eventually struck down the West Virginia decision for apparent bias, but that it was the four judicial conservatives, Roberts, Scalia, Thomas and Alito, who voted to uphold the judgment. They may also now know that, thanks to a subsequent Supreme Court ruling, Massey need no longer channel its subventions through its chairman: it can donate to judicial re-election campaigns corporately and without limit. What is still uncertain is whether the *Caperton* decision means that corporations are likely to be wasting their money because the bare fact of their donations will disqualify the beneficiaries from sitting on their cases, or whether (as the majority judgment suggested) disqualification on this ground is going to be confined to facts as extreme as those in *Caperton*.

The seeds of Supreme Court abstentionism were sown long ago in the US. Justice Kennedy, writing for the *Caperton* majority, put it this way:

'It is axiomatic that "[a] fair trial in a fair tribunal is a basic requirement of due process." As the court has recognised, however, "most matters relating to judicial disqualification [do] not rise to a constitutional level." The early and leading case on the subject is *Tumey v. Ohio*. There, the court stated that "matters of kinship, personal bias, state policy, remoteness of interest, would seem generally to be matters merely of legislative discretion" ... As new problems have emerged that were not discussed at common law, however, the court has identified additional instances which, as an objective matter, require recusal. These are circumstances "in which experience teaches that the probability of actual bias on the part of the judge or decision maker is too high to be constitutionally tolerable."'

The *Tumey* case was, at least to our eyes, another case in which there was a manifest risk of bias: it concerned a mayor with judicial powers whose municipal funds were swelled by any fines he imposed. It echoed the early decision of Chief Justice Coke in *Dr Bonham's Case*. Justice Kennedy explained:

'The *Tumey* court concluded that the Due Process Clause [of the constitution] incorporated the common-law rule that a judge must recuse himself when he has "a direct, personal, substantial, pecuniary interest" in a case. This rule reflects the maxim that "no man is allowed to be a judge in his own cause; because his interest would certainly bias his judgment, and, not improbably, corrupt his integrity."'

Those last words are Madison's, writing in the *Federalist* in 1787, and they put in crystalline form what is still today the essential logic on both sides of the Atlantic. It's their application which is fraught with difficulty. The first main difficulty is to decide what makes someone else's cause the judge's own. The second, which is far from being merely technical, is who decides and how.

The dissenting judgment in *Caperton* sets out a list of 40 questions allegedly begged by the majority opinion, a list too long and in places too contrived to reproduce here. But all the questions drive at a single object: to demonstrate that once the test for recusal is set at any but the highest constitutional level, the grounds for removing judges from the court, and with them the spate of motions for recusal, will be unending. That is a serious consideration, and one which the British courts, which set the bar much lower, are already having to face up to. But serious as it is, it cannot be decisive. As Chief Justice Holt said three centuries ago, when the same argument was advanced in the great election corruption case of *Ashby v White*, if wrongs are multiplied, remedies must be multiplied.[2]

Even so, as Justice Scalia remarked in a pointed dissent:

The court's opinion will ... [add] to the vast arsenal of lawyerly gambits what will come to be known as the *Caperton* claim. The facts relevant to

---

[2] *Ashby v White* (1703) 2 Ld Raym 938.

adjudicating it will have to be litigated—and likewise the law governing it, which will be indeterminate for years to come, if not for ever. Many billable hours will be spent in poring through volumes of campaign finance reports, and many more in contesting nonrecusal decisions through every available means.

Britain, like other countries in the Commonwealth, has already embarked on this road. But, at least in countries where judges are appointed and not elected, the road has not turned out to be a highway to hell. Neither, however, is it a yellow brick road to contentment. It is a tortuous and sometimes stony road which is worth following even if its destination is uncertain.

MR DIMES AND LORD COTTENHAM

When does somebody else's cause become the judge's own? When the judge has a private interest in that person's prosperity, plainly. The case which set the tone in Britain, in 1848, involved the then Lord Chancellor, Lord Cottenham. Cottenham turned out to hold shares in the canal company in whose favour he had decided a case brought by a litigious solicitor named Dimes, who had bought a piece of land in order to hold the canal company to ransom for crossing it. Dimes had litigated without much success for more than ten years when luck delivered Cottenham into his hands, and he finished by pocketing the £700 which the canal company finally had to pay him to go away. The turning point, however, was not as neat or sharp as my account may have suggested.

Cottenham, on appeal, had affirmed an order made against Dimes by the Vice-Chancellor, the senior judge of the chancery division of the High Court, restraining him from interfering with the canal. When Dimes finally petitioned to have Cottenham's order set aside, Cottenham correctly recused himself and handed the decision to the Master of the Rolls, Lord Langdale. Langdale was able to duck the issue on the ground that an appeal from the Vice-Chancellor lay to the Lord Chancellor and nobody else, so that disqualifying him was impossible. It was only when Dimes resorted to sabotaging the canal and its towpath, and Cottenham had to issue injunctions against him, that Dimes was able once again to challenge Cottenham's jurisdiction. This time the House of Lords took the case. Dimes got nothing out of it, since the striking down of the Lord Chancellor's decision left the Vice-Chancellor's decision standing. But, although Lord Campbell went out of his way to say that 'no one can suppose that Lord Cottenham could be in the remotest degree influenced by the interest that he had in this concern', the Lords held that he should not have sat.

It now seems that Lord Cottenham's stake in the Grand Junction Canal Company was quite substantial. But the principle of recusal which Dimes established had nothing to do with the extent of the judge's interest: it had to do solely with the fact of it, and the Lords took trouble to emphasise that the principle applied from the highest to the lowest tribunal in the land.

Pecuniary interest, precisely because it is completely unrefined, is therefore the simplest and most radical ground of recusal. It appears to operate independently of the will of the parties, rendering a decision void even if a party raises the matter only after finding it has lost. As a result, judges who recognise that a party to a case in their list is a company in which they hold shares make sure routinely that the case is tried by somebody else without waiting for an objection. But it has not been unknown in modern times for a judge, typically in the chancery division, to mention to corporate parties that he or she holds shares in one of them and to have the objection summarily waived, as often as not with a polite expression of hope that 'your Lordship's shares will prosper whatever the outcome.' Trouble may be in store there.

GENERAL PINOCHET AND LORD HOFFMANN

Fast forward 150 years from Lord Cottenham to Lord Hoffmann in 1998, sitting as a member of the appellate committee of the House of Lords on the prosecutors' appeal against the High Court's decision to quash the Spanish extradition warrants against General Pinochet on the ground of sovereign immunity. A group of individuals and organisations including Amnesty International were allowed to appear by counsel as interveners. By three to two the law lords held that Pinochet could be extradited to Spain. One of the three composing the majority, Lord Hoffmann, was chairman of a trust which conducted Amnesty International's charitable work in the UK, and his wife was an employee of the organisation itself.

Pinochet's lawyers applied to the House of Lords to set aside its own judgment on the ground of apparent bias, and a differently composed appellate committee, in a still controversial judgment, acceded to the application. The law lords for the most part stressed that simply supporting a cause was not a disqualification: it was

Lord Hoffmann's active role as a trustee of an organisation that was siding with the prosecutor which made the difference. But Lord Goff of Chieveley pushed the door wider open: there could be cases, he said, where 'the interest of the judge in the subject matter of the proceedings arising from his strong commitment to some cause or belief ... could shake public confidence in the administration of justice'.

This seems to some observers a step too far. If the editors and public moralists whose views pass for public opinion are to be believed, the trouble with British judges is that (unlike editors and public moralists) they live lives remote from the real world. If every judge who supports a good cause is to be regarded as a partisan and disqualified from sitting on cases which touch on its subject matter, it will be hard to find a competent tribunal to try a controversial case.

AFFINITY AND THE REASONABLE OBSERVER

What rings a clearer bell, and in fact became the law of the early Scottish courts, is the brightline rule of the early canon law against adjudication by a judge linked to a party by consanguinity, affinity, friendship, enmity, or previous retainer as a party's advocate. Like other early church laws, it was much honoured in the breach. When Urbain Grandier, the curate of Loudun, was accused in 1634 of bewitching and seducing the nuns in the local Ursuline convent, Cardinal Richelieu, whom he had displeased, made sure that a member of the court that retried and convicted him after an initial acquittal was a relative of the mother superior. You can see poor Grandier's ashes to this day in the local museum. When a juror was challenged in 1572 because he was related in the ninth degree to a party, the court was driven to say: 'All the inhabitants of the earth are descended from Adam and Eve and so are cousins of one another [but] the further removed blood is, the more cool it is.'

The principle is nevertheless a sound one even if in practice it is frequently unnecessary or occasionally unenforceable. (In an appeal against Shell and BP in 1980 about the lead additives in their petrol, the registrar of civil appeals was unable to assemble three judges who had no shares in either defendant.[3]) The common law world today, however, casts the recusal net much wider. In one form or

---

[3] *Albery-Speyer and Budden v BP Oil Ltd and Shell Oil Ltd* (1980) 124 Sol Jo 376 (CA).

another it asks whether a sensible observer, knowing what the case was about, who the parties were and what connection the judge had with any of them or with the issues in the case, would think that the judge might be influenced by these things. The trouble with any such simple formula is that it immediately demands fuller detail. How cautious or suspicious is a sensible person? What kind of link will he think matters? How robust will she expect the judge to be?

The minority in the *Caperton* case set store by the last of these questions. The hypothetical observer needs to be aware that the judge on taking office has sworn a public oath to do right by all manner of people without fear or favour, affection or ill-will. How is the observer to gauge the risk that such a judge will break his or her oath? Indeed why, the *Caperton* dissenters asked, should the sensible onlooker expect it at all?

The first answer is that in the case of a pecuniary interest, the law itself presumes it. The second is that judges are human. The third is that, whatever the reality, appearances matter, and nowhere more so than in the administration of justice.

The problem of freemasonry illustrates the second point. Lord Irvine, when he became Lord Chancellor, let it be known that he was minded to require judges to disclose whether they were free-masons. It was pointed out by objectors that this could well be an invasion of the right of association guaranteed by Article 11 of the European Convention on Human Rights. But what was more to the point, though never so far as I know acknowledged, was that it matters not at all if one person in court is a freemason. The problem arises if two freemasons are present and one is the judge, because masons are bound by oath to help one another. So seen, the problem is not difficult to solve: any judge to whom a litigant or witness sig-nals membership of the freemasons is obliged by the judicial oath to stop the trial. The judge is also, I would think, entitled to make a party who has sought favour in this way pay the costs of the conse-quent adjournment, and is probably bound to report the attempt to pervert the course of justice to the DPP.

DEALING WITH CONTEMPT

Such judicial robustness is not always needed. The judge whose court is disrupted by abusive or violent conduct may be compelled to use his or her contempt powers on the spot. But in the absence of a pressing need to act, courts on both sides of the Atlantic recognise that the right course is for the offended judge to back off and to send the contemnor for trial by another judge. As Chief Justice Roberts said in his dissent in the *Caperton* case:

> 'It may also violate due process when a judge presides over a criminal contempt case that resulted from the defendant's hostility towards the judge. In *Mayberry v. Pennsylvania*, 400 US 455 (1971), the defend-ant directed a steady stream of expletives and *ad hominem* attacks at the judge throughout the trial. When that defendant was subsequently charged with criminal contempt, we concluded that he "should be given a public trial before a judge other than the one reviled by the contemnor."'

It may be that at least in this regard some of the judges in this country have the edge. One circuit judge some years ago was called a four-letter word by a defendant on whom he had just passed sentence. The judge had him brought back into the dock. 'In a short while,' he said, 'I am going to go home to a good dinner. I shall spend the evening reading in front of the fire before retiring to a comfortable bed with my wife. You, thanks to your own greed and stupidity, are going to be taken in a van to a prison where you will have to slop out every day, eat prison food and stare at the same blank walls for the next two years. Now which of us would you say was the … ?'

LAY TRIBUNALS

So far I have mentioned only professional judges. Clearly, however, all this applies to the lay magistrates who try more than 95 per cent of our criminal cases. But they are not the only lay judges in our system. In all serious criminal cases, and in some civil cases and coroners' inquests, the judges of fact are a jury of 12 ordinary people. How do these principles apply to them?

One of the principal justifications for the jury, at least in Britain, is its randomness. The abolition of the right of peremptory challenge in 1988 was a recognition of this. Unless some good reason for objection to an individual juror is apparent, both sides face judgment by 12 effectively anonymous individuals. We have never had, as the Americans have, a right to cross-question jurors-in-waiting in order to see whether there is cause for recusing them. But our random system brings its own problems. A juror may know the accused or a witness, or may have heard things about them from neighbours, or may work for a company involved in the case. He or she may have fixed opinions about something on which the jury is going to need an open mind. Yet without allowing questioning there is no way of finding out.

The way most trial judges deal with this is to bring all the jurors in waiting into court, let them know who is to be tried, tell them what the case is about and get the court clerk to read them the list of witnesses. If any of the names or events are known to a potential juror, that juror is stood down. But this leaves gaps. I recall one juror, who had rightly said nothing when asked if she worked for the company whose property the defendant was accused of damaging, at the last minute raising a hand and asking whether it mattered that she and her husband had shares in the company.

This kind of direct personal or economic connection, however, is only the fringe of the problem. The real difficulty is what you might call institutional prejudice. Until 1973, jury lists included the jurors' occupations; but in the 'flying pickets' trials which followed a prolonged and bitter building workers' strike, the defence lawyers found that by using the seven peremptory challenges to which each of the accused were entitled they could get a jury composed wholly or mainly of workers from the local steel mill. This produced a series of acquittals until the Lord Chancellor, Lord Hailsham, directed that jurors' occupations should be deleted from the printed lists. But, while the Crown's right to stand jurors by (that is, to exclude them) was rarely arbitrarily exercised, some defence counsel went on using peremptory challenges to get rid of jurors wearing suits, jurors carrying the *Daily Telegraph* or the *Guardian*, young jurors, elderly jurors, female jurors—whatever happened to bump up against some idiosyncratic notion entertained by the accused or their lawyers—until that too was first limited and then stopped by legislation. The result is that, names apart, we genuinely and designedly do not know now who is sitting on a jury. And since the implementation of the Auld Report almost all the exclusions from jury service (other than for convicted criminals) have gone. Judges, police officers, prison officers, lawyers who defend, lawyers who prosecute can all sit as jurors.

In consequence the criminal division of the Court of Appeal has had to consider whether it should quash a verdict of guilty brought in by a jury which included two police officers and a prosecuting lawyer. It had already had to consider what, if anything, was to be done about the near certainty that one or more jurors would go home after the first day of a trial and google the defendant and anything or anyone else whose name had come up. Research carried out by Professor Cheryl Thomas of UCL suggested that something approaching one juror in eight was doing this, and the Appeal Court has made it clear that if any really prejudicial material finds its way by this means into the jury room, it is likely to vitiate the verdict. But the equally important principle of the sanctity of the jury room means that it is only by chance that the introduction of such material is likely to be revealed.

Nevertheless, judges have from time to time taken what precautions they can with a jury. In 1969, after the Kray twins had been convicted, with massive publicity, of murdering two rival gangsters, George Cornell and Jack 'the Hat' McVitie, they had to stand trial again for murdering Frank Mitchell, the Mad Axeman. The trial judge agreed that the adverse publicity was not going to do much for a fair trial this time round, and to everyone's surprise allowed the defence to question the prospective jurors about what they knew of the Krays. Within half an hour they had a jury of 12 citizens who apparently never read a newspaper or watched the television news.

15

The Right to Die

This article considered the state of the case for legalising assisted dying as it stood in the autumn of 2015, and pretty much as it still stands as this book goes to press. Both the legislature and the courts had reached a point of stasis, raising the unnerving prospect that the deadlock will one day be broken for the worst of all reasons: the sheer pressure of an increasingly aged and infirm population on public resources.

WHEN SUICIDE WAS decriminalised in 1961, assisting suicide continued to be a crime. This was in part an acceptance of the theological view of suicide as murder, but it was also a recognition of the difficulty in many cases, with the main actor by definition unable to testify, of distinguishing assisted dying from culpable homicide. The simple binary system that resulted, however, failed to take account of cases in which the deceased's wish to die was explicit, considered and rational, and the need for help in accomplishing it demonstrable.

Article 8 of the European Convention on Human Rights, which since 2000 has been given domestic effect by the Human Rights Act, guarantees respect for individual autonomy except where an interference is permitted by law and is proportionate. In 2002 the Strasbourg court held in Diane Pretty's case that the crime of assisting suicide was a proportionate limit on the right to die, since it protected 'the weak and vulnerable and especially those who are not in a position to take informed decisions'. This again left out the case of patients who were in none of these categories but wished for good reason to be helped to die. For such patients the court accepted that the discretion of the Director of Public Prosecutions to refrain from bringing to trial those who helped them afforded a sufficient safeguard. But because the DPP's discretion has to be exercised not only lawfully but consistently, the law lords, when Debbie Purdy's case came before them in 2009, required that the DPP formulate and publish the policy by which his discretion would be guided. That policy, when published, exempted relatives who act out of compassion, but not medical professionals who do so.

When, in 2013, the cases of Tony Nicklinson and two others came to the Supreme Court, challenging the compatibility of the policy and the law with Article 8 (Nicklinson, in desperation, had starved himself to death, leaving his widow to continue his claim), four of the panel of nine justices (Sumption, Clarke, Hughes and Reed) held the legislation and the policy to be compatible with the Convention. Of the five who considered the legislation incompatible, two (Hale and Kerr) were prepared to make a declaration of incompatibility; but the remaining three (Neuberger, Mance and Wilson), forming a majority within the majority, held that any declaration of incompatibility should be deferred for long enough to give Parliament a chance to get its legislation into conformity with the Convention, failing which the court might intervene. The European Court of Human Rights has since declined to take the case any further.

At the time the Supreme Court judgment was given, in June 2014, Lord Falconer's Assisted Dying Bill was before the House of Lords. It sought to give legal protection to medical professionals, as well as relatives and close friends, who helped a rational patient with a life expectancy of six months or less to die, provided two doctors confirmed that it was a settled, informed and voluntary decision and a high court judge was satisfied that all was in order. It was thus minimalist, omitting the hardest cases—patients in unendurable pain or distress with no predictable end in sight; but it was seen both by its opponents and by many of its supporters (though not by Falconer himself) as a first step on a longer road.

The second reading of Falconer's bill in the Lords in 2015 prompted a debate in which the former Archbishop of Canterbury, Lord Carey, broke ranks with the mainstream religious lobby to support it. With the prospect of a substantial majority in its favour, the bill was sent on without opposition to the committee stage, where it survived attempts to sabotage it by hostile amendment; but it sank with the dissolution of Parliament for the general election. That seemed to be that for the immediate future. Then the top place in the private members' ballot in the new House of Commons was won by Rob Marris, who introduced Falconer's bill in the Commons. The bill, which opinion polls suggested had the support of more than 80 per cent of the population, was given its second reading in the Commons in September 2015. But anyone who expected a vote that echoed public opinion will have been disappointed.

There are several reasons. David Cameron, who was known to be opposed to the measure, declined to make parliamentary time—ie time allocated by the government whips—available for it.

This meant that Marris had to run the gauntlet of the private member's bill procedure. These bills are debated on a Friday, the day most MPs try to get away to their constituencies or to their homes. Those who are there at the start of the debate may drift away, possibly making the House inquorate, unless constituents persuade them to stay. The debate may be filibustered by individual MPs who want to push subsequent private members' bills off the order paper. MPs opposed to the measure may keep their supporters outside the chamber in order to lure the mover into a fatal vote or, if they know they are facing defeat, try to block a vote by refusing to appoint tellers. Even when a private member's bill secures a majority on its second reading, it may be talked out by a single determined opponent at the report stage.

Despite all this, a private member's bill which has drawn first place and which deals with an issue of public importance has a better chance than other bills of being seriously debated, as Marris's bill was, though the standard of debate in the Commons fell short, as it often does, of that in the Lords. The bill was defeated by 330 votes to 118. In Scotland, where opinion polls showed a comparable level of public support, an Assisted Suicide (Scotland) Bill, containing a different regime from Falconer's, had been defeated earlier in the year by a margin of more than two to one.

Why are MPs so out of kilter with public opinion? Part of the reason, familiar to US politicians, may be MPs' fear for their seats. Any electoral votes to be won by support for assisted dying are eclipsed by the damage that can be done by the hate campaigns it provokes. Evan Harris, the Liberal Democrat MP for Oxford West and Abingdon from 1997, a thoughtful and decent man, lost his seat in 2010 after a campaign cheer-led by the *Daily Mail*, which dubbed him Doctor Death (he is medically qualified) because of his support for legal abortion and assisted dying: 'Zealous, obsessive and self-righteous ... fanaticism and lack of social grace ... unmarried and without children ... Though of Jewish origin, he is an aggressive secularist ... his tone of pious ideological certainty ... baseless rumours about his sexuality.' It takes nerve to run the risk of this kind of public trolling.

By deliberate but arguably unwise choice, both bills concerned only patients with a life expectancy of up to six months, irrespective of their degree of suffering. When the next case reaches the Supreme Court of a rational patient who needs a doctor's help to put an end to a life that has become an indefinite torment, the judges may be invited to live up to their *King Lear* moment in the *Nicklinson* case.

Assuming that the randomised constitution of the court does not produce a new majority which rejects the *Nicklinson* decision (a tricky legal issue in itself), the court may have to declare that both the statute law that indiscriminately criminalises assistance in dying and the DPP's policy which seeks to mitigate some of its most inhumane effects fail to meet the standard of personal autonomy vouchsafed by the Human Rights Act.

Such a decision will render the DPP's present policy unlawful and require it to be reformulated. Whether the DPP can do this without breaching the embargo placed by the 1689 Bill of Rights on the dispensing power of the Crown is uncertain. So far as the 1961 Suicide Act is concerned, the declaration of incompatibility which is all the court is empowered to grant will call on Parliament to return to an issue for which it has little appetite. What notice MPs and peers take in that event of the judicial reasons for finding one act of Parliament incompatible with another, and what—if anything—they choose to do about it, may open a new chapter in the UK's constitutional history.

16

The Brexit Case

The unaccountable determination of ministers to give notice of withdrawal from the European Union without Parliament's assent provoked a major piece of constitutional litigation and some historic press abuse directed at the High Court. Because much of the rhetoric in favour of leaving the EU had turned on giving the final say on questions of law to the UK's own Supreme Court, the government's decision to obtain the Supreme Court's ruling left little room for a fresh attack on the court's competence or motives if, as happened, it found against the government.

WHEN THE GOVERNMENT decided to appeal to the Supreme Court against the High Court's ruling that ministers could not lawfully use the royal prerogative to leave the EU, many lawyers, myself included, thought it a hopeless enterprise. A court of three judges—the Chief Justice, the Master of the Rolls and Lord Justice Sales (who had been standing counsel to the government when at the bar)—had held on cogently reasoned grounds that the prior authority of an Act of Parliament was required. Nevertheless the Supreme Court sat in full, all 11 members, to hear what even the sober Constitution Unit was calling the case of the century. Well, the appeal failed, and by a decisive margin of eight votes to three. But the margin conceals what was jurisprudentially a closer-run thing than the numbers suggest.

For well over 400 years British monarchs and their ministers have contested the claims of Parliament to have the last word on matters of state. The judges have arbitrated between them, laying down as part of the common law what ministers can lawfully do in the exercise of the royal prerogative—declare war, make peace, sign treaties, grant honours, govern colonies—and what requires the authority either of the common law or of Parliament. Over these centuries it has been the rolling back of ministerial claims to arbitrary power, exercised by the use of the royal prerogative, that has shaped the British constitution.

In 1636 a London trader called Richard Chambers sued the mayor for having wrongfully imprisoned him for refusing to pay ship money. His case was that the tax was itself unlawful, having been levied by the Crown without the authority of Parliament. The court refused to hear the argument. 'There is a rule of law,' Justice Berkeley said, 'and a rule of government, and things that may not be done by the rule of law may be done by the rule of government.' It took the rest of the seventeenth century—a civil war, the king's execution, the implosion of the republic, the restoration of the monarchy and the coup d'état we know as the Glorious Revolution—to establish that government enjoyed no such extra-legal power.

In 1685 the Duke of York, who had been brought up in exile as a Roman Catholic, succeeded his brother Charles II as king and became ex officio head of the Church of England. On any view this was going to be a problem, and James II as he now was, egged on by his theological advisers, made the worst of it. Among other unwise moves he declared the Test Acts, which barred Catholics and dissenters from public office, to be of no effect, allowing him to commission Catholics as army officers at a time when the major threat to the nation was considered to come from the Catholic states of Europe. He then packed the 12-judge court which was going to decide the legality of what he was doing. The consequent finding in favour of a regal power to suspend or dispense with Parliament's legislation brought a hurricane of political protest that culminated in the collusive invasion of England by a Protestant army and in James's abdication and flight. In 1688 Parliament reconstituted itself and offered the Crown to the invader, William of Orange, on terms spelled out in a Bill of Rights that is still the foundational statute of the British state. Its second article reads: 'That the pretended power of dispensing with laws or the execution of laws by regall authoritie as it hath been assumed and exercised of late is illegall.' For Scotland, the Claim of Right replicated the prohibition: 'All Proclamationes asserting ane absolute power to Cass [quash] annul and Dissable lawes ... are Contrair to Law.'

The regal authority or absolute power in question was the royal prerogative, the residue of monarchical powers by which executive government is conducted by ministers and their departments. The powers are residual for more than one reason. When in 1611 Chief Justice Coke held that 'the King hath no prerogative but what the law of the land allows him', he was echoing what his predecessor Sir John Fortescue had written in the fifteenth century: the king had no power to alter the law (that was for Parliament) or to administer it (that was for the judges). He was also reacting to what the law reporter John Hawarde had noted in 1597: the habit of the Queen's privy counsellors—in effect her ministers—'to attribute to their councils and orders the vigour, force and power of a firm law, and of higher virtue and force, jurisdiction and pre-eminence, than any positive law, whether it be the common law or statute law'.

Although the ambit of the prerogative has been constricted over time, it still importantly includes the United Kingdom's entry into and withdrawal from treaties, a function which accordingly falls to the Crown's ministers—in substance, the foreign secretary. But because ours is a dualist system, treaties have no effect in domestic law unless and until Parliament decides to adopt them. Thus the 1950 European Convention on Human Rights had no direct effect here until 2000, when the Human Rights Act 1998 came into force. To withdraw from the convention by diplomatic act would have no effect on the legislation giving it domestic effect, whereas repeal of the Human Rights Act would leave the convention without any domestic purchase.

All of this boils down to a simple proposition: to use the royal treaty-making prerogative to stultify primary domestic legislation is to do exactly what the Bill of Rights forbids—to dispense with laws by regal authority. It makes no odds whether the law concerned is the Dangerous Dogs Act, which somehow got into the argument before the Supreme Court, or the 1972 European Communities Act with its more recent add-ons: the executive cannot use the prerogative power to undo what Parliament has done.

Given all this, it was hardly surprising, despite the footstamping of newspapers whose conception of British values seemed not to include the country's constitution,[1] that when the Prime Minister let it be known that her government intended to trigger the Article 50 leaving mechanism without legislative authority, her proposal was challenged in court. The critical reasoning of the majority in the Supreme Court was this:

'Withdrawal is fundamentally different from variations in the content of EU law arising from further EU treaties or legislation. A complete withdrawal represents a change which is different not just in degree but in kind from the abrogation of particular rights, duties or rules derived from EU law. It will constitute as significant a constitutional change as that which occurred when EU law was first incorporated in domestic law by the 1972 Act. And, if Notice [under Article 50] is given, this change will occur irrespective of whether Parliament repeals the 1972 Act. It would

[1] It included the *Daily Mail*'s now notorious front page denouncing the three High Court judges as 'enemies of the people'.

be inconsistent with long-standing and fundamental principle for such a far-reaching change to the UK constitutional arrangements to be brought about by ministerial decision or ministerial action alone. All the more so when the source in question was brought into existence by Parliament through primary legislation, which gave that source an overriding supremacy in the hierarchy of domestic law sources.'

This looks pretty impregnable until you turn to Lord Reed's dissenting judgment. Standing by the principle of parliamentary supremacy, Reed argues that what Parliament enacted in and after 1972

'is inherently conditional ... on the UK's membership of the EU. The Act imposes no requirement, and manifests no intention, in respect of the UK's membership of the EU. It does not, therefore, affect the Crown's exercise of prerogative powers in respect of UK membership ... If Parliament chooses to give domestic effect to a treaty containing a power of termination, it does not follow that Parliament must have stripped the Crown of its authority to exercise that power ... Withdrawal under Article 50 alters the application of the 1972 Act, but is not inconsistent with it. The application of the 1972 Act after a withdrawal agreement has entered into force (or the applicable time limit has expired) is the same as it was before the Treaty of Accession entered into force. As in the 1972 Act as originally enacted, Parliament has created a scheme under which domestic law tracks the obligations of the UK at the international level, whatever they may be ... If Parliament grants rights on the basis, express or implied, that they will expire in certain circumstances, then no further legislation is needed if those circumstances occur. If those circumstances comprise the UK's withdrawal from a treaty, the rights are not revoked by the Crown's exercise of prerogative powers: they are revoked by the operation of the Act of Parliament itself.'

What the disagreement comes down to is that the majority see diplomatic withdrawal from the EU as an illicit act of the Crown, draining the statutes governing EU membership of meaning and effect, while Reed and the two judges who supported him see it as one of an indefinite range of contingencies that the legislation is explicitly designed to accommodate. Using a metaphor that recurs in the judgments, the minority see the legislation as a conduit which may, and does, change repeatedly in what it carries and which may run dry for political reasons that are not the courts' business. The majority see it as the means prescribed by Parliament by which EU law is introduced into domestic law: 'So long as the 1972 Act remains in force, its effect is to constitute EU law an independent and overriding source of domestic law.'

From these two approaches flow either of two consequences. One, supported by the majority, is that the executive is constitutionally forbidden to stifle a source of law which has been created by statute and which will therefore continue to flow until Parliament decides otherwise. The other is that the Crown's ministers, in conducting the UK's foreign affairs, are free to turn off the EU tap, leaving Parliament's legislation empty but intact. If three more judges had taken the latter view, the government would have won.

Lord Carnwath, one of the other dissentients, based much of his agreement with Lord Reed on ministerial responsibility to Parliament as a sufficient check on executive action. Leaving aside the fact that ministers are frequently not MPs but peers and do not actually have to be members of either house (the trade-union leader Frank Cousins was a rare instance[2]), he may have forgotten what Lord Justice Farwell said in *Dyson's Case* more than a century ago:

> 'If ministerial responsibility were more than the mere shadow of a name, the matter would be less important, but as it is, the courts are the only defence of the liberty of the subject against departmental aggression.'

Despite Lord Reed's astute reasoning my vote would have gone with the majority on the ground I began with. Since 1689 the Crown has been stripped of the power of 'dispensing with laws or the execution of laws'. Whether diplomatic withdrawal from the EU treaties is regarded as turning off the tap or dismantling the plumbing, its purpose and effect would be to dispense with extant legislation which makes EU law part of the UK's legal system. That is something which on principle only Parliament has authority to do.

One of the majority taking this view was Lord Sumption, whose critique of the judiciary for meddling in politics drew a good deal of attention when he was appointed directly from the bar to the Supreme Court.[3] So Lord Reed can be forgiven his parting shot: 'It is important for courts to understand that the legalisation of political issues is not always constitutionally appropriate, and may be fraught with risk, not least for the judiciary.' But the *Miller* case was not about the legalisation of political issues: it was about the politicisation of legal issues.

***

If the government's appeal had succeeded, another troublesome issue might have arisen: whose advice is the monarch required to take in deciding how her prerogative should be exercised? In the

---

[2] So, more remarkably albeit more briefly, was a Prime Minister, Sir Alec Douglas-Home.
[3] See Ch 35 below.

ordinary way the cabinet of the day, basing itself on the theory that the Queen is to be advised solely by her ministers, either deputes the decision to an appropriate department or takes the decision itself. But constitutionally it is exercising the function of the Privy Council, which at present consists of about 670 individuals who have held high office in the state as cabinet ministers, judges, diplomats, archbishops or whatever. We shall never know whether, had Lord Reed secured a judicial majority, the law would have required the summoning of a body which nowadays confers in plenary session only to name the successor to the throne or (according at least to some) to sanction the marriage of a reigning monarch, in order to tender its collective advice as to whether the UK should leave the EU.

***

The Supreme Court's judgment was handed down on 24 January 2017. On 8 February, practically without opposition, the House of Commons passed a bill the operative part of which reads in its entirety: 'The Prime Minister may notify, under Article 50(2) of the Treaty on European Union, the United Kingdom's intention to withdraw from the EU.' The petulant and ungrammatical wording, alongside the use of an acronym rather than the name of the European Union, is a curiosity. Notifying usually involves notifying somebody of something. Thus in the treaty, Article 50 requires any member state which 'may decide to withdraw from the Union in accordance with its own constitutional requirements' to 'notify the European Council of its intention'. You might have expected UK legislation, which is generally punctiliously written, to adopt a corresponding formula; but somehow the use of words acknowledging the status and authority of the European Council seems to have stuck in the legislative craw. Instead we have two lines of bad English, so unlike the usual prose of the parliamentary drafter that one wonders whether it was taken from the back of a ministerial envelope.

Perhaps more important, if this could be done now, why could it not have been done before? All the government needed to do when permission was given to Gina Miller to bring her case, or at the latest when she won it in the High Court, was to put the issue beyond doubt by securing legislation, as it has now done. Instead, having chosen at considerable public expense to die in a legal ditch in defence of the royal prerogative, the government has now ended up legislatively where it could have started.

17

The Supreme Court

An op-ed written for the Financial Times *in the wake of the Brexit case.*

THE SUPREME COURT'S inauguration in 2009 was welcome and long overdue. Although the law lords had been a distinct professional elite since the 1870s, they had an anomalous status as both legislators and judges which mocked the separation of powers. I doubt whether I am the only former barrister who can recall the Lords' Appellate Committee adjourning when the division bell rang in order to go and vote on a law reform measure in the House.

The creation of the Supreme Court, suitably located on the far side of Parliament Square, was anticipated by the abolition in 2003 of the Lord Chancellor's judicial functions—another sensible measure, debased by the crudity of its execution (Lord Irvine was in effect dismissed by press release) and by the licence it has given Prime Ministers to appoint non-lawyers to an office which is now a spare-time job for the Secretary of State for Justice. The pointed failure of Liz Truss, who as Lord Chancellor had a statutory duty to uphold the independence of the judiciary, to do anything to defend the three senior judges abused by the right-wing press for their initial ruling against the government in the Brexit case is evidence enough of the fragility of judicial independence.

So far, however, the Supreme Court has flown above the storm. It was initially populated by simply moving the law lords from the Palace of Westminster, and thereafter by making appointees titular lords without making them peers. No public fuss was made, as it might have been, when the judicial appointments panel which sat to fill the first vacancy included the judge the appointee was to succeed. And yet by 2017 there was still only one woman— Lady Hale—on the court[1] in spite of the availability of excellent

---

[1] With the appointment of Lady Black, there are now two.

female candidates, both on the bench and at the bar, and no sign of anyone from an ethnic minority. Why is this?

The independent Judicial Appointments Commission, which was set up in 2006 for England and Wales as part of the new dispensation (Scotland has its own commission) and which rightly makes all appointments solely on merit, has not, or at least not yet, redressed the imbalance. It has a mix of lay and professional members who sit in panels to make routine appointments. For appointments to the Supreme Court, which covers the whole of the United Kingdom, a small panel chaired by the president of the court is used. It is required by law to consult a considerable number of high-ranking judges and office-holders. Although something like half the Supreme Court's cases now involve issues of public law, only three of its permanent judges are specialists in the field.

Of the promotions made, more than one has caused surprise—but surprise is one of the by-products of judicial independence. Think of Earl Warren, a Republican politician appointed chief justice as a reward for giving Dwight Eisenhower a clear run at the presidency, who led probably the most liberal reforming court in US history; or the former KKK member Hugo Black who, in the phrase of an anonymous contributor to *Time*, began life by putting on a white robe and scaring black folks and ended by putting on a black robe and scaring white folks. But none of this is any kind of reason for moving to an American system of political Supreme Court nominations. When British judges are described, as they repeatedly are, as unaccountable (which they most certainly are not: everything they decide is explained by them in detail and at all but the highest level is appealable), the subtext is that their critics would like politicians to be able to dismiss them for giving unpopular decisions. That way tyranny lies. Appointment to the UK Supreme Court, whatever its faults, would not be improved by making it subject to either a political or a popular vote. I once suggested to a member of the US Supreme Court that it enjoyed its status and respect not because of but in spite of its mode of selection. To my surprise, he agreed.

A particularly ill-judged omission from the legislation is the eligibility of senior academics for direct appointment to the Supreme Court. While academics can and do double as practitioners and may secure appointment to the bench in that way, and while familiarity with practice is needed in order to be a trial judge, it should not be necessary for a member of the Supreme Court, which functions on a quite different plane, to have practised. One has only to consider how much error the great academic criminal lawyer Sir John Smith would have prevented had he been among the law lords (few of whom knew much about crime) in the 1960s, 1970s and 1980s.

Another opportunity missed on transition was to change the format of judgments. As law lords, the first members of the court had been accustomed to delivering what were both in form and in substance speeches, either reasoning out their individual conclusions or expressing laconic agreement with others. On occasion this caused uncertainty about what principle had actually been decided by the House. The move to the new court was an opportunity to change all this—not to the kind of monolithic text promulgated by the Court of Justice of the European Union, representing an often Delphic lowest common denominator, but—or so I would suggest—to the format used by the European Court of Human Rights. This adopts a single text, produced after discussion by the *juge rapporteur* and commanding the support of the whole or a majority of the court, to which each judge is free to add either a concurring or a dissenting judgment. From this, at least in principle, the law can be read off with reasonable confidence, while concurrences may add worthwhile points, and while dissents, if cogent, live to fight another day. At least, under Lord Neuberger's presidency, there has been a visible shift (possibly determined as much by workload as by principle) towards group judgments.

No court deciding major issues of public law is going to escape controversy, but the Supreme Court, with a decent record so far of resisting executive claims to unbridled power, still enjoys respect.

18

Arbitration

A review of Early English Arbitration *by Derek Roebuck.*

WHEN THE ARCHBISHOP of Canterbury suggested in a lecture in 2008 that there was room within national legal systems for some degree of religious law for members of particular faiths, the country shook with indignation—not at what the prelate had actually said, but at the menacing story the broadcast and print media extracted from it. The *Sun*'s uniquely helpful contribution was a 'Bash the Bishop' campaign, corroborating Martin Amis's suggestion in *Yellow Dog* about the way the red-tops view their readers.

All Rowan Williams was trying to argue was that a universalist doctrine of human rights does not demand what he called 'an unqualified secular legal monopoly' but leaves space for religious inputs. He was clear that these could not include a licence to undercut fundamental rights or general laws. He was not endorsing or advocating the dualist systems of places like Iran, Afghanistan, Pakistan and northern Nigeria, where Sharia courts are permitted to administer sometimes appalling forms of sectarian justice within or alongside a formal constitutional system of law. What he was describing was actually our system as it has been for many years.

One of the least remarked ways in which particular communities, not only religious ones, have for centuries been able to apply their own law to their own members is by arbitration. This has not happened by stealth or accident. Legal systems, our own included, positively welcome consensual private forms of dispute settlement, and traders commonly find them cheaper, quicker and more alive to practical realities. The courts in consequence will abdicate in favour of a binding arbitration agreement, and the law will lend the winning party the state's power to enforce the award. What is more, the parties can choose the law by which the arbitrator is to determine the dispute. In commercial arbitration agreements this usually means stipulating which country's laws are to apply. But there is nothing to stop the parties to a dispute agreeing that it is to be privately determined by some other code of law, which may be a religious one. A good many religious organisations and sects require this of their members, and a good many more permit or encourage it.

This is not to say that private arbitration within religious communities is without problems, as the archbishop might have done well to recognise. It may be entered into less by free will than by moral coercion. It may well subject some members, often women, to disadvantage or indignity. And disputes not infrequently arise between the priests and scholars of a religious community as to what its law actually is. For these and other reasons the legal system of the host society needs to be ready to step in. But the likelihood is that arbitration and mediation in one form or another are a great deal older than the legal systems of the states in which they now exist.

The reason is simple enough. A court before which the wronged and the indignant can haul their antagonists requires an organised state with ascertainable laws and an adequate apparatus of adjudication and enforcement. Simple societies and small communities, lacking this, need other ways of preventing resort to self-help and violence each time a dispute arises. Communal pressure on the parties to find a compromise is one way, akin to modern methods of mediation. Another is to encourage or permit the parties to find their own judge or judges and to agree to abide by their decision: that is, to go to arbitration. The later Romans recognised both methods: the state's adjudicative power was exercised by a *judex*, consensual adjudicative power by an *arbiter*, though the two were not always clearly distinguished.

It's easy to overlook the chronological overlap between Roman and early British society. The *AngloSaxon Chronicle*, begun towards the middle of the fifth century, antedates Justinian's code by about 90 years. Indeed, Justinian's code, still taught as a primary source of Roman law, is the law of a nascent feudal society which had long since been driven eastwards out of Rome and Italy. But there is very little evidence in Britain of cultural overlap. The institutions and practices exported by the Romans to their colonies were almost certainly confined to imperial enclaves and do not appear to have outlived Roman hegemony. The Latin element of the English language entered with the Normans; but William the Conqueror, far from imposing a new legal order as an aspect of regime change, took pains to assert that the laws of England were to remain those of

Edward the Confessor. It is with Henry II and the first foundations of a modern legal system in the mid-twelfth century, as a regular court begins to sit in London and the king's justices ride out on circuit carrying the common law with them, that Derek Roebuck's *Early English Arbitration* ends.

We possess the texts of a good many Anglo-Saxon laws, translated here by Roebuck into readable modern English; though there are some words that won't translate—for example, *domas*, which means both a law and a judgment, becomes doom, leaving him no escape from 'deeming a doom'. But until Edgar, in the tenth century, ordered his laws to be copied and distributed, royal dooms were little more than instructions to local arbitrators, telling them such things as how much they should exact for a stabbing (knife crime seems to have been a problem in early English society) depending on the injury. For the rest, customary law prevailed: in cases of adultery, the Domesday Book reveals that, in Kent at least, the king took the fine paid by the man and the archbishop the fine paid by the woman. (This probably seems quite rational at a time when the Treasury wants judges to be paid out of court fees.) The typical arbitral proceeding, not only here but throughout early society, seems to have been a communal assembly at which priests or elders would attempt to mediate a settlement or, failing that, make an adjudication. In either case, the characteristic penalty for noncompliance was not enforcement or incarceration but (as in some parts of the world it still is) expulsion or ostracism.

Until Roebuck set about it, nobody had attempted a panoptic history of arbitration. Since his retirement from a succession of chairs of law—in Australia (where he was teaching when I first met him), Papua New Guinea and Hong Kong—he has produced volumes on arbitration in ancient Greece and in the Roman Empire, and on English arbitration down to (so far) the seventeenth century. The ancient societies are far better documented than early and medieval England (the only evidence we have that the Romans invaded Britain in 55 BC, for example, is that Caesar says they did), to the extent that much of Roebuck's material about Britannia comes from Roman sources. Thus some evidence for an early legal profession in these islands comes from Juvenal in the second century CE: 'Gallia causidicos docuit facunda Britannos', rendered here as 'Fluent Gaul has taught the British advocates', though it could also be 'France has taught British advocates eloquence'. Neither translation means much until one adds to it the fact, noted by Roebuck, that there were Roman schools of rhetoric in Marseille, Toulouse, Bordeaux and Trèves, and the further fact, noted by Juvenal, that these schools had Athenian origins.

But there is no evidence that the Greco-Roman tradition of advocacy, or indeed any recognisable legal system at all, survived the departure of the Romans. There is only one hard piece of evidence of the way law might have worked in practice, and that is the much studied Fonthill Letter. It was written in about 920 CE by an arbitrator, Ordlaf, who was not chosen by the parties but appointed by the king and so was more nearly an ad hoc judge than a consensual arbitrator (Roebuck characterises this method as public, as opposed to private, arbitration). The letter reports to the king that Ordlaf, in return for a piece of the action, secured settlement of a long-running land dispute by establishing which of the hard-swearing parties was 'nearer the oath'—that is to say, which of them held a document of title to corroborate his oath. While Roebuck reserves the possibility that this was an atypical procedure, it is likelier that the Fonthill dispute is an example of a monarch lending his authority to a respected individual to procure or impose a resolution of a potentially explosive quarrel—a precursor, arguably, not of arbitration but of litigation.

In the unsurprising absence of much other hard evidence of earlier dispute resolution, at least before the eleventh century, Roebuck's method is an engaging series of polymathic raids into the territory of geographers, ethnographers, linguists, lawyers, historians and archaeologists, fetching back the kind of data that reminds you there is no such thing as useless information, and assembling it into tentative shapes. But he has to accept the fuzzy character of the shapes:

> 'First, the definition [of arbitration] by distinction from litigation is irrelevant when there is no litigation, properly defined, with which to contrast it. Secondly, the requirement that arbitration be consensual … is anachronistic when applied to societies where such emphasis on individuality was unknown.

> There is no evidence of professional arbitration in England as there is in contemporary Ireland, where the *brithem* was a legal expert who regularly heard disputes. Nor is there any sign of the *bonus homo*, the single private arbitrator of Roman law, even in Roman Britannia … When the Anglo-Saxon for *boni homines*, *god man*, is found, they are acting as "witnesses", a role which there included representing the whole assembly.'

Some scholars might have been daunted by such incertitudes. But if the book is consequently a history less of arbitration than of dispute resolution, and one mapped less by landmarks than by intersecting lines, it is an engaging rattlebag of facts and notions. Of course, speculation, as Roebuck reminds himself, has its limits, though they do not stop him having a shot—not necessarily any wilder than the standard druidic and human sacrifice explanations—at appropriating the standing stones of Avebury as a site of early dispute resolution.

More relevantly, he is fascinated by a polished flint object, a stylised human head with open mouth, found not in England but in Ireland and dating from the fourth millennium BCE. Archaeologists have decided it was the head of a warrior's mace. But it is too small and light to have been the business end of a weapon, and Roebuck suggests that it was more probably the head of a speaking-staff, an analogue of the mace of the Speaker of the House of Commons, an object described in the *Iliad* ('one after another took the *skeptron* … in their hand and adjudicated') and still used today by, among others, some Australian aboriginal communities. It may not add much to the history of arbitration, but it is reassuring to reflect that preventing everyone talking at once has been an art form for as long as there have been arguments, and that human communities have recognised for a long time that facilitating argument is a better use for a mace than breaking heads.

19

Detention without Trial

AWB Simpson, who died in 2011, was a legal polymath. This review of his 1992 book In the Highest Degree Odious: Detention without Trial in Wartime Britain *is a small tribute to him.*

E VERY SO OFTEN, poking around in the law's attic for something you need, you come across a piece of legislation or a report of a case which still has enough grass and twigs sticking to it to hint at the life behind it. Researching a case some years ago about public rights of access to Fylingdales Moor, it dawned on me that behind the opaque language of the successive Defence Acts and Military Lands Acts which from the 1840s onwards had handed huge tracts of land to the military for practice and manoeuvres lay a widespread struggle, in and outside Parliament, to keep the commons open. It resulted in the inclusion of a proviso forbidding the predecessors of the Ministry of Defence to close off any rights of common, and it gave the Greenham women the satisfaction of striking down the bye-laws under which they had repeatedly been prosecuted for entering land in breach of prohibitions which, it turned out, had been illegal. It also gave the Lord Chief Justice, Lord Taylor, an example, for his 1993 Dimbleby lecture, of the law's ability to play a straight bat.

A book may be lurking there, as it must be in many other corners of the legal attic. Brian Simpson himself embarked on such an enterprise some years ago with the nineteenth century case, known to every law student, of *R v Dudley and Stephens*[1]—the captain and mate of the yacht *Mignonette* who survived a ship-wreck by eating the cabin boy and were convicted of murder when they got home. What was so good about Simpson's *Cannibalism and the Common Law* was that it went much wider than the one earlier book on the case, Donald McCormick's *Blood on the Sea*, trawling in great social

---

[1] *R v Dudley and Stephens* (1884) 14 QB 273 (DC).

and nautical circles and retrieving wonderful things. His book on wartime internment in Great Britain does the same, with the deliberate result that the historic case which internment threw up, *Liversidge v Anderson*,[2] ranks not as the centrepiece but simply as one episode in a Byzantine, absorbing and in one respect important piece of history.

Like the rest of us in the law business, Simpson first learnt about the case as a student. 'Subsequent work', he comments, 'has made it clear to me that, like the judges involved in that great case, we had only a very shaky notion of what it was all about.' In recent years the law lords themselves have publicly repudiated their predecessors' majority decision in support of arbitrary executive power, holding that it does not represent the law of this country and that Lord Atkin's famous dissenting speech on that occasion does. In this situation Simpson's critique and contextualising of the case becomes more, not less, relevant, for he does not adopt the adulatory view of Atkin's judgment which is now the conventional wisdom among lawyers.

Every state needs or believes it needs emergency powers for times of crisis. In 1914 the British Parliament, which in 1911 had rushed through the first Official Secrets Act, rushed through a Defence of the Realm Act, drawing on much experience in Ireland and the colonies and giving ministers wide powers to govern by regulation. By 1915, MI5 had procured a regulation, 14B, permitting detention without trial of persons suspected of enemy associations. A German-born British subject, Arthur Zadig, who was detained under it, challenged in the courts whether it lay within the power of government to introduce such a fundamentally unconstitutional procedure without clear legislative authority. At each level the judges upheld the executive. Only the Scottish law lord, Shaw of Dunfermline, stood out against what he called 'a violent exercise of arbitrary power'. Lord Atkin ran with the pack on this occasion. It is sobering to find a scholar as good as Simpson writing: 'From 1917 onwards British judges have, with the rarest exceptions, consistently upheld the progressive erosion of British liberty in the name of good government.' He calls Zadig's case 'a sort of watershed between the world of Victorian liberalism and the world of the vigilant state'.

His meticulous search through public and private records and recollections—for many of the actors are still alive—enables Simpson

---

[2] *Liversidge v Anderson* [1942] AC 206 (HL).

to make his thesis three-dimensional. The blimps and pompous asses he finds and quotes at every level of government give force to his suggestion that it was a wave of misjudgment, confabulation and rhetoric rather than any soberly appraised emergency which swept both government and judiciary along. This may be right, but I am not so certain that it swept them from a principled Victorian liberalism to a Machiavellian statism. The world of mechanised warfare and instant communication into which the cavalry generals and civil servants had been gradually blundering ever since the Crimean war made alarming demands that promoted a combination of authoritarianism and arbitrary government. The Defence and Military Lands Acts of the nineteenth century were an example. But the world of Victorian liberalism to which Simpson looks back was actually one of constant state intervention, characterised both by the installation of statutory commissions to oversee and regulate the chaos of mercantile enterprise in areas of public utility and by a judicial interventionism which enabled entrepreneurs—as still happens in the United States—to tie up and tie down state bodies with litigation about the legal scope of their powers.

It was also the judges who in the new century shifted from a hands-on to a hands-off attitude towards departmental government. Why they did so is an important piece of history that has yet to be written,[3] but it cannot be explained solely in terms of capitulation to the panic-stricken demands of government in wartime. Simpson is therefore right not to call Zadig's case more than a watershed, for the process of judicial abdication which resulted in the long sleep of judicial review of government action between, crudely, the second and seventh decades of the twentieth century had much to do with the Northcote-Trevelyan transition to government through and by an Oxbridge-led professional civil service in whom the judges by and large thought they could repose their confidence and trust. The line between judicial control of the executive and judicial interference in government remains sensitive, but the fact that today it is contentious at all is evidence of a new constitutional mood that contrasts dramatically with the supine jurisprudence of the period of the two world wars which is Simpson's subject. His view that there has been a progressive judicial betrayal of British liberty in the longer term is another question.

---

[3] For an attempt, see S Sedley, *Lions Under the Throne* Ch 1, 'Lions in winter'.

Regulation 18B was made by the Privy Council under a new Emergency Powers Act passed on the same day in May 1940. Its target was principally Mosley's British Union of Fascists, the only visible and audible nucleus of an anticipated fifth column; though collaboration throughout Europe was already showing that an organised fifth column was not a necessary condition for the emergence of the enemy within. Simpson chronicles with an uncharacteristic lack of curiosity the hesitancy of the Home Secretary, Sir John Anderson, to strike quickly and hard at the BUF. He records a paper submitted by Anderson to cabinet a few days before regulation 18B was made, arguing that drastic action was premature, and he quotes the cabinet minute of the ensuing discussion, which recorded Anderson explaining at length 'the difficulty of taking any effective action in the absence of evidence which indicated that the organisation as such was engaged in disloyal activities'. Anderson, Simpson comments, respected legality.

Churchill, by contrast, supported by the Chiefs of Staff, wanted a major sweep of communists and fascists—'and very considerable numbers should be put in protective or preventive internment, including their leaders', he wrote. Then, in late June, a new regulation 18AA gave the executive power to ban organisations. It took Anderson two weeks to ban the BUF under it. 'Although difficult to believe, were it not documented, this delay was not an oversight', says Simpson, quoting a fine departmental example of Cornford's principle of unripe time to show why. He does not consider whether Anderson's heart was in it.

In his colonial service autobiography *A Mole in the Crown*, Michael Carritt describes working under Anderson when he became Governor of Bengal in the mid-1930s.

'He had been sent to Bengal as a strongman, a trouble-shooter, to cope with a quick succession of terrorist assassinations and an increase in Indian nationalist militancy. He had had experience in this role in Ireland after the First World War and had there acquired the nickname "Black-and-Tan Anderson". He was authoritarian and ruthless, but at the same time an extremely competent administrator … We who worked under him respected his efficiency but distrusted his avowed approval of the Fascist regimes.'

Carritt was the secretary of a conference of Bengal regional commissioners held in 1937.

'The conference was addressed by Sir John who stressed that his remarks were in confidence, then proceeded to advocate legislation like that in

Nazi Germany for the suppression of trade unions and political parties
and the wholesale arrest of their leaders.'

Curiouser and curiouser. The cabinet in which Anderson served
was initially Chamberlain's, but Churchill kept him on until he took
a peerage. Ultimately it was Churchill who insisted that regulation
18B be scrapped (the title of the book, *In the Highest Degree Odious*,
is a phrase he used in 1943 about detention without trial, character-
ising it as 'the foundation of all totalitarian government'), while the
communist Left, pleased that the regulation had resulted in Mosley
and not its own leaders being locked up, campaigned to lift the ban
on the *Daily Worker* and to keep Mosley in gaol.

Meanwhile, however, the judiciary had sided not with Churchill's
eventual view but with the executive's demand for unquestioned
power. The reasoning of the majority of the law lords in *Liversidge
v Anderson* was cogently ridiculed by the dissenting member, Lord
Atkin, in a speech which eventually received the accolade of inclusion in Louis Blom-Cooper's anthology *The Law as Literature*. Atkin
mortally offended his colleagues by drawing on Lewis Carroll to
characterise their semantics. Regulation 18B started with a conditional clause: 'If the Secretary of State has reasonable cause to
believe any person to be of hostile origin or associations and that
by reason thereof it is necessary to exercise control over him ...'
The majority held that whether the Home Secretary had reasonable
cause to believe any such thing was not their business. Atkin in his
dissent said:

'I view with apprehension the attitude of judges who ... when face to face
with claims involving the liberty of the subject show themselves more
executive-minded than the executive ... In this country, amid the clash
of arms, the laws are not silent. They may be changed, but they speak
the same language in war as in peace ... In this case I have listened to
arguments which might have been addressed acceptably to the Court of
King's Bench in the time of Charles I.

I know of only one authority which might justify the suggested method
of construction: "When I use a word," Humpty Dumpty said in rather a
scornful tone, "it means just what I choose it to mean, neither more nor
less" ... After all this long discussion the question is whether the words,
"If a man has" can mean "If a man thinks he has", I am of opinion that
they cannot, and that the case should be decided accordingly.'

This is stirring stuff; it still cheers lawyers and judges up when
the system comes under criticism, and it kept judicial morale stirring through the long sleep of judicial review. But what was it that

Atkin actually proposed should be done to protect the liberty of the subject?

'In my opinion the appellant in this case was clearly right in asking for particulars. If the respondents were able to satisfy the court that they could not give particulars in the public interest, the court would either not order particulars or, if the objection came after the order, would not enforce it.'

In other words, the executive could have made the whole issue go away by speaking the magic words 'national security'. It is only in more recent years that the courts have tried to develop a principle of judicial invigilation of such claims.

Arguably the major contribution of Simpson's book to modern jurisprudence is what he has found under the stone of executive discretion and judicial compliance. He shows that internment orders were being signed by the Home Secretary without consideration of evidence, and that many were being made effectively without evidence. Of the eight short paragraphs of the report which resulted in Liversidge's internment, all but one were a combination of anti-semitism and character assassination.[4] A single paragraph read: 'The said Liversidge was associated from time to time with Germans and with those associated with the German Secret Service.'

Whether this was an isolated case or part of the official ethos can be gauged by a passage, which Simpson quotes, from Lord Denning's memoirs:

'Most of my work in Leeds was to detain people under regulation 18B ... As an instance I would tell of the Nazi parson in a village in Yorkshire. He often spent his holidays in Germany ... Although there was no case against him, no proof at all, I detained him under 18B. The Bishop of Ripon protested, but we took no notice.'

Brian Simpson deserves credit for playing Ezekiel to the bones he has disinterred. We need to watch them anxiously as they dance.

---

[4] See Tom Bingham, *The Business of Judging* Ch V.3, 'Mr Perlzweig, Mr Liversidge, and Lord Atkin'.

20

Originalism

The claim of loyalty to the original language and intent of the US constitution has served as a figleaf for some highly innovative and politically driven lawmaking. Jack Balkin's Living Originalism, *published in 2012, was an attempt to lure originalism out of its shell and into a real world where, I argue in this article, it was already very much at home.*

L IVING ORIGINALISM? THE heart sinks. Is this going to resemble a treatise on tabloid ethics or some other well-meant oxymoron?[1] To a degree, the despondency is justified. How can you breathe life into a text if its meaning remains what it was in 1787 or 1868? Jack Balkin, who holds one of America's premier chairs of constitutional law, argues that you can. He is not seeking to recruit diehard originalists to the cause of creative interpretation of the US constitution, or to persuade them and their antagonists that they are all really in the same business. What he sets out to do is to offer an account of modern American constitutional adjudication which, while keeping the fundamentalists at bay, begins with fidelity to the text but recognises that, if it is to continue to be the basis of a living polity, it has to be creatively bodied out as time goes by.

It is a troubling comment on the state of America's constitutional law and politics that such an enterprise is considered necessary. Its equivalent in Britain would be a book explaining why Magna Carta, while still seminal, does not have the significance it had in 1215. The reason for the difference is that the politicisation of the US Supreme Court, which has the final word on what is constitutional, has collapsed a major part of the distinction between law and politics in the United States and significantly realigned the separation of powers. This was not the doing of the framers of the constitution. It was the Supreme Court itself which, in 1803 in the historic case

---

[1] A letter from Professor TJ Reed of Oxford rightly reproved me for using secular spirituality as a similar contradiction in terms.

of *Marbury v Madison*,[2] held itself to have the power to determine the constitutionality of congressional legislation. The ambit of the court's jurisdiction has never been seriously challenged since then. Balkin's endeavour is to redefine the consequent geometric model— a pyramid with the people at the bottom, state and federal legislatures above them and the federal courts at the top—as an organic democracy in which, almost cyclically, each element respects and influences the others.

To do this, Balkin breaks down constitutional interpretation into the ascertainment of meaning (for example, what 'speech' in the First Amendment embraces) and constitutional construction: how do you apply your interpretation? I believe this to be a false dichotomy. You cannot ascertain the meaning of words except in relation to known or supposed facts. The question of what 'speech' means in the First Amendment can be discussed only if you ask it in relation to, say, flag-burning. In fact Balkin himself implicitly recognises this by adopting a protean mode of constitutional interpretation that embraces both meaning and application. To do this he uses the word 'construction' to correspond with the verb 'to construct' rather than 'to construe'. By so doing he not only compounds but exploits the incomprehension that has beset generations of law students, whose teachers rarely start by explaining that the construction of contracts or of statutes means taking them apart, not putting them together.

Thus Balkin suggests that from 'interpretation-as-ascertainment' one proceeds to 'interpretation-as-construction', 'implementing and applying the constitution using all of the various modalities of interpretation: arguments from history, structure, ethos, consequences and precedent'—arguments from everything, in fact, except current intent as embodied in whatever happens to be the Supreme Court majority. When in the hearing of the challenge to Obama's health-care legislation Justice Antonin Scalia asked the Solicitor General whether the statute satisfied the constitutional 'necessary and proper' formula ('I get that it might be necessary, but is it proper?'), it is doubtful whether he was thinking of what the word 'proper' meant in 1787—which was 'appropriate' rather than 'desirable'— and probable that he had in mind his own standard of propriety.

The idiosyncrasy is revealing because Balkin's underlying enterprise is to allow as much literalism as possible into the creativist

---

[2] *Marbury v Madison* 5 US 137 (1803).

tent. The total process, he suggests, 'involves far more than developing doctrines and precedents': it culminates in 'activities which build out the American state over time'. Such a collaborative enterprise looks like liberalism on the back foot, which is pretty much where liberalism is at the moment in the US.

Balkin is firm, nevertheless, about keeping conservative originalists out of the tent. These were the people who succeeded for a time in blocking Roosevelt's New Deal legislation, and who later opposed liberal rulings on civil rights, contraception, abortion and so forth, on the ground that the constitution said nothing in terms about them. But their modern successors are not stupid. The cleverest of them, Justice Scalia, as Balkin acknowledges, has shrewdly declared himself 'a faint-hearted originalist', accepting as he does such developments as the constitutional recognition of centralised economic power which the New Deal cases eventually brought about, despite the certainty that the framers of the constitution would have fallen off their chairs at the idea.

This is in truth a school of legal conservatism, familiar throughout the common law world, which, because it sets high store by precedent, finds itself eventually regarding as authoritative and orthodox decisions it originally denounced as activist and heretical. Balkin rightly points out its intellectual shakiness; but it is actually only slightly shakier, at least in Balkin's scheme of things, than Earl Warren's influential stance that the true constitutional mandate to the courts was to preserve both democracy and individual rights, not to comb through the text in a theological belief that it must contain all the answers. Balkin, however, is less ecumenical than this. He sets out to cede as much ground as he decently can to the originalists, provided the originalists will allow him to build a living constitution by constructing it rather than merely construing it.

But originalism can play creativity at its own game. Scalia, discarding appeals to the framers' actual or supposed intentions, argues for the original meaning of the words on the page as a bulwark against moral slippage. The object of the constitutional prohibition of cruel and unusual punishments, he contends, is to stop a future generation introducing punishments even more cruel that those used at the end of the eighteenth century—no mere fantasy, you might think, in the days of Bagram and Guantánamo. Liberal lawmaking has to face the possibility that what was regarded as cruel in 1791, when the Eighth Amendment was adopted, will not be considered cruel in, say, 2091, and so will be granted legitimacy by a living originalism.

Whether you describe the true judicial enterprise as a search for the framers' original intent or for the constitution's original intended application, the attempt at interpretation repeatedly turns out to be a mare's nest because it has to be carried out in a factual and political context undreamed of by the framers. Indeed, the search is itself question-begging: why would the framers not have intended and expected that their instrument should be flexibly used and adapted by a future society of whose nature and problems they knew they had no conception? The question was asked by Leonard Levy in his classic debunking of originalism, *Original Intent and the Framers' Constitution* (1988), a book not discussed by Balkin.

One of the things Levy pointed out was that Reagan's Attorney-General, Edwin Meese, was repeatedly using originalist arguments in order to expand presidential prerogative powers and keep them from being controlled by Congress and the Supreme Court. The last Bush administration, Vice-President Dick Cheney especially, thrived on this doctrine, which some academics are developing into a meta-doctrine of executive supremacy that marginalises both the legislature and the courts.[3] Balkin confronts this problem in his final section, 'The Problem of Constitutional Evil'. In the past, he says, 'lawyers have used legal-sounding arguments to defend the legality of slavery, Jim Crow and compulsory sterilisation'. Why only 'legal-sounding'? These were legal arguments; not only that, they succeeded. Chief Justice Taney's lead judgment in the *Dred Scott* case,[4] whose denial of citizenship to slaves and their descendants helped to spark the Civil War, contains perfectly tenable legal logic founded on originalist principles and what seemed to the Court to be self-evident truths about race. The torture memos produced by Bush's office of legal counsel are ignoble, immoral and arguably plain wrong; but they are legal arguments.

What then, Balkin finally asks, if a politically packed bench, using such arguments, cedes huge tranches of power to an unreviewable presidential prerogative? He postulates this scenario in the wake of a succession of Bush-type administrations, but it could happen in many other ways. Can the system ever correct itself? 'Ultimately it is a question of design and faith in that design', he writes, 'whether the system of living constitutionalism we have generated through

---

[3] See A Vermeule and E Posner, *The Executive Unbound: After the Madisonian Republic* (Oxford University Press, 2010).
[4] *Dred Scott v Sandford* 60 US 393 (1857).

years of construction is a worthy successor to the framers' idea of separation of powers and checks and balances.'

Here perhaps is the real issue. Originalism, like the concomitant assault on judicial activism, has always been a stalking-horse. Along with what the historian Lawrence Kaplan called 'Founder hagiolatry', it developed during the Cold War as a riposte to the progressivist critique which had dominated the first part of the twentieth century and viewed the constitution as an elitist arrangement made by propertied men in their own interests. In the last two generations originalism has been a form of resistance not to judicial lawmaking but to the law that judicial liberals make. With the swing of the judicial pendulum to the right, originalism, as Scalia's diffidence about it foreshadowed, may well become an embarrassment. If it is now being discarded, Balkin has missed the party.

The great political accident of Eisenhower's nomination of Earl Warren to the post of Chief Justice in 1953 (in return for Warren's clearing the way for Eisenhower's presidential campaign), followed by a series of overtly liberal judicial appointments, gave the Supreme Court a lawmaking impetus, commonly characterised as activism, which carried it into the early years of this century. One of the intellectual obfuscations of these years, on both sides of the Atlantic, has been the repeated counterposing of activism to self-restraint, as if self-restraint were something different from deciding the same case the other way. Abstaining from redressing a wrong is about as interventionist as it gets.

Where self-restraint does have real meaning is in keeping appellate judges from deciding constitutional questions that they do not need to determine in order to decide the case before them. In 2009, the US Supreme Court, its right wing newly reinforced, took advantage of an appeal brought by Citizens United, a non-profit corporation, to determine whether corporate spending restrictions applied to a campaign they wanted to run, by taking it on themselves to reconsider the constitutionality of the legal limits on corporate interventions in elections. Nobody had asked them to do this, but the outcome has been cataclysmic. In January 2010—by when Balkin's text must have been completed, since the decision is not mentioned in it—the court handed down a 5–4 decision holding that the First Amendment forbade any restriction on 'independent' interventions in federal elections, and opening the door to a federal circuit ruling that the sums collected and spent for this purpose could not be capped. To accomplish this, the Supreme Court abandoned one of its own precedents (concluding that it was 'not well reasoned') and provoked a *New Yorker* cartoon showing an attorney, arms spread, submitting plaintively to the nine justices: 'If you prick a corporation, does it not bleed? If you tickle it, does it not laugh?'

More recently that magazine described the *Citizens United* decision as 'baby brother to the *Dred Scott* and *Bush v Gore* atrocities'. It could also be described as an essay in living originalism.

21

Colonels in Horsehair

This was a review of a volume of sceptical essays[1] written in 2001, when the ink of the Human Rights Act was barely dry. It considers the relationship between the state and judiciary when fundamental rights are in issue, and ventures a forward look which, I think, has proved broadly correct.

T HE UNITED KINGDOM is without doubt a good place in which to assemble a book of sceptical essays about human rights, but was 2001 a good year in which to do it? True, by then Scotland and Wales had operative devolution statutes which obliged their governments to observe the European Convention on Human Rights in all they did; and some interesting decisions had already been thrown up north of the border. But the big one, the UK's Human Rights Act, although enacted in 1998, had been put on a slow fuse to enable the country to get ready for it, and it was not until October 2000 that it was brought into force.

By then all hats were in the ring: liberal opinion had hailed a new dawn, and conservative opinion, both left and right, had predicted a bonanza for cranks and lawyers. It was a safe bet that neither would be proved wholly right, but there was no hope as yet of assessing whether the new system had significantly changed the way the country was run. This volume of sceptical essays thus sits uncomfortably on the millennial cusp, looking back at a past which is now over and forward to a future which has barely begun.

According to the mission statement riskily disclosed by the editors, the essays critically examine 'the extensive shift of political authority to the judiciary'. Now what extensive shift would that be? The judge who held that the Home Secretary was violating Louis Farrakhan's Convention right of free speech by denying him entry to Britain was told by the Court of Appeal that the Home Secretary

---

[1] T Campbell and KD Ewing (eds), *Sceptical Essays on Human Rights* (Oxford University Press, 2001).

was the best judge of these things. The court which concluded that
the town and country planning system lacked independence at its
apex and so failed to afford fair hearings was patiently told by the
House of Lords that the whole point of the planning system was to
give policy the last word so long as it stayed within the law. And the
nascent right of privacy which some of us thought we heard drawing breath was still in the incubator with an uncertain prognosis.[2]

If you look at what has happened elsewhere, you start to see why.
How much or little judges make of human rights seems to have
not a lot to do with the tools the legislature hands them. We know
that since its 1982 Charter of Rights and Freedoms came on stream,
Canada's polity has been profoundly altered both by the decisions
of the courts about what legislatures can't do, and by legislators' and
administrators' fears of what will happen if they try. Judy Fudge's
thoughtful and factual piece tracks the jurisprudential politics of
two decades of Charter litigation. She points out how early Charter
liberals have become disillusioned as a fightback by the well-heeled
National Citizens' Coalition has resulted in federal elections being
fought without effective legislative restraints on political advertising, with outcomes much to the satisfaction of the advertisers.

'There you are,' a sceptic looking at Canada would say, 'Give the
judges a bill of rights and they take over the country.' But Canada
had an earlier Bill of Rights, passed in 1960, under which the courts
managed to decide little more than that a First-Nation Canadian had
as much right as a European to be drunk in the Old Stope Hotel,
Yellowknife. By the 1980s something new had stirred in Canada's
judicial ethos; possibly the same thing as in Australia where, in
the early 1990s, the Federal High Court discovered in the country's
1901 Constitution, which provides for elections but says almost
nothing about human or civil rights, a power to strike down in the
name of free speech legislation which imposed controls on political advertising in the run-up to elections. Since then the Australian
courts have been in partial and—Adrienne Stone's essay contends—
disorganised retreat towards an ill-defined middle ground.

It's only if you stand back, with the variegated experiences of
Canada, Australia, South Africa and New Zealand (to take just the
Commonwealth examples) in your hand, that you start to see that
there is probably little direct causal correlation between a bill of
human rights and judicial interventionism. New Zealand acquired

---

[2] For its subsequent development, see S Sedley, *Lions Under the Throne* pp 202–205.

in 1990 a Bill of Rights Act which is modest in the extreme, giving not even an interpretative nudge, much less a judicial override on existing legislation; but in the hands of judges who wanted to make a reality of human rights it has taken wing. A peevish essay by James Allan criticises them for deciding that, even though they cannot interfere with incompatible legislation, they can at least declare that it is incompatible. For such critics I doubt whether judges can do anything right.

As to South Africa, which, with the demise of the apartheid regime, created a constitution with an advanced Bill of Rights and a court of high calibre with full powers of enforcement, Saras Jagwanth has the candour to start by saying: 'It is difficult to be sceptical of the South African experience of entrenching a justiciable Bill of Rights.' I know of nobody who seriously suggests that South Africa would be better off without constitutional adjudication. One of the constitutional courts' early decisions both in South Africa and—Wojciech Sadurski tells us in a useful essay on modern Eastern Europe—in Hungary was to strike down the death penalty. It's no good saying that this is a political, not a legal, issue. Abolition of the death penalty is one of the hot potatoes that lose politicians votes, and it is they—the elected representatives of the people— who in more than one country have with relief left it to the courts to sack the hangman.

The truest note is struck by the American scholar Mark Tushnet, who always has something sane to say in this area. The US experience of judicial review, he concludes, 'is nothing to get excited about one way or the other. The Supreme Court has not done much that could not have been accomplished, in perhaps a slightly longer period, through ordinary political action. But what it has done has not interfered much with democratic self-governance.' What most matters, he concludes, is who gets put on the bench, and I'll return to this.

Oddly for a book about the United Kingdom, what none of the essays addresses is the pivotal relationship between the European Court of Human Rights and our own courts.[3] The Human Rights Act enjoins our courts to take into account the decisions of the Strasbourg Court; and they would be foolish anyway not to do so, since non-compliant court decisions may put the UK in breach of its international obligation to observe the convention. Even so, on such

---

[3] See Ch 10 above.

issues as enforced self-incrimination the UK courts have been willing to plough a deviant and (as I have argued in the past[4]) welcome
furrow. But it became apparent very early in the operative life of the
Human Rights Act that our stream of human rights litigation was not
going to be anything like Canada's whitewater torrent, and the reason, looking back, should have been obvious. In Canada the sky was
initially the limit of legal argument. A colleague on the Manitoba
bench said to me in 1987: 'Don't talk to me about the Charter. Every
two-bit crook without a defence cites the Charter.' But the UK in
1998 was not introducing an open-ended rights instrument: it was
buying into an established body of jurisprudence which had already
worked out and set limits to most of the fundamental issues thrown
up by the convention. In the countdown, judicial and professional
training was able to focus on two quite specific things: the method-
ology of convention adjudication and the hard-law decisions it had
already produced.

It was the first of these that was to have the deepest and—perhaps
unexpectedly—the most positive effect on our law. I will give a
single example: the concept of proportionality. Many of the rights in
the convention permit encroachments if they meet specified objec-
tives and are 'necessary in a democratic society'. One of the book's
editors, Keith Ewing, complains in his uncompromising critique
that there is no guidance in the act or the convention as to what
'a democratic society' means. But the Strasbourg Court realised a
long time ago that it should not be lured into making socio-political
choices of this sort. Instead, it developed the juristic response that a
democratic society was one which would interfere with recognised
human rights only if there was a pressing social need which the
interference answered rationally and directly and without overkill:
if, in other words, the interference was proportionate.

A good many of our laws do interfere with convention rights. The
law which entitles a lessor to evict a residential lessee, whether
absolutely or conditionally, is an interference with the right to
respect for one's home. Courts are generally allowed by statute to
make such orders when they judge it reasonable to do so. The effect
of the Human Rights Act has been to focus the sometimes fuzzy
concept of reasonableness through a lens of proportionality, and so
to make judicial reasoning about it both more structured and more
intelligible. The liberal use of restrictive bail or parole conditions,

---

[4] See S Sedley, *Ashes and Sparks* Ch 9.

for example, has now to be thought through in terms of proportionate restraints on freedom of movement. Courts and public administrators have had to get accustomed to this reorientation. It does not make headlines, but it affects hundreds of thousands of people every year, and to them it matters a great deal.

In addition to the hands-off decisions I have instanced there were also some significant hands-on ones. The Court of Appeal used the Human Rights Act to widen the 'exceptional circumstances' escape route in the Act which in 1997 introduced the two-strikes-and-it's-life sentencing system, so that it was only where a repeat offender was a proven danger to the public that the system could be triggered. The family court used the Convention to stop the tabloids hounding the youths who killed James Bulger when they were released. One would have liked the authors of a book of sceptical essays to think about unsexy but quite important issues like these, but neither of these two early and important Human Rights Act decisions is discussed in the book.

A sceptical piece about the jurisprudence coming from Strasbourg would also have been interesting: how, for example, the margin of appreciation (a meaningless bit of translationese but a deadly legal device) has been used by majorities on the European Court of Human Rights to uphold intolerant national decisions on blasphemy and obscenity.[5] Many of these essays manifest an attitude towards change with which Albert Steptoe would have had an immediate sympathy. Their constant theme is the handover of power to unelected and unaccountable judges. The mantra is so mesmeric that it deserves a moment's reflection. Certainly, judges in this country, as in most countries, are unelected. So are monarchs, permanent secretaries, bishops, chief constables, generals and ministers. Yes, ministers. Like senior judges, they are appointed by the Crown on the advice of the Prime Minister, and they don't have to be members of either house of Parliament (two of Harold Wilson's ministers belonged to neither). If you want elected judges, look at those American states where candidates for the bench raise campaign funds from law firms.

Then there's 'unaccountable'. Ministers of course are accountable to Parliament: those who are MPs answer to elected representatives; those who are peers to, well, other peers. Judges have to account in public for effectively everything they decide: they give reasons, and

---

[5] See Ch 6 above.

if their reasons don't stack up there are two tiers of appellate courts ready to say so. If the end result is unacceptable to the electorate, Parliament always has the last word—for one of the achievements of the drafters of the Human Rights Act has been to forbid any judicial override of primary legislation which cannot be read conformably with the convention, and instead to include a neat mechanism, the declaration of incompatibility, by which the problem is passed to Parliament for solution.

I do not imagine that the unelected-and-unaccountable critics want judges who have to be voted in or can be voted out. A judge who can be removed from office by a government or an electorate which he or she has displeased lacks the central attribute of judicial office, independence. Tushnet, faced with the Hobson's choice of appointment by political deal and election by political campaign, goes for the intelligent high ground of secure but finite appointments. What other contributors are posing is something different: the need to keep political decisions in the hands of politicians. But this raises unaddressed questions—for in an important sense every decision of legal principle is a decision about how the country is to be run and is, in that sense, political.

Of all the sceptical essayists, it is Sandra Fredman who at least gets the questions straight; and it is not a coincidence that she starts an incisive essay on labour law and human rights by asking whether we ought not to be sceptical about scepticism. If there is a single area in which there is good historical reason not to trust the judges, it is labour law; yet as Fredman points out, it is precisely because this was an area in which no basic rights were ever enacted that for many years the judges' power to make law was untrammelled.

> 'Far from enhancing the power of the judiciary, a bill of rights can in fact constrain that power, provided the legislature retains proper control over the content and interpretation of the rights.'

Fredman suggests that litigation and legislation are more nearly symbiotic than mutually exclusive, and correctly counsels against seeing the one as a substitute for the other. And she focuses, at last, on why diversity on the bench matters: not because people in judicial office will vote for their own class or race or gender but because the breadth of understanding and experience of the bench in its present narrow composition cannot match that of a truly diverse bench. With this, of course, go serious issues of public perception and individual equality of opportunity. The evidence, incidentally, points not to fundamental failings in the judicial appointment process (its secrecy is a separate issue) but to deep-seated discrimination within the legal profession through which all judges have first to make their way. I wonder, however, where the final epithet comes from in Fredman's characterisation of the bench as 'largely populated by relatively elderly, white, middle-class Christian men'. I've no idea if figures exist for this country, but an American lawyer friend recently heard a veteran local judge explode on hearing that there was a Jewish nominee for a state supreme court vacancy: 'There ain't enough foreskin on the supreme court to bait a fishhook.'

Fredman's scepticism is reserved for the real weaknesses of the present system: the failure to reach behind formal equality to substantive inequality; the limiting to the individual 'victim' of the right to litigate a breach of human rights; the idea that the tradition of 'negative' rights—that you are free to do anything the law doesn't forbid—is somehow a substitute for, indeed an improvement on, positive rights. To these I would add reservations of my own which antedate the Human Rights Act and which will not be resolved, if they ever are, for many years: the capture of rights litigation by the already powerful; the view of society as a billiard table where individuals' rights simply cannon off one another; the casting of the state in the role of the individual's natural enemy; the need to protect individuals from violations of their rights by non-state entities often more powerful than the state.

All of these are addressed in places in the book, but most commonly as part of a jeremiad directed not at the deep structures of law but at the modes of its administration. Yet even in these early days some shapes are emerging. Almost osmotically, seepage from public to private law relationships is happening—most literally where Parliament has required statutes, including those governing private law relationships (I mentioned landlord and tenant), to be read into conformity with the convention; most ineluctably in family law, where the right to respect for family life permeates every argument about the care of children; most interestingly where the gate *is* pushed open by wealthy and powerful people (Michael Douglas and Catherine Zeta-Jones, for instance, suing a magazine for publishing unauthorised photographs of their wedding), and through it in their wake come vulnerable people like Venables and Thompson.

I used to argue that the advocates of the convention resembled the Brooklyn woman who came out with chicken soup for a man lying inert in the road, and when a bystander said 'Lady, it won't help,' replied: 'Mister, it won't hoit.' Now, I confess, I am less sure. There are still ways in which the new dispensation is capable of doing long-term as well as short-term harm, not least by judicial abstention; but there is also good, some of it unexpected even by the advocates of reform, which it is now clear that it is capable of doing. A judicial hijack remains, no doubt, a possibility; but there is little empirical support so far for the prognostications of a coup by colonels in horsehair which resonate in these essays. The emergence of the people and authorities of the UK, hand in hand, on to sunlit uplands of human rights protection will stay in the realm of wish-fulfilment; but the downside scenario is unlikely to be worse than Conor Gearty's chapter suggests—that the Human Rights Act 'will be buffeted on waves of litigation, thrown back and forth between various litigants, sometimes doing good, sometimes doing bad, occasionally being washed up on useless analytical islands where it will be stuck for years on end until a rescue by some tidal wave of fresh thinking'.

In any event, like the weather, the Human Rights Act is there and has to be lived with, and while scepticism will remain a useful posture in relation to it, negativity will not.

22

The British Constitution

A review of Martin Loughlin's Very short introduction *to Britain's constitution.*

WRITERS ON THE British constitution have always faced the problem that it cannot simply be held up to the light and admired. Our constitution is simultaneously a description of how, for the moment, we are governed and a prescriptive account of how we ought to be governed. In both respects (the former much more than the latter) it undergoes constant change; and there are concerns that the process may be accelerating into a critical and damaging phase.

Oxford University Press has managed to get one of the most sophisticated British scholars of modern public law to produce a brief and readable account of the interpenetration of these two constitutional functions. Take Magna Carta, successively lauded as a charter of English liberties, then dismissed as a carve-up between a tyrannical monarch and his predatory barons, due for yet another reappraisal on its 800th anniversary. Martin Loughlin gets it in one:

> 'By establishing the principle that acts of the king had an official character exercisable through certain forms, the charter constituted a landmark in the emergence of English governing arrangements.'

What followed was, as he says, messy. It took a long time for king and Crown to become visibly distinct,

> 'but it is from this concept of the crown—the king in his official capacity—that our understanding of government has evolved.'

In fact, it's more than just our understanding of government: for more than three centuries it's been the reality of the British state. While, as Loughlin points out, similar Continental charters in the thirteenth century made barons sovereign within their fiefs, the English charter gave the nobles a toehold in an already centralised state. It did so in part by forbidding taxation 'except by the common counsel of our realm': less an early outbreak of democracy than a recognition that the assent of the second estate, the nobility, and the co-operation of the third estate, the burgesses and knights of the shire who represented the commons, was necessary if taxes were to be gathered for the Crown. By the third decade of the seventeenth century it was estimated that the commons could have bought the lords twice over: the Civil War and Britain's experiment with republicanism were on their way.

One of the principal contributors to this long and uneven process was, of all people, Henry VIII, who repeatedly resorted to Parliament for legislative authority for his divorces and his break with Rome. The establishment of a state church, with a hereditary monarch as its spiritual head, was a novelty which only an act of Parliament— an institution which Dicey was later, rashly, to boast could do anything except make a man a woman or a woman a man—could even purport to accomplish. To build on or to modify what Henry had done, his successors had again and again to resort to Parliament.

Loughlin comments that the 1689 settlement, establishing the Crown-in-Parliament as the supreme authority in the state, 'fudged the finer points of constitutional principle'. It is true that the British bill of rights has a back-of-an-envelope look to it, but little more so than the constitutional shopping list contained in its US counterpart a century later. What is no less important is that in 1653 the Instrument of Government (Britain's first and only written constitution, as Loughlin points out) had created what is today recognisable as an American-style presidency, installing a head of state, Oliver Cromwell, who was to be not a figurehead but a chief executive, whose powers of taxation were subject to Parliament's override, and who was forbidden to suspend or dispense with its legislation:

> 'The laws shall not be altered, suspended, abrogated or repealed, nor any new law made, nor any tax, charge or imposition laid upon the people, but by common consent in Parliament.'

The debt of the 1689 bill of rights to the Instrument of Government (which itself reflected some of the radical demands of the Civil War) is palpable:

> 'That the pretended power of suspending of laws ... without consent of Parlyament is illegall ... That the pretended power of dispensing with laws or the execution of laws by regal authority ... is illegall ... That levying money for or to the use of the Crowne by [pretence] of prerogative without grant of Parlyament ... is illegal.'

Although it took a while to settle in (monarchs continued purporting to suspend legislation into the early eighteenth century), the essential purpose and effect of the bill of rights were to make the Crown, which had long since been forced—in principle at least—to delegate its judicial authority to the judges and was shortly to begin devolving its administrative authority to ministers, subordinate to Parliament. In return, the state undertook to conduct all three core functions in the monarch's name.

Thus far we have the structure, but very little of the content, of the British constitution. Blackstone, in the late eighteenth century, took its content to be assured by three institutions: Parliament for the redress of grievances, jury trial for the protection of the innocent and habeas corpus for the restriction of state power, the latter two springing from Article 39 of Magna Carta and assured by a judiciary whose independence had been guaranteed by the 1701 Act of Settlement. It was Dicey, a century after Blackstone, who sought to encapsulate the content of the constitution in what he called the rule of law: the idea that because the constitution itself derived from the rights of individuals, its fixed purpose was to guarantee those rights by the equal application of the same law to everyone from the prime minister to the postman.

Not only is Dicey's paradigm a long way, as Loughlin points out, from the modern practice of prescribing rights by tabulation; it was erroneous from the start because, at a time when a sophisticated system of judicial review of official action existed in Britain, Dicey's hostility to civil law systems in general and to France in particular led him to insist that in England 'we have no *droit administratif*'. Loughlin notes the curious (and under-studied) decline of judicial interventionism in the first part of the twentieth century, as the negative freedoms which preoccupied Blackstone and Dicey were supplanted by the positive but paternalistic freedoms of the managerial and welfare state; and the hesitant but finally confident regrowth of judicial review in and after the 1960s into a system which 'brought the administrative powers of government under the overarching supervision of the common law courts'. To do this the courts had to recognise, in defiance of Diceyan orthodoxy, 'a conceptual distinction between public law and private law'.

Loughlin uses the *Malone* case[1] as a barometer of the constitutional changes we have undergone. Malone was an antique dealer who was charged in 1977 with handling stolen property. At his first trial, which ended inconclusively, it emerged that the police had

---

[1] *Malone v Metropolitan Police Commissioner* [1979] Ch 344 (DC); *Malone v UK* (1985) 7 EHRR 14.

been tapping his telephone pursuant to a warrant issued by the Home Secretary. No law allowed this, but no law forbade it. To prevent the use of the intercept evidence at his retrial, Malone sued the state for a declaration that the phone-tap violated his legal rights. He failed in the English courts on the ground that there was at that date no law against phone tapping, but won resoundingly in Strasbourg on the ground that under the European Convention on Human Rights the UK could violate his privacy only as prescribed by law.

One result has been a statutory surveillance regime shrouded in secrecy, part of a growing constitutional model which has led some of us to wonder whether the tripartite separation of powers—legislature, judiciary, executive—conventionally derived from Locke, Montesquieu and Madison still holds good. The security apparatus is today able in many democracies to exert a measure of power over the other limbs of the state that approaches autonomy: procuring legislation which prioritises its own interests over individual rights, dominating executive decision-making, locking its antagonists out of judicial processes and operating almost free of public scrutiny. The arbitrary use of sweeping powers of detention, search and inter-rogation created by the (pre-9/11) Terrorism Act illustrates a long-term shift both in what is constitutionally permissible and in what is constitutionally acceptable. The former may be a matter for Parlia-ment, but the latter is still a matter for the rest of us.

Despite all this, access to justice remains, in principle at least, a pillar of our constitutional law. Without it, the rule of law lacks sub-stance. The long-standing constitutional convention that the Lord Chancellor should be a senior lawyer was not a mere genuflection to the judges. It reflected the fact that the separation of powers prop-erly denies the judiciary a voice in government, so that unless a senior cabinet minister speaks for the justice system the equilibrium between the limbs of the state is jeopardised. The problem was that, until 2005, the Lord Chancellor wore three hats: speaker of the Upper House, cabinet minister and head of the judiciary. Because there was one day going to be trouble in Strasbourg over a politician presid-ing in a member state's highest court, the Blair government took the opportunity to dismantle the system overnight. It made sense to make the Lord Chief Justice head of the judiciary, but making the lord chancellorship a secondary occupation of the new Secretary of State for justice was more than a simple consolidation of tasks: by depriving the judiciary of a voice in cabinet, it exposed the legal system to the vagaries of politics and policy, with profound implica-tions for the rule of law. We are now seeing the consequences.

23

A New Constitution?

Perceptions of constitutional change do not fare too well on time's whirligig. This article, written in 2009 when the drama of Brexit still lay the better part of a decade away, cast a not wholly misplaced shadow ahead of it. The attack on the Human Rights Act proved to be no more than a stalking horse for the grand design of leaving the EU. With the referendum result in the bag, repeal of the HRA dropped off the agenda.

THERE'S AN EPISODE of *The Wire* in which the intellectual drug baron Stringer Bell, trying to launder his gang's profits by legitimate real estate development, finds the project stalled by bureaucratic delays. He is tactfully advised by his contractor that it takes money in the right place to get things moving. Bell is outraged; but, as the contractor explains, it's 'democracy in action'. The day after I had laughed aloud at this, I read that one of the London boroughs was considering introducing such a system: if you want your planning application dealt with promptly, it will cost you, while for everyone else the wait will get even longer. The difference is that this system will be entirely above board.

Is it constitutional for a public authority to offer different standards of public service in return for premiums? Fifty years ago it might well have been doubted. But the postwar notion that the state provided service according to need, and that if queues formed they were not to be jumped, has given way to an entrepreneurial model in which, subject to a safety net at one level or another, you pay for what you get and you get what you pay for. Each concept has acquired constitutional legitimacy in its time—for, as John Griffith famously observed, the constitution is what happens.

So when you pick up a book called *The New British Constitution* and ask what new constitution that might be, one answer is that the British constitution, because it is always changing, is always new. But the veteran political scientist Vernon Bogdanor goes further. His thesis is that since the election of the Blair government in

1997 the pace and depth of constitutional change have increased to a point where a new shape of the state, though still fuzzy in outline and incomplete in detail, can be discerned and described with some confidence.

Riskily, however, Bogdanor takes the cornerstone of the new constitution (the metaphor is his) to be the 1998 Human Rights Act. His starting point is, as it has been for the whole of his generation of political scientists and my generation of constitutional lawyers, the writings of Bagehot and Dicey. Bagehot, in his bright and energetic prose, went out of his way to stress how little separation actually existed in mid-Victorian Britain between the executive and legislative powers of the state located in cabinet and Parliament. He was right to point it out but wrong to support it. The dominance of Parliament by ministers and their departments was and remains a major issue for parliamentarians.

Bagehot's sound account of the organic nature of the constitution stood and stands in sharp contrast to Dicey's iconic reverence for the arrangements he chose to see and describe. Leaving aside his xenophobic and counterfactual insistence that Britain, unlike France, had no body of administrative law, Dicey's doctrine of parliamentary supremacism stood firm until Home Rule came up: then he changed his mind and argued that there were some things that even Parliament couldn't do. This apart, Dicey's was a classic endeavour to enshrine what happened (or what he claimed happened) as what ought always to happen. Bogdanor is generous to describe Dicey's account of the Victorian constitution as 'perhaps … reasonably accurate'.

His argument, however, is that that was then, and that what has now happened has made much of it irrelevant. This is the clean break he needs if he is to make good his 'new constitution' thesis. Is it really there?

The first turning point, Bogdanor suggests, was the enactment in 1972 of a UK statute making European Union law superior even to Parliament's legislation. The statute has certainly operated at that radical level, but what is perhaps equally important is that it is no more than an act of Parliament and can still be repealed by a simple majority. That does not necessarily suggest a constitutional measure. Nor does the occasional use since 1975 of referendums, admittedly a measure of direct democracy even if heavily mediated by the way the question is put; nor the introduction of proportional representation for European elections. But Bogdanor's big argument is that since 1997 constitutional change has gone into overdrive.

He lists 15 measures, starting with the withdrawal of the Treasury's hand from the Bank of England's monetary policy, running through the devolution of major central powers, the increasing use of PR and the introduction of mayoral government, to the partial reform of the House of Lords, the Freedom of Information Act, the regulation of political parties and their funding, and the recasting of the judicial system.

The last of these is without doubt a real shift in the shape of the constitution. The law lords in 2009 ceased to be members of the legislature and became a distinct supreme court. The umbilicus linking judiciary and cabinet had already been severed when the Lord Chancellor ceased to be head of the judiciary and became a rank and file minister, while an independent commission took over his role of appointing judges. But Bogdanor makes the cogent point that if, instead of the disorderly and protracted way in which these changes have been introduced, they had been carried out in a single methodical swoop, the arrival of a new constitutional order would have been all but undeniable.

That may be; but it may equally be said that the very disorderliness of the process, the toe-in-the-water approach to reform of the Upper House, the resort to referendums to decide whether cities shall have mayors, the use of PR for some elections but not others, are examples of much the same kind of organic development as Bagehot was describing. If one were determined to locate a constitutional moment between the Victorians and us, the postwar institution of the welfare state might be a stronger candidate, realigning as it did the relationship of state to individual, and bringing in its wake the eventual reassertion of judicial oversight of executive and local government.

The high point of Bogdanor's conspectus is also, through no fault of his, the most tantalising and least conclusive. It is now widely accepted, and Bogdanor does not dispute, that the doctrine of parliamentary supremacy is itself an artefact of the common law, growing out of the historic compromise between the three limbs of the Crown—legislative, judicial and executive—which was reached in the course of the seventeenth century and has been developed in modern concepts of the rule of law. Off parade, one or two senior judges have in the past considered the consequent possibility that if parliamentary legislation were to violate fundamental constitutional norms it might be the duty of the courts to disapply it. But more recently, on parade in the case challenging the hunting legislation, three of the law lords took the opportunity to spell it out.

Bogdanor cites the storm warnings given by Lord Steyn, Lady Hale and Lord Hope. Hope, one of the Scottish law lords, said:

'Parliamentary sovereignty is no longer, if it ever was, absolute ... Step by step, gradually but surely, the English principle of the absolute legislative sovereignty of Parliament ... is being qualified.'

He went on to locate the ultimate constitutional control Hart's rule of recognition—in 'the rule of law enforced by the courts'.[1]

This is potent and pregnant stuff. The outcome of the hunting ban case didn't depend on it, but, not long before, the government had been forced to drop a clause in an asylum bill which would have shut off all judicial review and appeal to the courts. Ronald Dworkin in a lecture in Cambridge had called on the judges, if it was passed into law, to hold it unconstitutional and to treat it as invalid. His suggestion brought into sharp focus the allocation of power between Parliament and the courts, a polarity that Bogdanor identifies as the site of a potential constitutional crisis. For what would happen in real life if the higher courts treated such a withdrawal of their jurisdiction as unconstitutional, ignored it and allowed an asylum seeker's appeal? The Home Secretary, not recognising their jurisdiction, would proceed with deportation, and the court would arraign him or her for contempt. How would it end? We do not know, and most of us would prefer not to find out.

In any event, a constitutional moment of truth is nowhere near as imminent as Bogdanor suggests. He thinks there is a conflict, created by the Human Rights Act and developing at what he calls remarkable speed, between the judges on one side and government, Parliament and the people on the other. This is an analysis which owes more to tabloid journalism than to constitutional reality. The reality is that, without taking the last word away from Parliament, the Human Rights Act has given the courts a voice in determining the compatibility of legislation with the convention, and Parliament and government have had the wisdom to heed the courts' advice on the relatively few occasions when it has been negative. The law lords' holding that the indefinite detention of foreign nationals on security grounds was contrary to the convention was accepted, albeit through gritted teeth, and different legislation introduced.

[1] In an interesting footnote, Bogdanor relates Scottish scepticism about the absoluteness of Parliament's sovereignty to the longstanding view that the 1707 Act of Union left the Scottish legal system and Presbyterian church beyond the reach of Westminster.

That is not conflict: it is part of a major constitutional shift, initiated not by the judges but by Parliament, by which the judicial functions of statutory interpretation and protection of fundamental rights have been dovetailed with the legislative process. Inevitably, the media's badmouthing of the Human Rights Act has succeeded in obscuring this constitutional achievement, but it is a pity that Bogdanor buys into it. That there remain areas of law in which the judges are frustrated with Parliament (the proliferation and complexity of criminal justice statutes, for example) and others where ministers are fed up with judges (for example in areas of asylum law) is not a harbinger of crisis or breakdown: it's what happens under the rule of law in a democracy. It might be otherwise if Bogdanor's assertion that 'the judiciary is the only one of the three branches of government to hold unchecked and unaccountable power' were correct; but to believe this you would need never to have read a reasoned judgment, and to have forgotten that Parliament has not only final legislative power but sits on ethical questions as judge in its own cause.

The still larger question, whether constitutional change has now acquired a critical mass or is simply happening as it always has done, may be less important than the fact that no constitution, except perhaps that of a moribund state, stands still, and that ours is and for some time has been, as Bogdanor says, changing before our eyes. The devolution of major state powers to Scotland in particular is a true constitutional change, both because it is in practice irreversible without the consent of the Scots and because it is capable of having opened the door to a unilateral declaration of independence.

The changes to the judicial system are also probably irreversible, despite their not inconsiderable problems. The requirement to apply for all judicial posts is no doubt an advance on the tap on the shoulder from a Lord Chancellor who has been taking private soundings from senior judges—itself an advance on Lord Salisbury's belief (cited by Bogdanor) that an unwritten law dictated 'that party claims should always weigh very heavily in the disposal of the highest legal appointments'. But the self-promotion that applications involve does not necessarily reveal the best candidates. Nor has it done much so far to redress the imbalances on the bench of gender and ethnicity. This is not because the appointments commission has been less than conscientious in its efforts. It is because the legal profession itself does not give women and minorities the same chance to shine as their white male counterparts. The real stars may well shine anyway; but the critical difference is with the average—sometimes very average—white male practitioner who can still reach the upper tranche of the practising profession. You cannot constitutionalise this problem: it has legal aspects but it reaches deeper than law.

There is a further series of problems with recorderships—part-time judicial appointments. These are a requisite first step on the staircase to the bench, for which applications can now outnumber vacancies by a factor of 20 or more. The new system, recognising the hazards of self-promotion, moved from shortlisting on the basis of references, with its capacity for idiosyncrasy, to a tickbox system which had the effect of excluding good candidates with atypical CVs, and from there to shortlisting by examination. This too is proving problematic: barristers who are at or close to the peak of an intellectually exacting profession, and whom the judges they appear before know to be outstandingly able, are failing the examinations which allow them to be shortlisted for interview as potential recorders. It would be ironic if a practice which, though indefensible in principle, delivered at least some of the goods had been replaced by a process which rewarded mediocrity at the expense of talent.

The effect of the changes to the judicial system, like the effect of devolution, is thus neither prescribed nor predictable. What, however, any reformed constitution must surely contain is an acceptable template of parliamentary conduct, something which three centuries of self-regulation have failed to create. The Committee on Standards in Public Life has a great deal to think about. Will modifying the allowance system answer the underlying problem of a parliamentary salary which many think incommensurate with the status and responsibilities of an MP? Will enhancing the salary be an acceptable solution if second jobs and employed relatives continue to be tolerated?

Then there are Parliament's own composition and procedures. Should it continue to be possible for a single MP to sink private members' bills which otherwise have the support of the whole house? Should a member of either house who has declared an interest be able, unlike a local councillor, to remain and vote? Are we ever going to resolve the West Lothian question? And what is to become of the Upper House? Election of its members will, on a strategic level, deprive Prime Ministers of ultimate control of its composition, and on a political level may challenge the legitimacy of the Commons. When at one point ministers settled on a four-fifths elected chamber, on what basis were the members to be elected?

If after 12 years of proposals and withdrawals we still did not know, it may have been less because of political hesitancy than because the issue was and is genuinely intractable. Bogdanor, a knowledgeable writer, is long on voting systems but short on these much bigger questions. Yet without answers to them any new constitution would be a lame thing.

By no means uniquely, the UK's constitution is not a fact but a process, a space to be watched. Ineluctably and unevenly, the old order changes; but to assert that it has become a qualitatively new dispensation is, at least for the present, to jump a gun which may never go off.

24

Freedom of Expression

Part of a paper given to the Faculty of Advocates in Edinburgh in 2015 on some of the perils of censorship.

IN 1909 MY Inn of Court, the Honourable Society of the Inner Temple, disbarred and expelled a barrister named Shyamji Krishna Varma. Varma was a prominent Indian nationalist who, like other nationalists, had found it possible to speak more freely in Britain than in India. He had written a letter to *The Times*[1] warning the British that their time as rulers and exploiters was coming to an end and that the end could be a violent one. His disbarment was moved by Master the Earl of Halsbury, the former Lord Chancellor, by then aged 86 but sufficiently incensed to take the lead in getting rid of a turbulent barrister. A motion to give Varma an opportunity to put his case against expulsion was defeated. A generation later, in 1922, Mohandas Gandhi was convicted of sedition in India and sentenced to six years in gaol. He too was expelled by the Inner Temple.[2]

Both Varma and Gandhi have now been posthumously reinstated: their heresy has become, if not orthodoxy, at least a respectable stance. Where Varma had incurred the benchers' wrath by writing that 'Indian nationalists regard all Englishmen in India as robbers', and that 'every Englishman who goes there for exploiting that country directly or indirectly is regarded as a potential enemy by the Indian Nationalist party', as respected a British historian as William Dalrymple has pointed out that Powis Castle 'is simply awash with loot, room after room of imperial plunder, extracted by the East India Company', whose governance had 'quickly turned into the straightforward pillage of Bengal and the rapid transfer

---

[1] *The Times*, 20 February 1909.
[2] See *Inner Temple Yearbook*, 2005/6 p 62. The expulsion took place within three days of the conviction.

westwards of its wealth', while Indian markets were flooded with British products.[3]

Varma's shade must have applauded; for one of the many risks of censure and censorship is that it will be the censor, not his victim, who is made by history to look foolish. In February 1803, during the brief cessation of hostilities which followed the Peace of Amiens, the Anglo-French writer John Peltier was prosecuted and convicted before the Court of King's Bench on a charge of seditious libel for publishing an attack (in elegant alexandrines) on the monarchical ambitions of Napoleon, who was momentarily the head of a friendly state.[4] Within the year Peltier had been proved right, but by then he was in gaol.

I have argued in the past,[5] and still think, that censorship is a pit with no bottom. But does it follow that there should be no limits on writing and speech? Most liberal societies adopt a harm threshold and criminalise speech or writing which transgresses it. I have little difficulty with this, even though it throws up a plethora of moral questions both about whether it is intent or effect which should be the crucial test, and about what constitutes harm. I have a great deal more difficulty with societies which use the harm test to criminalise religious heterodoxy by stigmatising it as blasphemy. I also have some difficulty with the law which, at least in England and Wales, has replaced the common law offence of blasphemy with a statutory offence of incitement to religious hatred, seeking to ringfence one particular class of belief or point of view against the winds of hostility which other beliefs and viewpoints—political, aesthetic, social—are rightly expected to put up with. A particular asymmetry arises where hatred is promoted on religious grounds against secular and therefore unprotected targets—notoriously homosexuality, but also apostasy or atheism.

Where we lawyers tend to lose the plot is where the discussion gravitates away from bans and penalties and towards simple civility—a form of soft law—as a control on free speech. A great deal of potentially offensive speech takes place in controlled or controllable forums—schools, universities, newspapers, broadcast media— which are able to make and enforce their own rules. For these reasons

---

[3] *The Guardian*, 4 March 2015.
[4] *Le 18 brumaire, an VIII* ('Que faut-il à ses voeux? un sceptre? une couronne?'). See *R (Buonaparte) v Peltier*, cor. Lord Ellenborough CJ (in KB, on AG's information), 21 Feb 1803.
[5] S Sedley, *Ashes and Sparks* Ch 38.

it may be legitimate to criticise a periodical such as *Charlie Hebdo* for giving unjustified offence—for incivility, in other words—without for a moment wanting to see it or any similarly pungent periodical penalised or banned. Correspondingly, the 'no platform' policies adopted by many tertiary education institutions and supported in general by the National Union of Students are intended to protect minorities in the student body from insult or isolation. But the price of this, the stifling of unpopular or abrasive voices, is a high one, and it is arguable that it is healthier for these voices to be heard and challenged. Challenge of course brings its own problems: is it legitimate to shout a speaker down? But these are exactly the margins of civility which institutions need to think about and manage. They are not a justification for taking sides by denying unpopular or abrasive speakers a platform.

Parliament, for its part, has sought to draw a legal perimeter around academic platforms, banning outright their use for the promotion of forms of extremism which may nurture terrorism. The aim is laudable, but the means are worryingly open to error and abuse, and the deliberate chilling effect on the exchange of ideas may do little to halt the serious proselytising which happens well away from public forums.

25

The Abuse of Power

This paper was delivered, in longer form, as the Commercial Bar Association lecture in 2011, shortly after my retirement from the bench. It considers, among other things, how a constitutionally supreme parliament or a constitutionally autonomous monarchy may abuse its powers.

NOBODY DOUBTS THAT power—any power—can be abused; and nobody is likely to assert that abusing it is a good thing. Like sin, we are all against it. We all know, too, that Lord Acton wrote 'Power tends to corrupt, and absolute power corrupts absolutely',[1] though why this casual remark in a letter to a bishop should have achieved such celebrity is something of a mystery. Even more mysterious is what was going on in the mind of the Dragon Lady, the late Madame Nhu, when she remarked half a century ago: 'Power is delightful, and absolute power is absolutely delightful'. Whether she was neatly parodying Lord Acton or naively misquoting him, she knew what she was talking about. As the wife of the South Vietnamese dictator Ngo Dinh Diem, Mme Nhu had accumulated powers which, according to one American commentator, were the equivalent of simultaneously running the CIA, the FBI, the Congress and the press.

But what constitutes an abuse rather than simply a use of power has to depend in the first instance on what the power is. An autocrat can do almost anything without exceeding his powers. In a state which acknowledges the rule of law, by contrast, there are multiple constraints on the exercise of power. Breaking these bounds may attract political or public censure but is not necessarily a justiciable abuse. Nor, however, is abuse of power necessarily deliberate or reckless. It may happen by pure inadvertence; it may be done, as it

---

[1] *The Life and Letters of Mandell Creighton* (Longmans Green, 1904), reproducing a letter of 3 April 1887.

most often is, for political advantage; very rarely its motive may be corrupt; or—as Mme Nhu reminded the world—it may be done, as arguably it was in *Wednesbury*, for the sheer satisfaction of doing it.

I want to consider such abuses, though without assigning any single motive to them, in two contemporary contexts, neither of them the now familiar context of judicial review. One is the possible misuse of Parliament's own constitutional supremacy. The second is the misuse by ministers of the royal prerogative

I need first, however, to excuse my failure to include the judiciary in this sweep of the searchlight. Having been part of this body for nearly two decades, I am not in an ideal position to take an objective look at it. But I am certainly conscious of its vulnerability to abuse. Sitting in Room 101 (presciently nominated by George Orwell as the place where the thing you most dread happens to you), I used regularly to be asked to grant injunctions to freeze the assets of claimants' business competitors who were alleged to owe them money—a form of order which, as claimants well knew, could put a small business swiftly on the rocks. The application, made in the nature of things in the defendant's absence, was commonly supported by an affidavit, sworn by or derived from an enquiry agent, containing complete details of the defendant's bank accounts. I began to make a practice of asking counsel for an assurance, on instructions, that this information had been lawfully obtained. If it had not been, I would refuse to make an order because the claimant had not come to court with clean hands. I never once received an affirmative answer to my question. The use, not only by lawyers but by journalists, of private investigators with ready access to corrupt officials and police officers is not new, and the legal profession bears blame for turning a profitably blind eye to it; but I think too that the judges could and should have done more to root it out.

Nor am I going to be saying much about the use by ministers of their status to attack judges whose decisions they dislike. When a Prime Minister, Tony Blair, feels free to attack a judge, Mr Justice Sullivan, for having 'taken leave of his senses' in his decision on the Afghan plane hijackers which was unanimously upheld by the Court of Appeal; and when a Home Secretary, Theresa May, with her own Prime Minister's backing, attacks the Supreme Court in very similar language over a cautious and balanced decision that not all sex offenders need necessarily remain on the register for life, something is going wrong with the rule of law and the separation of powers: far from judges seeking to influence the political process, politicians seem to be trying to influence the judicial process.

All that I propose to say about the culture of ministerial abuse is that its seriousness was recognised by the Select Committee on the Constitution in its 2007 report, which advised that the next revision of the Ministerial Code, which Downing Street periodically issues, should contain strongly worded guidelines about public comment by ministers on individual judges. But the Code still contains nothing about ministerial attacks on judicial decisions. One can speculate about the reasons for this omission, but they are unlikely to be divorced from the fact that ministerial attacks on judges play well with much of the press.

THE ABUSE OF PARLIAMENTARY POWER

Parliament's supremacy in our constitution is not today in question, though more than one academic commentator and more than one judge has suggested that its legislative power is not unlimited. But supreme power, whether or not subject to formal limits, carries a high degree of responsibility. One such responsibility is not to misuse the immunities which the parliamentary function necessarily attracts. Another is to maintain the separation of the state's powers, of which parliamentary sovereignty is one element only.

The latter of these obligations might at one time have been dismissed as mere aspiration, but since the enactment of section 3 of the 2005 Constitutional Reform Act ministers have been under an explicit statutory duty to uphold the independence of the judiciary. Who can say whether it may one day become necessary to test whether the duty is enforceable? All one can do for the present is note that in 2007 the House of Lords Select Committee on the Constitution, reporting on the wave of ministerial attacks on judges, spoke of:

> '... the need for an independent judiciary able to interpret the laws made by Parliament, particularly when Ministers do not appear to understand the constraints that apply to their policies, or indeed the full content of legislation that they proposed to parliament.'[2]

Article 9 of the 1689 bill of rights, one of the foundational documents of our democracy, forbids the impeachment or questioning in any court or place out of Parliament of 'the freedom of speech and debates or proceedings in Parlyament'. The protection that this

---

[2] HL Paper 151, 26 July 2007, para 55.

gave to a courageous member like Samuel Plimsoll in his campaign for safe merchant shipping, conducted in a parliament stuffed with shipping interests, has been amply justified.[3] But the necessary quid pro quo was, at least until recently, a reciprocal recognition by both Houses of Parliament that they were not to defy or impugn the decisions of the courts—something constitutionally distinct from the practice of ministerial briefings against individual judges. The reason was and is that it is the courts and not Parliament who have the sovereign function of interpreting and applying the law. If members object to the courts' decisions, their recourse is to persuade Parliament to change the law, possibly even retrospectively. If they consider a judge of the senior courts unfit for office, he or she may be removed on an address of both Houses of Parliament, but not otherwise.

In 1996 a junior minister and member of the Bar, Neil Hamilton, issued proceedings for libel against the *Guardian* newspaper. He also sued Mohammed Al Fayed, who claimed to have paid him substantial sums of money for asking parliamentary questions. (Evidently nobody had told Mr Al Fayed that if you have a sensible question for a minister your MP will ask it free of charge.) On a preliminary application, a Queen's Bench judge ruled that the case against the *Guardian*, as pleaded, could not be tried without infringing Article 9 of the Bill of Rights. There was no interlocutory appeal against the decision. Instead an amendment was moved to the Defamation Bill then before Parliament, permitting an MP or peer (or for that matter a witness before a parliamentary committee) who was involved in defamation proceedings to waive, 'so far as concerns him, the protection of any enactment ... which prevents proceedings in Parliament being impeached or questioned in any court ...'—in other words to disapply Article 9 of the bill of rights in his or her own personal interests.

Although the Lord Chancellor had moved other amendments to the bill, he did not move this one. On Lord Mackay's invitation it was moved by a law lord, Lord Hoffmann, and in spite of principled opposition in the Upper House from lawyers and historians, who pointed out that Article 9 was there to protect the legislature as an institution, not to give individual members a shield which they could use for their own convenience, it was passed in both Houses.

Neil Hamilton, having used the waiver to continue with his action against the *Guardian*, abandoned the case shortly before trial.

[3] See also Ch 2.

He went on to lose his libel action against Mohammed Al Fayed in circumstances which were both dramatic and ironic. Shortly before the jury trial, it came to the knowledge of Mr Al Fayed's lawyers that Mr Hamilton had a few years earlier been brought in as junior counsel to give Mobil Oil tax advice. He had then tabled an amendment to a finance bill which, although later withdrawn, would have improved the tax position of oil companies, and had subsequently asked for and been paid a fee of £10,000. A late amendment of the defence was allowed in order to plead the receipt of this money as a corrupt act, and the jury in due course returned an affirmative answer to the judge's question: 'Are you satisfied … that Mr Hamilton was corrupt in his capacity as a member of Parliament?' Whether the answer was based on Mr Al Fayed's allegation that Mr Hamilton had been collecting cash in brown envelopes in return for putting questions, or on the Mobil episode (which depended not at all on Mr Al Fayed's testimony), or on both, we cannot know for sure, though the Court of Appeal later took the view that Mr Hamilton's chance of weathering the Mobil evidence was slender.[4] But it would seem that, had it not been for Mr Hamilton's earlier decision to waive the Bill of Rights in his own interests, it would not have been possible for the crucial element of the Mobil episode, his tabling of a parliamentary amendment, to be called in question by Mr Al Fayed by way of defence to his libel proceedings.

Not long after the libel action, in 1999, the Joint Committee on Parliamentary Privilege advised that the provision which had been slotted into the Defamation Act should be repealed and any power of waiver be placed in the hands of each House; but, in spite of opportunities to reverse it, it was not removed from the statute book until 2015. If the reason was that, notwithstanding its distorting effect on the constitution, parliamentarians preferred to leave it there for a rainy day, they might have reflected that those who chose to live by the waiver of parliamentary immunity could also perish by it.

THE ROYAL PREROGATIVE

There is a second form of legislation, the Order in Council, which receives no parliamentary attention at all. Some Orders in Council are made under express statutory powers and rank as statutory instruments. Those providing for governance of the colonies,

---

[4] *Hamilton v Al Fayed* [2001] EMLR 394 (CA).

however, continue to be made by the Queen in Council—that is to say the Privy Council[5]—as an exercise of the royal prerogative. They form a major exception to the rule, laid down four centuries ago in the *Case of Proclamations*,[6] that the Crown cannot legislate without the advice and consent of Parliament. They thus represent a form of ministerial power which Mme Nhu would have recognised as absolutely delightful, for the Privy Council does not even meet to discuss them and the Monarch's assent to them is a constitutional formality.

In an article published in 1994, when he was still in opposition, Jack Straw wrote:

'The royal prerogative has no place in a modern western democracy ... [It] has been used as a smoke-screen by Ministers to obfuscate the use of power for which they are insufficiently accountable.'[7]

It has been one of the achievements of modern public law to bring the ministerial use of the royal prerogative within the reach of judicial review, starting in 1967 when the High Court asserted its supervisory jurisdiction over the first criminal injuries compensation scheme, which had been deliberately set up by the Home Office without enabling legislation, and culminating, ironically, in the confirmation by the House of Lords in the Chagos islanders' case in 2008 that judicial review ran to the prerogative power to legislate by Order in Council for the colonies.

I say 'ironically' because the Chagos islanders' case, like the *Wednesbury* case, failed to deliver on its legal promise. Having confirmed the view of the Divisional Court and the Court of Appeal[8] that prerogative Orders in Council are open to judicial review for abuse of power, a bare majority of the House declined to exercise the jurisdiction on facts which had seemed to seven other judges (potent among them Lord Bingham) to establish a clear and shameful abuse of power by the British government.[9] In 2000 a Divisional Court had struck down as ultra vires a local ordinance purporting to exile the Chagossians from their islands, and the Foreign Secretary, Robin Cook, had undertaken to Parliament that the wrong would

[5] See further S Sedley, *Lions Under the Throne* pp 132–34.
[6] *The Case of Proclamations* (1611) 1 Co Rep 74, 24 ER 646.
[7] A Barnett (ed), *In Power and the Throne: the Monarchy Debate* (Vintage, 1994).
[8] *Bancoult v Foreign Secretary* [2007] EWCA Civ 498, [2008] QB 365.
[9] *R v Secretary of State for Foreign and Commonwealth Affairs, ex parte Bancoult (No 2)* [2008] UKHL 61, [2009] 1 AC 453.

now be put right. For the time being, it was: the Chagossians were given a legal right of return. We still do not know what it was that four years later prompted some FCO officials to advise the Foreign Secretary to renege on his predecessor's honourable act and to do by Order in Council what the court had held could not be lawfully done by ordinance—exclude the Chagos islanders for ever from their homeland. But we do know that the Foreign Secretary who did it was Jack Straw.[10]

The Chagos islanders' case has a further bearing on my subject. In the *CCSU* case in 1984,[11] Lord Roskill listed a number of prerogative functions which in his view could never come within the purview of the courts: the making of treaties, the defence of the realm, the prerogative of mercy, the grant of honours, the dissolution of Parliament, the appointment of ministers. The Chagos islanders' case prompted the Court of Appeal to wonder whether in the light of modern experience these examples all held good. Would the courts be powerless if it was proved to them that an honour was being granted in return for payment? Or if some future government proposed to embark on what was, under the Nuremberg principles, a war of aggression? Or if a Home Secretary used the royal pardon, or an Attorney-General the power to abandon a prosecution, for an illegal or improper reason? Or if a future Prime Minister sought to appoint a convicted fraudster to ministerial office or refused to invite the Monarch to prorogue a Parliament which had run its course? If such things were able to occur without the possibility of intervention by the courts, people might think the law was deficient.

---

[10] See D Snoxell (2008) 36(1) *Journal of Imperial and Commonwealth History* and (2009) 37(1) *Journal of Imperial and Commonwealth History*.
[11] *Council of Civil Service Unions v Minister for the Civil Service* [1985] AC 374 (HL).

26

A Compensation Culture?

This commentary on what has since come to be known as fake news is taken from the same lecture as the previous chapter.

P RESS STORIES WHICH owe more to a combination of journalistic imagination and editorial or proprietorial agendas than to fact or research are ten a penny in the history of British tabloid journalism. Among these is the recurrent tale of the compensation culture which, as we all know, has come to blight our legal system and, through it, our society. We know it because the press has repeatedly told us it is so.

The expression 'compensation culture' seems to have originated in an article about welfare by Bernard Levin in *The Times* in 1993. Between 1996 and 2004 references to it in the press rose year on year from near-zero to over 450. It had some basis, without doubt, in the advent of conditional fee agreements and of claims management companies which were making a living by ambulance-chasing. But the House of Commons' Constitutional Affairs Committee in 2006 found no evidence that the growth of risk-aversion was related to these factors. Over the same period, although tribunal claims increased with the creation of new causes of action, the total number of claims in the courts steadily declined. Moreover, the great majority of awards that were made were small; and costs as a fraction of GDP, though in absolute terms embarrassingly high, were lower not only than in the US but than in much of Europe.[1]

This, naturally, had no effect at all on those for whom the existence of a compensation culture was the springboard for an assault on the Human Rights Act, the health and safety legislation, personal injury litigation and laws forbidding discrimination and restricting

---

[1] See James Hand, 'The compensation culture: cliché or cause for concern?'(2010) 37(4) *Journal of Law and Society* 569.

dismissal. The assault was supported—as it continues to be—by an unstoppable stream of news items about absurd claims, most of them allegedly human rights-based, showing how easy it now was to get compensation for anything. That few of them ever came to court, and that those which did generally failed, went pretty much unrecorded.

The two spectres at this feast of fabrication have been the insurance industry, which foots most of the bills both for litigation and for settlements, and the press itself, for whom privacy claims have now joined the financial risks of libel actions. But there is a more serious agenda than the urge not to relinquish a good story whether it happens to be true or not. A significant proportion of compensation culture stories are attributed, usually falsely, to the Human Rights Act. Prisoners, the public now believes, can sue under the act for not being allowed to vote or to access pornography; paedophiles and rapists can refuse on privacy grounds to register their electronic addresses and identities; robbers under siege by the police have to be supplied with Kentucky fried chicken and cigarettes; photographs of fugitive criminals cannot be publicised because of their human rights; acquiring a cat is now a complete defence to deportation ... the nonsense rolls on with very little to impede it.

In 2004 the Better Regulation Task Force subheaded their report on *Better Routes to Redress* 'Compensation culture: exploding the urban myth'. For they found that there was no such culture; what was causing problems was the belief that there was one. The report was welcomed by government and was acted on in the Compensation Act 2006, which regulated claims-management enterprises and restated the common law negligence test so as to protect desirable activities. But the flow of articles about the compensation culture actually peaked in the wake of the report.

The report, in the same year, of the Commons' Constitutional Affairs Committee, which I mentioned earlier, concluded that the UK was not moving towards, much less embedded in, a compensation culture. The problem, it found, was a culture of risk aversion which the myth was actually provoking. Enter a new government. The Prime Minister asked the veteran politician and entrepreneur Lord Young 'to investigate and report back ... on the rise of the compensation culture over the last decade, coupled with the current low standing that health and safety legislation now enjoys, and to suggest solutions'. Lawyers will admire the way the questions came armed with the answers: as every cross-examiner knows, you don't leave these things to chance.

Despite this, in his chapter captioned 'Compensation culture' Lord Young wrote:

> 'Britain's "compensation culture" is fuelled by media stories ... and by constant adverts ...
>
> The problem of the compensation culture prevalent in society today is, however, one of perception rather than reality.'

That, chiming as it did with all that had previously been established, seemed to be that. But turn back to the title page of the report, and you read that it follows a review of 'the operation of health and safety laws and the growth of the compensation culture'. Then turn the page and read the Prime Minister's foreword:

> 'A damaging compensation culture has arisen ...'

If the health and safety legislation is to be cut back as an excessive burden on employers and their insurers, and the legal aid system as an excessive burden on the Treasury, the myth that these, along with the Human Rights Act, are fuelling a culture of extravagant claims and personal irresponsibility is too useful to shelve simply because it isn't true.

People

The following chapters are about individuals I have encountered either in my working life or as historical figures.

Those on Rudy Narayan, John Warr (whose writings I co-edited in 1992), Lord Scarman and Lord Bingham come from my entries on them in the *Oxford Dictionary of National Biography* (which may be consulted for sources and personal details). The chapter on Lord Diplock, also from the *ODNB*, was written jointly with the late Sir Godfray Le Quesne QC.

The chapter on Lord Denning comes from the obituary I wrote for the *Guardian*.

The chapters concerning Thomas More, Lord Mansfield and Lord Sumption were published in the *London Review of Books*, the first two as reviews, the latter as a response to a controversial lecture.

As no more than a historical curiosity, I have included the short reviews I wrote for *Tribune* of Bob Dylan's first two London concerts. A prefatory note explains a little more about them.

When, at the conclusion of a public interview recorded for the LSE judicial biography project in 2015, the interviewer, Sir Ross Cranston, invited questions from the audience, the first question had nothing to do with the law: it was what I thought of Ewan MacColl. By way of a fuller answer, I have added to this section the critical appreciation I wrote after MacColl's death.

27

Rudy Narayan

1938–1998

RAHASYA RUDRA NARAYAN—always known as Rudy—was born in British Guiana into a politically active Indo-Guyanese family, the ninth of ten children. He came to Britain as a teenager in 1953, and after a series of menial jobs, including washing dishes at a Lyons' Corner House and working night shifts at a soap factory, joined the Royal Army Ordnance Corps. He left the army in 1965, after seven years' service, with the rank of sergeant, and then read for the bar at Lincoln's Inn. There he helped to found the bar students' union, becoming its first president. He also captained the Inns of Court cricket club—a passion which never left him. He was called to the bar in 1968, and in 1969 married Dr Naseem Akbar, a medical practitioner with whom he had two daughters.

In advocacy Narayan found his métier. He was a fluent, powerful and persuasive speaker and, when he needed to be, a sound lawyer. He defended with remarkable success in a series of high-profile trials arising out of confrontations between black people and the police. But he encountered, like other black and ethnic minority barristers, the glass panel beyond which lay the steadier work and heavier briefs which were his due. After learning finally that clients who asked solicitors to brief him were being told he was not available, and angered at the apparent over-sentencing of black defendants, Narayan went public. It is improbable that a more temperate assault on the legal establishment would even have been noticed; but Narayan's protest, loud and uncompromising, was not only noticed—it resulted in the first of the three disciplinary adjudications which finally drove him from the bar. This one, in 1974, for bringing the administration of justice into disrepute (by alleging that Birmingham solicitors, counsel, and judges were racist), was followed in 1980 by a reprimand for discourtesy to a judge. In 1982 he was acquitted by the Bar Council of professional misconduct in issuing an extravagant press statement about the Attorney-General and the Director of Public Prosecutions (accusing them of 'collusion with the National Front and fanning the flames of racial hatred'), but his accusations were found 'scandalous and contemptuous' and he was suspended for six weeks after being found guilty of four other, unrelated, charges. By then he had become a heavy drinker and was lashing out at the nearest target.

Narayan achieved high-profile successes in the trials arising out of the Bristol riots of 1980 and the Bradford petrol bomb case of 1982. Nevertheless in 1984 he was expelled from his chambers in the Inner Temple after assaulting the chambers' head, Sibghat Kadri, at a conference. He announced his intention of qualifying as a solicitor, but failed the Law Society examinations. Then, back at the bar, in 1988 he put himself in the wrong by accepting briefs in two contemporaneous trials. Although he attacked the all-white disciplinary tribunal which heard his case, he was suspended for two years (a fate, he pointed out, which did not invariably await counsel who got themselves overbooked). In the following year he polled 177 votes standing as an independent in the Vauxhall by-election in protest at the Labour Party's 'outrageous and blatant exclusion of black candidates for a constituency made safe for Labour by black votes'.

His first marriage having ended in divorce, in 1988 Narayan married Saeeda Begum Shah. This marriage, too, ended in divorce. In 1991 he returned to Guyana, where little went his way. He returned to Britain three years later, an activist now without roots, an advocate turned demagogue, an anti-racialist stained with antisemitism, and now a terminal drinker. The series of disciplinary adjudications culminated in 1994 in his disbarment for professional misconduct. The following year a minor riot followed his speech outside Brixton police station following the death of a black man in custody.

Rudy Narayan died in 1998 in London of cirrhosis of the liver. He left behind him far more than a trail of failures. The Society of Black Lawyers, which he played a leading part in founding in 1973, remained as a necessary voice for an important professional minority. His books *Black Community on Trial* (1976), *Black England* (1977), *Barrister for the Defence* (1985), and *When Judges Conspire* (1989) may one day be revisited as more than memorials to his self-regard, though they are certainly that. The Lambeth Law Centre, of which he was the first chairman and where he held regular surgeries, survived him in a pivotal role in the south London community.

Above all, it was the waves made by an individual who was too volatile and too intransigent ever to coast to success on them himself which in Narayan's lifetime began to erode the bar's and the legal system's self-assurance about racial discrimination. The setting up of the Bar Council's race relations committee in 1984, and the continued concern which produced an amendment of the Race Relations Act to outlaw race discrimination in the legal profession, and then, in 1995, the bar's own equality code, all owed something—possibly a good deal—to the attention which Narayan had drawn to a legal profession which had much to be embarrassed about. That he had done so extravagantly and intemperately, alienating many other ethnic minority lawyers on the way, may be less a criticism of him than an illustration of the fact that it tends to be only when an angry member of a disadvantaged group exposes him or herself to fire that things begin to change. In his assault on the English legal system Narayan sacrificed his reputation, his practice, his bearings, and his health; but through the breach he made, younger black advocates have since passed.

28

John Warr

fl. 1648–1649

A MONG THE LEGAL and political polemicists of the English Civil War, John Warr stands out both for his radical thinking and for his elegant and vivid prose. 'Even truth itself,' he wrote perceptively, 'will jostle its adversary in a narrow pass.'

His three surviving pamphlets, all published within the space of two years by the Leveller bookseller Giles Calvert, constitute all that is known about him. They give evidence of a classical education and some experience of litigation; but his contempt for the legal system—'when the poor and oppressed want right, they meet with law'—makes it unlikely that he was a lawyer. A John Warre is found in the 1650s buying up sequestrated royalist estates; but, although such a trajectory would not have been unique among civil-war radicals, there is no evidence that this was the same man.

Warr's stance in the contest between monarchy and parliament was that neither of these forms of government would offer the common people freedom. That must come from the natural reason that every individual possessed:

'There are some sparks of freedom in the minds of most, which ordinarily lie deep and are covered in the dark as a spark in the ashes'.

But the constitutional foundation of freedom, he argued, using a phrase that did not come into its own until the age of the French and American revolutions, was neither monarchical authority nor a property-based franchise but 'people's rights'.

Warr's first known publication, *Administrations Civil and Spiritual* (1648), although on the face of it a theological tract, begins to grapple with the conflict between what he calls the 'darkness' of formal religion and imposed social order and the inner light of spirituality and reason. In it he invokes the Everlasting Gospel, the twelfth-century millenarian heresy that had resurfaced in the

German peasants' revolt of 1525 and was to re-emerge in William Blake's epic poems, forecasting an era of human equality and justice. In this, Warr perceptibly follows the road, well-trodden in the English Civil War, from spiritual to secular radicalism.

It was in his next and arguably finest pamphlet, *The Priviledges of the People*, published about the time of the execution of Charles I in early 1649, that Warr completed the transition. Although he acknowledged 'a beauty in monarchy, duly circumscribed, as well as in other forms of government', he now argued that the natural and rational order of society was egalitarian, not authoritarian. The purpose of law, he argued, was not to constrain the common people but to liberate them by constraining 'the mighty':

'Tis not possible for a people to be too free.'

Between rulers and ruled there was

'an irreconcilable contest … which will never cease till either prerogative and privilege be swallowed up in freedom or liberty itself be led captive by prerogative'.

Warr no longer looked to a divine scheme. Nor did he believe any longer in an ordained outcome:

'He which hath the worst cause may sometimes have the best success.'

From authority and equality Warr turned in his third pamphlet, *The Corruption and Deficiency of the Laws of England*, published in the summer of the same year, to the law. The view of the legal system as a ruinous snare for ordinary people was widespread in this period; but Warr, while adding his voice to the denunciations, went beyond and behind the present state of things, memorably locating the demand for rational laws in

'a spirit of understanding big with freedom and having a single respect to people's rights'.

Warr does not slot readily into any faction. His antipathy to land tenures—'slavish ties and badges upon men'—as well as his use of botanical imagery may suggest an affinity with Gerrard Winstanley and the Diggers. His egalitarianism echoes that of the Leveller Thomas Rainborough in the Putney debates of 1647. But Warr's work is better seen as one elegant strand in a long skein of English radicalism, reaching back to the mysticism of the Everlasting Gospel and forward, through the great democratic revolutions of the eighteenth and nineteenth centuries, to the universalism of democratic theory and human rights.

More immediately, when in 1657 Cromwell was reinstalled as Lord Protector his oath of office included 'the maintenance and preservation ... of the just rights and priviledges of the People'. Warr, if he was still alive, must have enjoyed the irony of Cromwell appropriating his vision of turning privilege, and the world with it, upside down.

29

Lord Diplock

1907–1985

IN SPITE OF having left Oxford with a second-class degree in chemistry, Kenneth Diplock's colossal legal learning and intellectual power were apparent to everyone. At the bar, to which he was called in 1932 (with a 4-year break for war service, in which he reached the rank of squadron leader), these qualities made him a formidable advocate, methodical, quietly spoken, meticulous and deadly. On the bench they made him an equally formidable tribunal, but his consciousness of his own ability made him dismissive of ideas at which his own fast brain had not arrived first. Those who were able to pick up his *sotto voce* comments in court (smoker's emphysema made his voice weak) would hear a well-known textbook greeted as 'The boy's book of income tax'. Anticipating the weak points of an argument, he would mine the advocate's path with Socratic questions the answers to which would in due course, as he knew, destroy the case.

Light moments in the court of a judge whose leisure reading was the works of Sir William Holdsworth were not numerous, but he was able in one of his later judgments to admit wryly that his use in an earlier case of the word 'synallagmatic' had been regarded as 'a typical example of gratuitous philological exhibitionism'.[1] Moments of bonhomie tended to be characterised on his long and boyish face by what a colleague later described as 'a smile that would have done credit to any shark'. But it was not only advocates who feared Diplock. The disdain he found increasingly difficult to conceal for judicial views contrary to his own sometimes stifled discussion and

---

[1] *United Dominions Trust (Commercial) Ltd v Eagle Aircraft Services Ltd* [1968] 1 All ER 104 (CA).

dissent. It was to this, as much as to policy, that the tendency of the House of Lords when he was in the chair to limit decisions to a single speech may have been due; but that the single speech was as often as not Diplock's was more of a tribute to his phenomenal industry than to his personal dominance.

It was not, however, simply intellectual arrogance which drove Diplock. He had both a panoptic knowledge and comprehension of the law and a scientist's desire to rationalise it. His most conspicuous contribution was to constitutional and public law. The constitutions created in the post-war years for former British colonies and protectorates included chapters defining and protecting fundamental rights and freedoms. Appeals arising from these chapters soon reached the judicial committee of the Privy Council, which thus became involved in constitutional interpretation and enforcement 40 years before the United Kingdom itself had any statutory source of equivalent rights. Diplock and his contemporaries Wilberforce and Scarman were the leading figures in this process.

Diplock gave an extensive interpretation to constitutional definitions of individual rights, following the principle, originally proclaimed by Lord Wilberforce, that such measures should receive 'a generous interpretation avoiding what has been called "the austerity of tabulated legalism", suitable to give to individuals the full measure of the fundamental rights and freedoms referred to'.[2] At the same time Diplock held that these definitions, thus widely interpreted, had to be observed, and constitutional rights were not to be pressed beyond them.

The same balance is displayed by Diplock's judgments on constitutional remedies. The special jurisdiction, created by a number of constitutions, to apply to the court for redress when invasion of a fundamental right occurred or was likely was, Diplock said in one case, 'an important safeguard of those rights and freedoms'.[3] On the other hand, the ordinary law was not superseded. If it provided an appropriate remedy for an unlawful administrative act, resort to the special constitutional procedure was not justified. These principles have had lasting importance in guiding the courts of a number of countries, particularly in the Caribbean, from which came most of the constitutional cases in which Diplock sat.

[2] *Minister of Home Affairs v Fisher* [1980] AC 319 (HL).
[3] *Harrikissoon v A-G of Trinidad and Tobago* [1980] AC 265 (PC).

Diplock's decisions on appeals in capital cases were sometimes said to show that he was a hard man. His judgments do not necessarily support this view. What characterises them is their intellectual integrity. He held that the task of a judge faced with a written constitution was to reach the proper interpretation of the constitutional language (the concept of 'a' proper interpretation was not within his mindset) and apply it. With the desirability of the result he was not concerned; that was the responsibility of the legislative arm of government, not the judicial. To this he adhered with complete consistency, even in a case in which a statute of Singapore imposed a mandatory sentence of death for trafficking in very small quantities of heroin. Diplock emphasised in his judgment that:

> 'in their judicial capacity [judges] are in no way concerned with arguments for or against capital punishment or its efficacy as a deterrent to so evil and profitable a crime as trafficking in addictive drugs. Whether there should be capital punishment in Singapore and, if so, for what offences, are questions for the legislature of Singapore'.[4]

Other approaches to such matters, deriving more from humanitarian than from juristic concerns, gained currency after Diplock's death,[5] and his reputation suffered, some would have said unfairly, in consequence.

In parallel with his pioneering work in the privy council, Diplock—alongside Lord Denning—had the acumen and the learning to anticipate and encourage the post-war regrowth of English public and constitutional law. As early as 1967, as a puisne judge, observing that the royal prerogative was the last unclaimed prize of the constitutional conflicts of the seventeenth century, he held that how ministers deployed it was now subject to judicial review for consistency and fairness. Almost two decades later as a law lord he was able to describe the modern development of public law as perhaps the greatest achievement of his judicial lifetime.

It was a development to which Diplock contributed probably more than any other judge. In 1982, however, he used the occasion of an attempt to exploit public law in lieu of private law remedies to set up by judicial decision a rigidly binary system of recourse, much criticised from the start by academics and finally abandoned by his successors.[6] But it played the part that he had intended of

---

[4] *Ong Ah Chuan v Public Prosecutor* [1981] AC 648 (PC).
[5] See Ch 31 on Lord Bingham.
[6] *O'Reilly v Mackman* [1983] 2 AC 237 (HL).

announcing that, from a post-war base of almost zero, a coherent and comprehensive system of remedies against the abuse of state power had grown to maturity. When in 1985 the challenge to the government's ban on trade union membership at the government communications headquarters came before the house, Diplock—ever the scientist—took the opportunity to classify the principles of public law as they had so far developed and to sketch the lines of further growth.[7] It says something for his sense of history that, as the century ended, the patriation of the European Convention on Human Rights had finally brought into Britain's public law the concept of proportionality to which he had looked forward in the early 1980s.

Diplock himself was clear that it was the changes in the contemporary state which had prompted and necessitated the growth of English public law. The rules of standing, he said:

> 'were made by judges, by judges they can be changed; and so they have been over the years to meet the need to preserve the integrity of the rule of law despite changes in the social structure, methods of government and the extent to which the activities of private citizens are controlled by governmental authorities, that have been taking place continuously, sometimes slowly, sometimes swiftly, since the rules were originally propounded. Those changes have been particularly rapid since World War II'.[8]

His espousal of public-law rights and remedies was in this sense a judicial response to long-term political and social changes at home, much as his decisions on Commonwealth cases were in part a response to the handing over of political power in the former empire.

Public and constitutional law were no more than a segment of Diplock's judicial work. His incursions into some specialised fields, equity for example, were not always well received; but in field after field of law—crime, contempt of court, intellectual property, restraint of trade, defamation, commercial and maritime law—his judgments became benchmarks of organised and logical jurisprudence, rationalising concepts that were or had become historically and intellectually confused. His decisions on the interpretation of statutes creating criminal offences were morally rigorous, tending always to hold individuals answerable for the consequences of their actions. These attracted academic criticism and have not always

---

[7] *CCSU v Minister for the Civil Service* [1985] AC 374 (HL).
[8] *R v IRC, ex parte National Federation of Self-Employed* [1982] AC 617 (HL).

stood the test of time; they also contributed to his reputation as a hard man. But his rigour shut out intellectual dishonesty, and he accorded considerably more importance to the body of precedent than his more populist contemporary Lord Denning. Diplock would never 'cheat' in order to reach a desired conclusion.

Nevertheless, where precedent went one way and reason the other, Diplock would say so. As early as 1965 he had urged that the notorious discrepancy between libel damages and personal injury damages, though entrenched, was indefensible; but it was not until 30 years later, a decade after his death, that the courts finally broke the mould and set out to bring libel damages into a proportionate relationship with damages for physical or mental pain and suffering. It was not untypical to find a speech of his which began: 'I understand your Lordships to be at one in holding that both of these appeals must be dismissed. I am of the same opinion—reluctantly, because I do not think that this outcome is either sensible or just.'[9] Thus his chosen role as a jurist was to consolidate and to rationalise the law. It fell to others, albeit in his wake, to reform it.

Diplock's second main role, and the one to which his name became permanently attached, was as a safe pair of hands for governmental inquiries. The Diplock courts of Northern Ireland were set up on the advice of a three-man commission which was set up under his chairmanship in October 1972 to consider the problem of jury intimidation in cases involving terrorism. By December he had recommended the introduction of trial by judge alone in specified classes of case. Not only was the system adopted in the Republic of Ireland as well as in the north, but by replacing jury verdicts with reasoned judgments open to scrutiny on appeal it resulted in more acquittals. While the outcome might not have been what he envisaged, it would not have induced him to go back on his scheme.

From 1971 to 1982 Diplock was chairman of the permanent security commission, charged with inquiring into failures of state security, among them the Sir Roger Hollis affair. He was also called upon in 1976 to report on whether the Foreign Enlistment Act of 1870 was of continuing use. The context of the inquiry was the recruitment of British personnel as mercenaries for the civil war in Angola, and Diplock's advice that the act was ineffectual and obsolete, though both contested at the time and called into question by later events, was welcome to government at the time. For some years he led a

---

[9] *Gammell v Wilson* [1982] AC 27 (HL).

British team, very successfully, in exchanges with senior American judges and lawyers.

Diplock was a passionate and surprisingly reckless horseman and fox-hunter. The guest list for the Middle Temple's 'grand day' in 1974, the year of his treasurership, included the Duke of Beaufort and seven masters of hounds. It was said that when he was a barrister he had a horse which he named Circuit, so that his clerk could truthfully tell enquirers that Mr Diplock was unavailable because he was out on circuit. He attended at least one sitting of his commission adorned with a black eye, the result of a fall from his horse, and went on riding until later in life than Lord Chancellors would have liked.

Diplock's final attendance at the Privy Council must be unique in judicial history. A special sitting was held during the long vacation of 1985, to deal with an urgent civil case from Trinidad and Tobago (not, as legend has recreated the story, a capital punishment case). Diplock, who was suffering from complications of severe and long-standing emphysema, took part in the hearing in a wheelchair, sustained by an oxygen cylinder. He died a month later.

30

Lord Scarman

1911–2004

O NE OF THE long-term processes which the twentieth century witnessed in the legal system of England and Wales was the transition from the common-law-dominated system of the nineteenth century to the statute-dominated system of the twenty-first. Scarman's life, which spanned and helped to shape this historic shift, was simultaneously the orthodox legal career of his generation and a breaking of the judicial mould.

Leslie George Scarman was the son of a Lloyd's underwriter and his Scottish wife, Ida—in Scarman's words a 'fierce and lovely' woman to whom he later attributed the streak of conservatism with which he was sometimes reproached. Certainly his early years gave little sign of the radicalism which came to be associated with him, though late in life he admitted having been a schoolboy Liberal and added: 'Maybe I still am.' Open scholarships took him to Radley College and on to Brasenose College, Oxford, where he took a first in classics and went on as a Harmsworth scholar to the Middle Temple. He was called to the bar in 1936.

The outbreak of the Second World War in 1939 rescued Scarman, as it did many of his generation, from the tedium of waiting for briefs which were slow to come. Having joined the RAF volunteer reserve and initially found himself stuck behind a desk in Abingdon, he eventually saw service in north Africa, Sicily, Italy, and northern Europe on the staff of Sir Arthur Tedder, the commander-in-chief of Mediterranean air forces, reaching the rank of wing commander. Although he saw no fighting, he was awarded the Order of Battle Merit of the USSR in 1945, and an OBE in 1944, the latter possibly in recognition of the skill which he had deployed earlier in the war to prevent Tedder's assignment to courts martial. Tedder, in retirement, recalled Scarman as 'the most intelligent and congenial civilian staff member I ever had'. Scarman was present when General Jodl surrendered to Tedder and Eisenhower at Rheims.

In the company of hundreds of other war veterans, many of them more scarred than he was, Scarman in 1945 returned to the bar. Although he claimed that he was by nature simply a hard worker who made up in industry what he lacked in talent, he rapidly displayed both. Where others were giving up and moving on, he began to develop a varied common-law practice, becoming sought after as a skilled cross-examiner.

As a barrister in these early post-war years Scarman began to display some of the intellectual courage which was eventually to mark him out. Arguing a Rent Acts case before a judge who was anxious to find for him, he was offered a point of law that would have won him the case but which he knew to be bad. Scarman refused to take it. Such adherence to principle did not earn universal admiration: some of his contemporaries regarded him as sanctimonious. The head of his chambers, Melford Stevenson, once remarked: 'Leslie helps solicitors on with their coats like Father D'Arcy elevating the host.' The comment was as astute as it was vitriolic, for it was typical of Scarman that he would not leave it to his clerk to help a solicitor on with his coat after a conference, and typical of the bar to notice such a breach of its class barriers. It was also true, however, that Scarman's long, gangling frame, his slight stoop, and his gravely courteous mien gave him the unctuous manner that the head of his chambers had guyed.

Scarman took silk in 1957. Four years later he was appointed a judge of the Probate, Divorce and Admiralty Division of the High Court, and was almost at once given the complex lawsuit over the multi-million pound Fuld estate to try. The writer Sybille Bedford observed him there:

> 'In ambles the lanky—gracefully lanky—figure of a youthful judge ... a most unusual face: enormous eyes deep-set between high cheek-bones and a jutting skull, a pale face, a hollow face with skin stretched taut, and yet the mouth is full and there show dimples in the sunken cheeks; it is an ascetic's face lit by charm, given the lie by a cherub's smile ... it is impossible to imagine him bullying anyone. Yet, he is held in respect: there is no doubt that authority flows from him.'[1]

It was as such a judge, first in the High Court, then from 1973 in the Court of Appeal, and from 1977 as a law lord that Scarman stood

---

[1] S Bedford, *As It Was* (Sinclair-Stevenson, 1990) pp 105, 108.

out among his contemporaries. It had been expected that he would succeed Lord Denning as Master of the Rolls, but Denning would not retire and Scarman was instead promoted to the Lords.

He was widely regarded as a model judge: courteous, learned, businesslike, humane; capable of being firm or generous as the case required in both the civil and criminal jurisdictions. His judgments, always lean and elegant, include some seminal expositions—of the law of contempt of court; of the necessary symmetry between the integrity of legal process and the right of free speech and comment; and of the developing area of public law by which the needs of the state and the entitlements of the individual were during Scarman's lifetime being rebalanced.

To have achieved even this much distinction in an era dominated by two other great judicial figures, Diplock and Denning, was no mean feat. Moreover Scarman, who yielded nothing to either of them in learning, possessed Diplock's acuity without his acerbity, and Denning's sense of policy without his partiality. On one occasion counsel arguing a major contempt of court case at the bar of the House cited a passage from Lord Shaw's speech in *Scott v Scott* (1913) on the importance of open justice. As counsel finished reading, Scarman said: 'You've just closed the book on one of the finest pieces of prose in the law reports. You should go on.' The passage, which Scarman must have known by heart, ran:

'To remit the maintenance of constitutional right to the region of judicial discretion is to shift the foundations of freedom from the rock to the sand.'

It was to be a keynote of Scarman's own work.

THE LAW COMMISSION AND THE PUBLIC INQUIRIES

In 1965 the Labour Lord Chancellor Lord Gardiner set up a permanent law commission, introducing a novel depth of research and breadth of policy into the process of law reform in England and Wales. Scarman, still in judicial office, accepted the chairmanship, and for seven years led a team of able and opinionated commissioners, listening to every point of view, taking great care not to impose his own, and showing a gift not only for strategic thinking but for detailed management. His ambition, no less real for being unrealisable, was to slim down the overweight statute book and to replace its bulk with simplified and, where possible, codified measures. The commission's work could have only as much effect as ministers and parliament were prepared to accord to it. But the Law Commission in Scarman's years of office produced 27 reports containing draft bills, every one of which reached the statute book—a record looked back upon by his successors with envy. Among the fruits were the radical reforms contained in the Divorce Reform Act 1969 and the Matrimonial Proceedings and Property Act 1970.

In these years the first chairman of the Australian Law Reform Commission, Michael Kirby, found Scarman, as well as being a good listener, to be 'sharp in analysis, brimming over with ideas, sweet in disposition, egalitarian in relationships, persuasive in advocacy and resolute in action. He became the example and beacon for institutional law reformers everywhere'. These, too, were the qualities that earned Scarman accolades as the chairman of a series of public inquiries instituted by government between 1969, when he was given the sensitive task of reporting on the disturbances in Northern Ireland, and 1981, when he was asked to report on the riots in Brixton. In these, and in his intervening inquiries—into the Red Lion Square disturbances (1975) and the Grunwick trade dispute (1977)—Scarman displayed what were by now his trademark qualities: approachability, open-mindedness, and procedural firmness. He initiated the inquiry into the Red Lion Square disorders with a statement that became a classic source of tone and content for later inquiries:

> 'This is an inquiry, not a piece of litigation … It is I and I alone who will decide what witnesses are to be called … I propose within limits to allow cross-examination of witnesses to the extent that I think it helpful to the forwarding of the inquiry, but no further.'

Scarman was clear, and made it clear to government, that in these extra-judicial roles he remained a judge, adaptable to the requirements of the job but not amenable to any political directions or pressure. He sharply and successfully opposed, as an invasion of judicial independence, a proposal to give the Law Commission a statutory duty to 'assist' government. In this way, repeatedly stationed on the boundaries between the divided functions of the state, Scarman was able to come to the aid of both the legislature and the executive without forfeiting his judicial credentials. What made him attractive to both government and the public were the judicial qualities he brought to his stewardship of the Law Commission and to his public inquiries. They eventually earned him the liking and respect of many members of the black community who had initially

seen the setting up of the Brixton inquiry as a whitewash, and both
there and in Northern Ireland his unconcern for personal security
and willingness to talk to anyone who approached him made him
many friends. He later described as 'traumatic' the realisation that
many of the people of the six counties were effectively without
rights.

Scarman's conduct of the Brixton inquiry was particularly influential. While praising the police for their conduct on the night of
the riots, he acknowledged that 'racial disadvantage' was 'a fact of
current British life', and called both for government action to tackle
the disproportionately high level of unemployment among young
black men and for a new emphasis on community policing to restore
trust between the black community and the police.

Even so, Scarman never rocked the political boat. His rejection
of the notion of institutional racism, and his conclusion that racists
in the Metropolitan police represented only a few bad apples in
the barrel, fell a long way short of what Sir William Macpherson's
inquiry into the death of Stephen Lawrence was later to conclude.

SCARMAN'S RADICALISM

Although as a judge Scarman's decisions were by no means always
socially liberal or politically left of centre, neither those who knew
him nor Scarman himself would have expected them to be. But
the reputation that came to surround him, and for which he himself was in large part responsible, was such that his admirers were
shocked when in 1979 he cast his vote with the other law lords
in favour of upholding the conviction of the editor of *Gay News*,
Denis Lemon, for the much-criticised common-law offence of blasphemy. Although in the case on trade-union recognition at GCHQ
in 1985 he set out a seminal statement of the modern amenability
of the royal prerogative to judicial review, he accepted the government's last-minute argument that once national security was raised
the courts were shut out. In fact Scarman very rarely dissented.
He made up the majority, in 1986, that rejected Victoria Gillick's
attempt to prevent doctors prescribing contraceptives for girls under
the age of sixteen, closing the door on the notion that children were
without rights. But he joined the rest of the Lords' appellate committee in striking down the Greater London Council's 'Fares Fair'
policy in 1981. It was this case that did most to damage Scarman's
liberal credentials. Although it ostensibly turned upon a dry issue

of statutory construction, everybody knew that the case was a political battle between Conservative-controlled outlying boroughs with already high rates and an addiction to private transport, and a Labour-dominated regional administration that wanted ratepayers to subsidise public transport in order to clear the roads of unneeded traffic. The leader of the Greater London council, Ken Livingstone, later called Scarman 'a two-faced old hypocrite' for his role in the decision. 'I'm not interested', he said, 'in people who get wonderfully progressive after they retire. He had his chance when he had power; he didn't take it'.

Scarman would not have endorsed any judicial decision that in his view sacrificed legality to politics, or even to policy; but he did become, in Livingstone's phrase, wonderfully progressive after he retired. Indeed he had moved markedly in that direction while still in judicial office. While chairing the Law Commission, he had defied the Kilmuir rules, which, until abandoned by a later Lord Chancellor, Lord Mackay, sought to prevent judges from speaking in public on matters of policy. Beginning with a series of factual broadcasts on the work of the Law Commission, he went on to take part in Michael Zander's Third Programme discussion series, *What's Wrong with the Law?* Later he followed his 1974 Hamlyn lectures with a four-part discussion on Radio 3 with Lord Denning (the latter's first but far from last broadcast); and in 1986 he debated Lord McCluskey's Reith lectures on radio with another Lord Chancellor, Lord Hailsham.

SCARMAN AND HUMAN RIGHTS

Although rejecting institutional racism in his Brixton report, Scarman had nevertheless recognised the toxic effects of racial discrimination and disadvantage in modern Britain, and he used his seat in the House of Lords to introduce the amendment to the 1984 Police and Criminal Evidence Bill which made racial discrimination by police officers a disciplinary offence. Then in 1985, just before he retired from the bench, he introduced in the Lords a bill to incorporate the European Convention on Human Rights into the United Kingdom's domestic law. His fellow peers passed it, but it was denied parliamentary time in the Commons and fell. It was another 13 years before a newly elected Labour government put the Convention on the statute book. Scarman's bill, however, was no flash in the pan. In his 1974 Hamlyn lectures, published as *English*

Law: the New Dimension, he had presented a full and cogent case, all the more arresting as time went by for the prescience of its arguments, for giving the powerless direct access to rights which the United Kingdom was willing for other peoples to have but less keen to vouchsafe at home. The lectures were a landmark in strategic thinking about the law.

Among many academic honours, from 1977 to 1989 Scarman was Chancellor of Warwick University. From 1973 to 1976 he chaired the Council of Legal Education and then from 1976 to 1979 the senate of the Inns of Court and the bar. In retirement he became president or patron of a series of charities and institutions, including the British Institute of Human Rights, the Constitutional Reform Centre, the Citizen Action Compensation Campaign, the constitutional reform group Charter 88 and the Public Law Project. While such largely honorific positions were perhaps to be expected of such a distinguished figure, what was unexpected was Scarman's championship, after leaving the bench, of a series of unpopular causes. He took up the cases of the Birmingham Six and the Guildford Four (gaoled on questionable evidence for alleged IRA terrorist activities), and the Tottenham Three (young black men convicted of the murder of a policeman during the Broadwater Farm riots in 1985), calling for an overhaul of the mechanism, which was at that time entirely a matter for the Home Secretary's discretion, for re-examining possible miscarriages of justice. As a judge Scarman had been responsible for quashing the three convictions in the *Confait* case, a historic miscarriage of justice that lay behind the eventual introduction of tape-recording of police interviews. He had satisfied himself in each case that something had gone seriously wrong, and the campaigns were all ultimately successful. In the same spirit he campaigned for a statutory right of access to official information and the repeal of the widely disliked section 2 of the Official Secrets Act. The creation, within his lifetime, of the Criminal Cases Review Commission and the passing of a Freedom of Information Act illustrated Scarman's capacity for wisdom before the event.

***

A tireless worker who often got up to work before dawn, a near-recluse who would not attend dinners except in his own Inn of Court, an admitted friend of change but an avowed enemy of disjunction, Scarman was someone whose private asceticism seemed incompatible with his outgoing public persona and his readiness to take on challenge and controversy. But if you add the fact that

as a young man he played the trombone, and that in later years he
became passionate about opera, you start to see the cultured man
who on one occasion politely interrupted a young barrister appearing before him who had casually attributed to Candide the view
that all was for the best in the best of all possible worlds, and said:
'I think you'll find it was Dr Pangloss.'

31

Lord Bingham

1933–2010

TOM BINGHAM'S FATHER was a Belfast-born doctor; his mother an American-born dentist. An only child, he was educated from 1947 at Sedbergh, an academically rigorous and physically spartan public school in Yorkshire, on the Howgill Fells. There he won a succession of literary and academic prizes and, with the encouragement of an inspirational teacher, developed an enduring fascination with English history, in particular the seismic events of the mid-seventeenth century and their central figure, Oliver Cromwell. Consistently with the wiry physique that was his throughout life, he disliked rugby but did well at fell running and took himself off on long and rigorous fell walks. Later, as an undergraduate, he climbed Mont Blanc in one of the fastest times recorded by an amateur, leaving some stranded climbers to be collected on the way back. 'I suppose I can be ruthless,' he admitted many years later.

At school Bingham developed religious beliefs that remained with him throughout his life, following his parents into the Anglican church and keeping a copy of the King James Bible by his bed. Late in life, asked about his ethical code, he said: 'I would hope that my own philosophy of life is largely coincident with the New Testament, however imperfectly realised in practice.' He also became interested, without pedagogic encouragement, in the politics of the Labour government that held office between 1945 and 1951, giving a paper on British socialism to the school forum in his last year at school, 1952. In later years he described his leanings at this time as Bevanite. The reason why he was still at Sedbergh in 1952 was that although he had already won an open scholarship to Balliol College, Oxford, he had stayed on in order to try, unsuccessfully, for a more prestigious award.

Before going up to Balliol (he stuck throughout his life to the traditional refusal to add 'college'), Bingham had to do two years' national service. While waiting for his papers he spent some time working in a concreting gang on a new runway at Gatwick airport. Given his father's background, when he received his call-up he joined the Royal Ulster Rifles, a regiment that despite its name was based in England and which swiftly selected him as officer material. He was commissioned as a second lieutenant in February 1953 with a merit award for passing out top of his intake, and was posted to Hong Kong. One of the military tasks that he found congenial was to act as defence officer before courts martial. He enjoyed his military service so much, and was so impressed by his commanding officer, that he gave serious consideration to signing up as a professional soldier. He decided in the end to take up his place at Oxford with a view to returning to the army, and remained in the Territorial Army for some years; but his military ambition had faded by the time he gained his degree. He had acquired in its place an indelible love of Oxford.

After two frustrating terms reading philosophy, politics and economics and finding much of the content sterile, Bingham made the decision to follow his first love, history. It was a subject in which Balliol was rich, having among its fellows the medieval historian Richard Southern and the leading historian of the seventeenth century, Christopher Hill, and as its Master the constitutional historian Sir David Kier. Bingham took his studies seriously, eschewing sport and debating. He was rewarded with a Coolidge Pathfinder award which took him during the long vacation of 1955 to the United States, where he was welcomed by both sides of his family. He spent time observing proceedings in several local courts, noting in the report he made on his return that the preponderance of black and east Asian defendants in the criminal justice system 'surely ... cannot be a coincidence'. The experience played a part in the later choice of 'Slavery and secession, 1850–1862' as his special subject for history finals.

In his third year Bingham was elected president of the Balliol junior common room, standing in his own right and not, as was common, on a party political ticket. But he became politically involved when, on his own initiative, he sent a message of support to a group of students who were preparing, without the college's knowledge, to take medical supplies to Hungary following the uprising there in the winter of 1956. A vote of censure on him failed: instead a collection of money was sanctioned by both the junior common room and the college. When he took his degree, the Master wrote to him: 'If only all undergraduates would put as much into the place as you did the sky would be the limit.' In his final year, 1957, Bingham won the university's Gibbs prize for modern history and then took first-class honours in history. The degree in turn brought him an Eldon law scholarship to enable him to read for the bar. His failure later in the year to secure a prize fellowship at All Souls College was a rare disappointment. In the event, he elected not to look to academia or to the army or to industry for his career but, with his mother's encouragement, to the law.

THE BAR

The choice of a career at the bar was not made arbitrarily: Bingham had joined Gray's Inn during his second year at Oxford. At that period the bar was not a graduate profession and its examinations could be passed by rote learning. The principal ordeal was having to eat three dinners a term for 12 terms. Bingham was not the only entrant to be dismayed by the poor academic standard required for access to one of the learned professions. But he was able, early in 1958, to travel out on circuit as marshal (a kind of educated factotum) to Mr Justice Finnemore, whom, despite his reputation for austerity, Bingham found generous and the experience rewarding. He also found, when in 1959 he came top in the bar finals, that intellectual prowess was after all recognised and rewarded by the profession: his success brought him two prizes, two scholarships, and—perhaps most valued of all—a dispensation from eating his remaining dinners. He was duly called to the bar by Gray's Inn later that year.

There followed the requisite 12 months' pupillage. Bingham was taken on as a pupil by Owen Stable in the prestigious commercial chambers that later moved from Crown Office Row, in the Temple, to Fountain Court. Not only did Stable pay Bingham to devil for him; the head of chambers, Leslie Scarman, after only a few months invited him to stay on as a tenant. A natural empathy between Bingham and Scarman, both of them humane liberal intellectuals and considerable scholars, might have been expected but Bingham thought Scarman sanctimonious and, surprisingly to those who knew both men, had a greater liking for Scarman's predecessor as head of chambers, the maliciously witty Melford Stevenson.

Bingham's practice began, as did most practices at the common law bar, as a knockabout succession of poorly paid briefs in undefended divorces, magistrates' courts defences and the like; but he rapidly began to attract serious and well-paid work, much of it in the fields of commercial and public law, which eventually brought him to the notice of Lord Denning, who as Master of the Rolls presided over the Court of Appeal. Since the heads of division had in practice a blackball on applications for silk, Denning's approval mattered, as did the support of Melford Stevenson. The result was that Bingham's name featured at the foot of the list of new QCs for 1972—the foot being the prestigious location enjoyed by the candidate who was taking silk at the earliest point of his career. Bingham was still only 38 years old.

There was nothing flamboyant or oratorical about Bingham's advocacy: he was quietly spoken, courteous and methodical, emphasising by understatement. But in silk, as before, his practice thrived as institutional clients (including the Department of Employment) and commercial clients sought to brief him. Increasingly, too, his sound judgment and dependability were recognised. In 1974 he served as counsel to the judicial inquiry into a fatal chemical explosion at Flixborough, demonstrating a detailed grasp of the plant's complex technology. Then in 1977–78 he conducted a major public inquiry into the supply of oil to Rhodesia in breach of UN sanctions, producing a penetrating report which did not draw back from finding that British civil servants had been complicit in breaching sanctions against the unlawful Rhodesian régime.

In his chambers pupils found that, unlike other barristers, he always took notice of them, involved them in discussions of legal problems, and made sure that they came along if the barristers went out for a drink at the end of a day. He quietly returned at least one pupil's 100-guinea pupillage fee by setting up a standing order for £10 a week to remunerate him for his assistance, first as a pupil and then as a junior tenant.

THE BENCH

In April 1980, at the age of 46, Bingham, now at the apex of his profession, was offered appointment to the Queen's Bench Division of the High Court, with the customary knighthood. Many years later, discussing his reasons for accepting the appointment despite the drop in income, Bingham reflected that practice in silk took a toll on advocates

'like heavyweight boxers who just can't bear to go back into the ring: as you get more senior the cases get longer, which makes them more burdensome and in a sense more worrying, particularly if they are going wrong. And I found I liked my clients less as time went by and they got richer. I got on very well with criminals in my early days'.

As a Queen's Bench judge, he was assigned to the Commercial Court, where he tried his cases with patience and civility. Almost all his decisions proved durable on appeal, but in one case[1] he was controversially overset by the House of Lords. The *Popi M* had been lost at sea, and her insurers refused to pay out because they did not believe that she had succumbed to an insured hazard. It was rumoured, but never established, that she had been scuttled. Bingham found that, of the several improbable explanations of the loss that were advanced, the least unlikely was a collision with a submarine. Since this was a finding of fact, the only way he could be overset was by faulting his logic, which is what the law lords did. Bingham, though not a vain man, did not take kindly to their lofty critique of his reasoning.

After six years as a puisne judge, Bingham in 1986 was promoted to the Court of Appeal, where he was able to deploy his clear brain on an endless variety of legal questions. Even his colleagues were impressed by the facility with which, with a few manuscript notes in front of him, he could deliver grammatically perfect extempore judgments. Here too, conformably with what he had once said about his own capacity for ruthlessness and contrary to what some later saw as his sentimental streak, he showed a capacity for hard-headed and unsentimental adjudication. In the litigation about the deaths of 16 members of the public and the injury of many more in the Abbeystead pumping station explosion of 1984, when a majority of his court upheld the finding of negligent engineering design and the consequent awards of damages, Bingham, showing a striking command of the scientific evidence and viewing the case as a test of the judiciary's duty to come to a decision without fear or favour, delivered a dissenting judgment which, had either of his colleagues concurred with it, would have sent the claimants away empty-handed.[2]

[1] *Rhesa Shipping v Edmunds* [1985] 1 WLR 948 (HL).
[2] *Eckersley v Binnie* [1988] 18 Con LR 1 (CA).

SENIOR LAW LORD

When in 1992 Lord Donaldson retired from the post of Master of the Rolls, Bingham was a natural choice to succeed him. He seemed comfortably settled into the job when, in 1996, the Lord Chief Justice, Lord Taylor, became terminally ill and the Lord Chancellor, Lord Mackay, decided to move Bingham to the apex of the judiciary. The decision was surprising, and Taylor himself opposed it, because of Bingham's lack of experience of criminal law; but Mackay persisted. His determination was vindicated by the assiduity and success with which Bingham undertook his new role. He not only mastered the growing complexity of statutory sentencing provisions but travelled out on circuit from time to time to regain the feel of trial and sentencing procedures.

Bingham had been in this post for four years when in 2000 the senior law lord, Lord Browne-Wilkinson, retired. Until then, the presiding role in the appellate committee of the House of Lords had been routinely taken by the longest-serving member, who would then have been Lord Slynn of Hadley, an able lawyer but not a dynamic leader. Lord Irvine, the Blair government's Lord Chancellor, took the opportunity to formalise the post of senior law lord in order to be able to appoint its incumbent, like the heads of all the other courts, on merit rather than seniority (a step advocated by Lord Diplock as long ago as 1984). Bingham, already eligible to sit as a law lord, was glad to be offered the post. He was by now finding the role of chief justice so burdensome, both because of the administrative workload it entailed and because of its heavy emphasis on crime, that he had been thinking of taking early retirement. It was a bold move and a shrewd one, for it placed in the chair of what was becoming the United Kingdom's constitutional court a jurist whose formidable intellectual competence sat with a courteous and attentive manner.

Irvine's confidence proved justified. In place of the months which his predecessors had been taking to produce the first draft of their judgments, Bingham would return from a weekend at his home in Wales with a judgment ready in manuscript—'leading without fuss', as a colleague put it. In this role, which carried with it the presidency of the judicial committee of the Privy Council, Bingham flourished, and it was as a law lord and privy counsellor that he made an enduring mark on the law. Its magnitude and depth are surveyed by Brice Dickson in his book *The Judicial House of Lords*; but in brief, Bingham brought to the office of senior law lord the leadership and management skills he had developed as Master of the Rolls and Lord Chief Justice; he piloted his two committees through the uncharted constitutional waters of human rights and devolution; oversaw the move to an independent supreme court; assembled a nine-judge panel for major cases, a step last taken in 1910; and with colleagues of the intellectual calibre of Baroness Hale, Lord Hope and Lord Hoffmann—although not always in agreement with them—positioned his court in the first rank of the world's supreme courts. As Dickson forecast, his act has proved extremely hard to follow. His contribution was recognised in 2005 when he was made a Knight of the Garter, the first judge ever to receive the accolade.

Both the law lords and the Privy Council customarily discuss their decisions in reverse order of seniority. Bingham's natural courtesy inclined him anyway to listen to others before expressing his own opinion. When he did so, and equally when conversing with colleagues, he would occasionally and unexpectedly decorate his prose with a four-letter expletive—a trait less out of character in light of his capacity in private life for impulsiveness, but one which did not seriously diminish his authority. One of Bingham's colleagues in the House of Lords, the New Zealand judge Lord Cooke of Thorndon, who had been a member of a variety of appellate courts in different countries, was once asked which judges he would put on his ideal court. 'I know exactly who they would be', said Cooke. 'I won't name them all, but I can tell you that Tom Bingham would be in the chair.'

Early in his tenure as senior law lord, Bingham, who regarded the Human Rights Act of 1998 as the Blair government's greatest achievement, had to consider the relationship of the common law to the human rights régime at a time when the latter had not yet come into force. In a case concerning a prisoner's entitlement to privacy for his legal correspondence, Bingham, rather than leave the issue to the still-nascent statutory regime, led the appellate committee in developing the common law in harmony with the European Convention so as to protect personal privacy against disproportionate interference by the authorities.[3] That he was prepared to do so in favour of an unpopular class of claimant was very much in character.

It was in the so-called Belmarsh case in 2004 that Bingham stamped his authority on the United Kingdom's constitutional law,

---

[3] *R v Home Secretary, ex parte Daly* [2001] UKHL 26.

holding the executive to account for unwarranted deprivations of liberty in the fraught and complex situation created by the 9/11 terrorist attacks on New York and Washington. The Home Secretary was detaining indefinitely in Belmarsh high security prison foreign nationals who, though suspected of terrorist involvement, could not be charged or tried for want of admissible evidence, nor deported because they would face torture in their home states. A nine-judge panel chaired by Bingham in December 2004 struck down the régime as an unlawful and discriminatory use of the state's immigration powers, holding that the executive's derogation from the European Convention in order to accommodate these measures had been an irrational response to the perceived threat to the nation's life. In a key passage of the leading speech Bingham took the Attorney-General to task for seeking to stigmatise judicial decision-making as undemocratic: the judges, Bingham pointed out, were enforcing law made by Parliament.[4] Writing about the case later, without referring to his own role in it, he described it as 'perhaps as serious a reverse as any of our governments has ever suffered in our domestic courts' but pointed out that it could not have happened without the same government's introduction of the Human Rights Act. Not long afterwards Bingham led the appellate committee in outlawing the use of evidence obtained by torture.

Bingham's swansong in the House of Lords was his dissenting speech in 2008 in the Chagos Islanders' case. The exiled islanders had succeeded before a unanimous High Court and a unanimous Court of Appeal in nullifying the ministerial order in council which purported to revoke their right of return. They lost by two votes to three in the House of Lords (where the opposition to Bingham was led by Lord Hoffmann); but Bingham, in a brief and penetrating judgment, stood by them. The royal prerogative, he held, could not lawfully be used to exile a population living under the protection of the Crown; and even if it was not void for this reason, the order in council was unlawful both because there was no tenable ground for making it and because it reneged on an unambiguous government promise to restore the right of return. The speech, one of Bingham's last, showed him at his moral and juridical best: principled, learned, astute, and humane.[5]

Bingham's critics pointed to two decisions in particular that were said to show a less liberal side to him. Presiding in 1998 as chief

---

[4] *A v Home Secretary* [2004] UKHL 56.
[5] *R (Bancoult) v Foreign and Commonwealth Secretary (No 2)* [2008] UKHL 61.

justice in the High Court, he allowed General Pinochet's appeal against extradition to Spain for crimes against humanity, holding that he was entitled to immunity as a head of state.[6] In a series of decisions which, though procedurally chaotic, attracted worldwide approval for their outcome, the House of Lords overset his judgment and authorised Pinochet's extradition on torture charges. Ten years later Bingham presided over a unanimous appellate committee in the Lords which, oversetting the High Court, held that the director of the Serious Fraud Office had been entitled to balance one public interest against another and had not surrendered his independent judgment when, with government encouragement, he discontinued an investigation into bribery in the arms trade because the Saudi government had threatened to halt its security and strategic co-operation with the UK if the investigation continued.[7] Bingham's answer to both critiques was that he was practising what he preached: adherence in the first case to orthodox principles of sovereign immunity, and in the second to executive autonomy within the law. He was entirely in favour of Pinochet's standing trial, but not by the means proposed; and his refusal to interfere with an exercise of prosecutorial discretion, whatever he might think of its morality, corresponded with his view of the separation of powers. It was where the law gave him the necessary space that Bingham's moral sensibility took charge, though, unlike his precursor Lord Denning, he would not bend facts or law to reach a desired goal.

THE PRIVY COUNCIL AND THE DEATH PENALTY

Of the appeals from those member states of the Commonwealth still accepting the Privy Council as their court of last resort, those concerning the death penalty and the use of life imprisonment were both the most dramatic and the clearest assertion of Bingham's humanitarianism. The United Kingdom itself had abolished the death penalty in 1965, but it had bequeathed capital punishment regimes to its former colonies. Prior to Bingham's presidency the judicial committee had halted the carrying out of executions after inordinate delay and had ensured that applications for clemency were considered lawfully and fairly; but in the subsequent cases contesting the use of the gallows in the Caribbean states, Bingham's

---

[6] *R v Bow Street Magistrate, ex parte Pinochet Ugarte* [1998] 3 WLR 1456 (HL).
[7] *R (Corner House Research) v Director of SFO* [2005] EWCA Civ 192; [2008] UKHL 60.

moral leadership came under sustained challenge. Having in 2002 led a unanimous five-judge panel that held the mandatory death sentence in Belize, St Lucia, and St Kitts respectively to be unconstitutional,[8] in 2004 he found himself outvoted by five to four in appeals on substantially the same issue: in a strongly worded judgment, the majority (for whom Lord Hoffmann spoke) declined to follow the earlier group of decisions and held that the constitutionality of mandatory death sentences in Barbados and Trinidad was unchallengeable.[9]

Two years later the balance was again reversed: with Bingham in the chair, the Privy Council distinguished the later decision, avoiding the need to challenge it directly, and held the mandatory death penalty for murder, this time in the Bahamas, to be unconstitutional as being an arbitrary deprivation of life.[10] The unanimous judgment, drafted and delivered by Bingham, contained a striking historical survey, drawn from both sides of the Atlantic, of the law's approach to excessive punishments from Magna Carta onwards. There is little doubt that Bingham would have sought to do away with capital punishment altogether if it had not been constitutionally entrenched; but his jurisprudence restricting its use, far from isolating the Privy Council, gave a lead that was followed not only by the newly-established Eastern Caribbean Court of Appeal and by the Inter-American Commission on Human Rights but by a number of former colonial states in Africa and Asia.

LAW REFORM

Bingham made no secret of his support for reform of the legal system. When in 1989 Lord Mackay proposed to open up High Court advocacy rights to solicitors, Bingham publicly warned that the greatest threat to the bar lay not in the proposal but in the bar's obstructive reaction to it. He became the first senior judge since Scarman to support the incorporation of the European Convention on Human Rights into the law of the UK, an objective achieved in 1998 with the Human Rights Act. He went on to support the abolition of judicial wigs, the use of plain English, and (despite his unfailing patience in court) the imposition of time limits on garrulous

---

[8] *Reyes v R* [2002] UKPC 11; *R v Hughes* [2002] UKPC 12; *Fox v R* [2002] UKPC 12.
[9] *Boyce v R* [2004] UKPC 32; *Matthew v R* [2004] UKPC 33.
[10] *Bowe v R* [2006] UKPC 10.

counsel. As Lord Chief Justice he opposed government proposals to introduce mandatory minimum sentences and argued against the mandatory life sentence for murder, contending in both cases that judges were best placed to decide appropriate punishments.

Bingham also endorsed the project to divorce the United Kingdom's final appellate court from the legislature, with the institution of a Supreme Court on the opposite side of Parliament Square. He took a detailed interest in the conversion plans and defended them against criticism. But time was not on his side, and when he reached retirement age in 2008 the Supreme Court was still a year from completion.

The unifying theme in Bingham's presidential work was the importance of judicial independence. With his acute sense of history, he always linked this with the judicial obligation, dictated by the separation of powers, to leave governance to government. But where law and politics clashed, he was clear in his insistence that unless legality took precedence the rule of law itself would stumble.

WIDER INTERESTS AND WRITINGS

Oxford remained an integral part of Bingham's life. He became visitor of Balliol in 1986, an office he held for 24 years, deciding internal disputes and giving advice. (He made the initial mistake of telling the porter on gate duty, 'I am the Visitor', and was told, 'Sorry, sir, no visitors allowed at this time of day'.) The university conferred an honorary degree of DCL on him in 1994 (one of ten honorary doctorates) and in 2002 appointed him to the office of High Steward. In 2003 he stood for election as chancellor of the university but was defeated by the better-known politician Lord (Christopher) Patten. Of the several portraits of Bingham, perhaps the best is the one (by David Poole, 2002) in Balliol, showing him seated in an armchair with a newspaper, in jeans and an open-necked shirt. Photographic portraits, by contrast, tend to show him squinting uncomfortably at the camera.

Of Bingham's many interests, all of which he pursued in depth, Samuel Johnson was perhaps the one that most absorbed him. As his lectures and essays testified, he knew a huge amount about this great and tormented scholar and had endless admiration for his single-mindedness and adherence to principle in a life of adversity. Johnson's opposition to slavery formed a link between Bingham's special subject for history finals at Oxford and the scholarly lecture he delivered during his time as senior law lord on the common law's eventual outlawing of slavery. That lecture, for its part, was no more than one brick in an imposing edifice of writings, many but not all delivered initially as public lectures, produced by Bingham in his last decade and remarkable for their range of subject matter, their depth of learning and their breadth of vision. To take a single instance, in a lecture delivered at Leicester University in 2009,[11] he not only gave an unparalleled account of the constitutional status of the House of Lords and its inbuilt anomalies but set out an innovative scheme for replacing it with a council of the realm which would do the one thing the house did well, namely revise measures coming from the Commons. That the proposal would not appeal to the political class did not worry him.

FAMILY LIFE

Tom Bingham's inseparable companion was his wife Elizabeth, who would travel out on circuit with him when she could. At the judges' lodgings, the butler's customary enquiry, '*Times* or *Telegraph*, my lord?', would be met with, '*Guardian*, please'. At home Elizabeth's first activity in the morning was to go out and buy two copies of *The Guardian* so that she and Tom each had their own copy. He never disclosed how he himself voted, though he displayed a touch of scepticism about judicial neutrality by quoting a senior judge who had opined that it was constitutionally improper for judges to use their votes and who had then added, 'Anyway, I don't need to: I live in Chelsea'. In later years, when Bingham chaired the Hay festival, he could be found rattling a collection bucket for the charity SOS Sahel to which Elizabeth devoted much of her time and energy.

In 1965 the Binghams bought a cottage in Powys, at Cornhill (near Boughrood). It was from here that Bingham in later life took the title of his barony, contrary to the widespread assumption in the legal profession that it was taken from the well-known street in the City of London. This was where he and the family spent every holiday. The house had been declared unfit for human habitation by the local authority, and so it remained: for 30 years there was no internal water supply or heating and no indoor toilet. Washing up was done out of doors, Bingham when necessary wearing an army greatcoat to do it. Between long and arduous family hill walks, he would help to grow and cook vegetables. He would also grapple with machinery,

---

[11] See T Bingham, *Lives of the Law* (Oxford University Press, 2011) Ch 7.

for which he had less aptitude. In the village he was known for his baggy tweed suits and eccentric socks. *En famille* he was the genial patriarch. In pub restaurants he would pre-empt individual study of the menu by announcing 'We'll *all* have the sausages'.

Family discourse was conducted in a version of undergraduate slang involving standardised prefixes and suffixes and impenetrable nicknames for inanimate objects. Meals (eaten out of doors unless the weather made it impossible) were congenial affairs, with wine and sometimes whisky, of which Bingham was both a connoisseur and a devotee. Christmas dinner would finish with songs, carols, and recitations. Bingham, an uninhibited singer, loved show tunes; he saw *Oh! What a Lovely War* seven times on its first run. Somehow the house also held books in quantity. Bingham would spend his mornings there writing lectures and judgments, his practice of using longhand making the absence of a word processor inconsequential.

LATER LIFE

Bingham retired, as he was obliged to do, on reaching the age of 75 in October 2008. Retirement, though not welcome, liberated him from the constraints of judicial office, and enabled him to begin his new life with a devastating critique, in the Grotius lecture at Lincoln's Inn, of the legality of the Second Iraq War. Somehow, too, he managed to find the intellectual and physical resources, as his health began to fail, to deliver the Hamlyn lectures in 2009, an extended conspectus of the uses of comparative law, and to write a short book on *The Rule of Law* (2010) which became an instant classic and won the Orwell prize for literature the following year.

In late 2009 Bingham received the devastating diagnosis of lung cancer. He refused to give in to it and went on speaking and writing while, as he put it, his batteries ran down. Some of his most interesting published work belongs to this period. His burial in September 2010 in Boughrood was followed by a packed memorial service in Westminster Abbey on 25 May 2011. As the liturgy ended, three loud bangs on a bass drum sounded in the choir and Bingham's favourite jazz band, the Adamant New Orleans Marching Band, came down the aisle playing, 'When the saints go marching in'.

* * *

Bingham's personality and achievements were garlanded both in and after his lifetime with superlatives. Those who knew and worked with him spoke repeatedly of his modesty and kindness. Those who sat with him respected his penetrating and compendious mind. Those who appeared before him found him attentive and courteous. Those who read his judgments found themselves admiring an unrivalled intellect. Those (including some of his colleagues) who considered him capable on occasion of letting sentiment eclipse legality were outnumbered by those who saw in him a judge for whom justice mattered at least as much as law. Those who considered him unequipped for the post of Lord Chief Justice were proved wrong, and those who regarded some of his decisions as unduly conservative had to accept that these were outweighed by his refusal, whenever he considered refusal to be possible, to lend the authority of the law to man's inhumanity to man.

32

Lord Mansfield

1705–1793

I N MARCH 1718, thirteen-year-old William Murray, the eleventh of Viscount Stormont's fourteen children, set off from the family seat at Scone, near Perth, on a pony. The journey to London, which he made alone, took him almost two months, and it is probable that he never saw Scotland again. Although it was a bare three years since the first Jacobite rising had attempted to place the Old Pretender, James Edward Stuart, on the throne, and although the Murrays were well-known Jacobites, the family was well enough connected to ensure that, when he reached London, William was able to enter Westminster School and then Christ Church, Oxford. At both he shone as a scholar.

Lord Mansfield, as Murray became, spanned the eighteenth century in more than simply years, though living from 1705 to 1793 was a good start. As chief justice of the King's Bench for 32 years, he modernised an antiquated system of common law and rationalised a diffuse system of mercantile law; he drafted statutes; he played a central role in politics as cabinet member, counsellor and confidant; he knew everyone from Boswell to Blackstone and Pope to Pitt; and at Kenwood in Hampstead he constructed a mansion, designed by Robert Adam, and a park which remain a high point of British design.

Norman Poser is not Mansfield's first biographer, but he is arguably the best so far. The first, John Holliday, wrote his not always reliable memoir shortly after Mansfield's death. Then came Lord Campbell, himself a chief justice, whose biographies of his predecessors became known as one of the new terrors of death, and whose *Life of Mansfield* contains at least one palpable fabrication. In the twentieth century two scholars, Edmund Heward and CHS Fifoot, produced good short biographies focused on Mansfield as a lawmaker; and James Oldham (the author of the excellent entry on

Mansfield in the current *ODNB*), with new access to a large cache of
Mansfield's trial notes, produced a scholarly cornucopia, the two-
volume *Mansfield Manuscripts*. Poser, with the further advantage of
access to the mass of Mansfield documents assembled over 22 years
by Arthur Vanderbilt, who died in 1957 just before retiring from his
post as chief justice of New Jersey, has now written the comprehensive biography[1] that Vanderbilt had planned to write.

The well-known engraving of Mansfield, taken by Bartolozzi from
the portrait that Reynolds painted of him at the age of 80, shows
what always seemed to me to be a thin-lipped and cruel face. It
is cheering to learn that the reason, according to Reynolds, is that
Mansfield had by then lost his teeth. Although Boswell in earlier
years had found his 'cold reserve and sharpness' repelling, earlier
portraits show a much more genial face. In parallel, the real-life
Mansfield can be read as a hard-nosed careerist and canny lawyer
whose wealth and connections enabled him to survive a good many
deserved and a few undeserved buffetings; or as a contradictory
and often inconsistent potentate, ruled as much by his heart as by
his head; or as both, depending on the situation in which he found
himself. Whichever it is to be, a judgment needs to go beyond the
simplistic contrast drawn by Poser between Mansfield's legalism
and his 'decency and sense of fairness'; or the amalgam, as Poser
perceives it, of an 'astute understanding of human nature with a
vigorous aspiration to achieve justice'. These are superficial, even
hagiographic, evaluations; but Poser's achievement as a biographer
is to equip others to form a fuller judgment.

On one level, Mansfield's was a model career and Samuel Smiles
wrote of him with reverence. His wife, Elizabeth, to whom he was
devotedly married for 46 years, was the daughter of an earl and
the granddaughter of a Lord Chancellor. A dutiful but not exces-
sively devout Anglican, he prospered at the bar, then entered Parliament and almost at once was appointed Solicitor-General. He
was promoted to Attorney-General, a position from which he was
able within two years to claim the vacant post of chief justice of the
King's Bench, the principal court of common law. More than once
he turned down the office of Lord Chancellor, aware that, in spite
of its grandeur, it was a post that was unlikely to outlast the current ministry. Unsatisfied with the barony that had been conferred

---

[1] Norman Poser, *Lord Mansfield: Justice in the Age of Reason* (McGill-Queen's
University Press, 2013).

on him when he was made chief justice (he took the title from one of the estates of his patron, the Duke of Newcastle), he bided his time and, following the first British victories in the American war, which Mansfield supported, asked the king for an earldom. By now he was an extremely wealthy man from his practice at the bar, from the huge salary and perks of the chief justiceship, and from shrewd mortgage londings which at his death were said to be bringing in £30,000 a year.

On another level, Mansfield was a child of fortune. Although insinuations of Jacobitism inevitably accompanied attacks on him—by Junius, for example, over his conduct of the trials of two publishers of the *Letters* for seditious libel, and repeatedly by his political antagonist Pitt—Mansfield's enemies never knew about the letters he had written at the age of 20 to his brother-in-law John Hay, an adviser to the Pretender in exile in Rome, offering 'my duty and loyalty to the king', that is to say to the Pretender. Much later in life Mansfield, reaffirming the oath of loyalty to the Protestant succession that was required of all university entrants, said: 'That a Protestant should reason himself into a Jacobite is as incomprehensible in politics as it is in religion that a man should reason himself into an atheist.' (That the latter process was by no means incomprehensible may be too modern an idea; it is unlikely that Mansfield was advancing a coded defence of Jacobitism.) But although the bare accusation was capable, particularly after the '45 and Culloden, of destroying a career, in Mansfield's youth, Poser points out, both Westminster School and Christ Church were seats of overt Jacobite sympathy. Many of the fellows of the college refused to take the oath of allegiance to a Hanoverian crown, and toasts to 'the king over the water' were drunk almost as regularly in Oxford ('a seminary of treason', Pitt called it) as in Edinburgh. Hostility to the Pretender, whose claim to the throne was practically unanswerable but for his Catholicism, was matched by hostility to a frequently absent German monarch whom the pursuit of a Protestant succession had shoehorned on to the British throne.

Mansfield's youthful offer of allegiance to the king over the water may therefore not have been just an emotional indiscretion, which is the way the king regarded it when an account of Mansfield's having drunk the Pretender's health as a youth was reported to him. There was for a time a more than fanciful possibility, stoked by the atmosphere of Oxford, that the British throne would revert to the Stuarts. If that had happened, it would have been a shrewd career move for Mansfield to have staked out a supportive position. Equally, there is no reason why Mansfield should not have genuinely altered his views about the succession as he became an ornament of the English establishment and eventually a trusted adviser to the Hanoverian monarchy, while the realism of a Stuart succession faded. But the critics of public figures are rarely content to allow them to change their minds, and the epistolary evidence of his early Jacobite leanings, had it emerged, could well have destroyed him.

When George III came to the throne in 1760, Mansfield, by now chief justice, was still sitting regularly in cabinet, a minister (as Poser says) in all but name. When the Whig ascendancy collapsed and the Tory administration of Lord Bute took office, Mansfield stayed on, earning himself opprobrium as a turncoat when he could as readily have been regarded as creditably non-partisan. More important, however, the king's initial hostility to him turned in the course of a few years to respect verging on admiration, giving Mansfield an enduring handle on the machinery of state. Legal historians tend to shrug at this gross violation of the separation of powers that Montesquieu and Madison purported to admire in the British constitution; but, even at the time, the crossover between justice and politics was a cause of concern: Poser quotes the comment of the *Public Advertiser* in 1777 that 'a man clothed with the robe of magistracy ought not to be a politician'.

Mansfield, however, found no embarrassment either in the multiplicity of his roles or in his personal connections with some of the litigants whose cases he unblushingly tried. He committed to a debtors' prison (where he died) the by then demented poet Christopher Smart whom in past years he had befriended and helped. When the Duchess of Kingston, a close friend of his former patron the Duke of Newcastle, was indicted before the House of Lords for bigamy, Mansfield took the unprecedented step of granting her bail and then met her privately and reassured her that she would not go to jail, before sitting as a member of the House to try her. And when Lord George Gordon was indicted for provoking the riots in which Mansfield's house and goods were destroyed, Mansfield had no hesitation in presiding at his trial for high treason (of which the jury acquitted him). Once again, it was left to the press to point out what was even then recognisable as an unacceptable conflict of interest: the *Morning Herald* tentatively suggested that Mansfield might 'from the point of delicacy absent himself ... lest the malevolent should, in case of ... conviction of the prisoner, attempt to slander his great name by insinuating that something more than a love of justice might have swayed his Lordship'.

The respectful tone of comments like this reflected another of Mansfield's achievements: the liberal deployment of the law of criminal libel to silence critics of the government and anyone who questioned the truth of Christianity. As Attorney-General he had prosecuted several such cases. He had also advised that Dr Johnson could be prosecuted for the definition in his newly-published *Dictionary* of excise as 'a hateful tax ... adjudged not by the common judges of property, but wretches [ie the commissioners of excise] hired by those to whom excise is paid'. Mansfield, experienced enough to anticipate what a jury of property owners would do with such an indictment, advised that it was better to threaten the Sage with prosecution if he did not modify the entry. Boswell, however, does not record that any such threat was received, and Johnson did not in any case alter his definition. But Mansfield, once on the bench, did not alter his mindset. He continued to hold that whether a publication was seditious was a question for the judge alone. It took legislation—Fox's Libel Act of 1792—to prise the question of libel or no libel out of the hands of the judges and give it to the jury.

When John Wilkes, known to be the editor and suspected of being the author of issue no 45 of the vehemently anti-government *North Briton*, was arrested along with 44 others on a ministerial warrant that blandly authorised the arrest of the authors, printers and publishers of the paper—leaving it, in other words, to the king's messengers to decide where to search and whom to apprehend—it was to the chief justice of the Court of Common Pleas, Sir Charles Pratt, not to Mansfield's court, that Wilkes's lawyers applied for a writ of habeas corpus. Mansfield, who despised Pratt (a good lawyer with a liberal track record at the bar), was angry that his court was being bypassed; but by the time the law officers managed to get the cases into Mansfield's court, the wind had changed and they got no help from Mansfield either. He dismissed the Crown's appeal against the award of £400 damages to the printer Dryden Leach, holding, as Pratt had done, that the law did not authorise the use of general warrants—a decision likelier to have reflected Mansfield's awareness of popular sentiment in favour of 'Wilkes and liberty' than respect for Pratt's jurisprudence.[2]

The culmination of this and other lawsuits, including Wilkes's, in historic judgments and heavy awards of damages against ministers and their staff for false imprisonment were, however, only

---

[2] See Ch 5.

part of the story. There were also successful prosecutions for seditious libel, in which Mansfield played a central role. He took it on himself to direct a jury that the *North Briton* was a seditious publication, making conviction of the printer inevitable. Wilkes too was convicted of seditious libel in absentia, having fled to France (and consequently been outlawed) in order to evade both this prosecution and a charge of blasphemous libel for having had printed *An Essay on Woman*, which salaciously parodied Pope's *Essay on Man* and its ponderous annotations by Mansfield's friend Bishop Warburton. On his return to England Wilkes surrendered himself to Mansfield's court to be sentenced on his convictions. Mansfield, again no doubt conscious of popular sentiment, managed to reverse the outlawry on a punctilio in the sheriff's writ, and left the sentencing to another judge.

Those who recall Mansfield's stirring dictum in the case of James Somersett, 'The air of England is too pure for a slave to breathe,' may wonder why there is no mention of it in Poser's book. The reason is that Mansfield never said it. The line appears to have originated in a decision of Star Chamber in 1569:

> 'One Cartwright brought a slave from Russia and would scourge him, for which he was questioned, and it was resolved, that England was too pure an air for slaves to breathe in.'

The earliest surviving account of the passage is in a contemporaneous account of the impeachment by the House of Commons in 1640 of the Star Chamber judges who three years earlier had had John Lilburne flogged through the streets, pilloried and jailed for refusing to give sworn answers to their questions. It was the parliamentary managers who drew the attention of the Upper House to the stirring dictum from *Cartwright*'s case, apparently in order to establish that flogging a gentleman, as opposed to a villein, was not lawful.

James Somersett, a recaptured slave, was being held aboard a ship moored in the Thames, about to be carried back to the West Indies. His abolitionist English godparents had habeas corpus proceedings issued on his behalf. When Mansfield, after some prevarication, was finally compelled to hear and decide the case, another of Somersett's pro bono counsel, the legal scholar and antiquary Francis Hargrave, quoted Cartwright's case in his argument (at least, he put it into the account of his argument in the report which he edited, admitting engagingly that it was not actually the speech he had delivered in court). But once the quotation was ringingly repeated by Somersett's leading counsel, Serjeant Davy, it became common currency.

It was in 1827 when Lord Stowell, refusing in the case of *The Slave Grace* to extend Mansfield's decision from England to the colonies, sarcastically ascribed to him the view that 'the air of our island is too pure for slavery to breathe in' that the attribution of the line to Mansfield took root, enabling Lord Campbell in his *Lives of the Chief Justices* to slot into Mansfield's judgment the peroration: 'Tho air of England has long been too pure for a slave, and every man is free who breathes it.' And there, in legal folklore, it has remained.

But the creditable fact is that Mansfield, who not many months before had refused to act on the verdict of a jury that another escaped slave, Thomas Lewis, was not the property of his former owner, refused now to accept that the slave-owner Stewart's return to the writ of habeas corpus, namely that Somersett was his property, was capable of justifying his detention. Mansfield was well aware of the domino effect that might follow if slavery were to be outlawed in England, and he said as much in his judgment. But he held—as in fact Chief Justice Holt had held in 1701 and again in 1706, only to be repeatedly overridden by advice given by the Crown's law officers—that

> 'the state of slavery is ... so odious that nothing can be suffered to support it but positive law. Whatever inconveniences, therefore, may follow from a decision, I cannot say this case is allowed or approved by the law of England; and therefore the black must be discharged'.

Although in later years Mansfield, and others, sought to limit the decision to preventing the export of slaves from England, its logic was far wider. The proposition that ownership of another human being was not a form of property known to English law—it had already been held to be outwith Scots law—dovetailed with Mansfield's judgment in *Campbell v Hall*[3] (a decision which played a part in the modern Chagos Islanders litigation) distinguishing between ceded colonies, which were subject to direct rule and therefore open to a common law ban on slavery, and settled colonies, whose legislatures were autonomous unless the imperial parliament overrode them. It was a distinction which could well have been built on by the American colonists in their bid for independence. But Mansfield, an influential hawk from the start, rapidly became a hate figure for them and their English supporters, not least by reason of the Quebec Act, which he may have drafted and which—consonantly

---

[3] *Campbell v Hall* (1774) 1 Cowp 204, 98 ER 1045.

with his religious liberalism—afforded a measure of toleration to Canada's Catholics.

It is his inclination towards religious tolerance and his affection for his black great-niece, Dido Elizabeth Belle, that begin to soften Mansfield's image as a conservative legal moralist and to hint at a conflicted and sometimes humane individual. Dido was born out of wedlock in the West Indies to his sea-captain nephew Sir John Lindsay and a black slave whose identity is lost. She went at an early age to live with the childless Mansfields at Kenwood as a companion to their great-niece Lady Elizabeth Murray, who had lived with them since the death of her mother. Zoffany's double portrait now hanging in Scone Palace, painted circa 1780 when Dido was in her late teens, shows two elegant young women with different skin colours but similar features.

Dido's life at Kenwood mirrored her ambivalent social status: she was not allowed to eat with the family but was permitted to join them for coffee. But she was evidently grateful, for she looked after the widowed Mansfield in his last years, and he left her a small legacy to add to the large one from her father. After his death Dido married, had three sons, and died in her early forties. She is sensitively portrayed in the recently released film *Belle*, which goes to great lengths to recreate time and place (much of it is set in the newly restored Kenwood House), but which is marred by one serious misjudgment: the lawsuit used to reveal the humanity beneath Mansfield's crusty exterior is not *Somersett*'s case, as it could well have been without overmuch dramatic licence, but the *Zong* case, which Mansfield heard 11 years later.[4]

The *Zong* was a slaver whose captain had jettisoned 150 captives on the voyage from West Africa when the ship's water ran low, and whose owners now claimed indemnity from their insurers for lost cargo, together with another sixty slaves who had died of thirst and forty who had thrown themselves overboard. A jury had found that the loss was occasioned by the ordinary perils of the sea, making the insurers liable. On appeal, Mansfield had a perfect opportunity to live up to his rhetoric in *Somersett* by throwing out the entire claim on the ground that the courts would not enforce a contract entered into for a purpose that was immoral or contrary to public policy. He had done exactly this in a number of cases involving oppressive loans or sharp transactions. Instead, accepting that slaves were

---

[4] *Gregson v Gilbert* (1783) 3 Doug KB 232.

insurable cargo, he washed his hands of the moral issues by order-
ing a retrial to investigate whether it had really been necessary to
throw them overboard. The case is as bad a blot as any on the law
of England and on Mansfield's reputation, and one is sorry to see it
sanitised in the telling of Dido's story.

While Mansfield's massive contributions to the rationalisation and
development of the law (Poser usefully catalogues them at the end
of the book) did not extend very far into the field of political liberty,
in relation to religious liberty his record was much better. The story
that he got a jury to acquit a woman of witchcraft by directing them,
not that the witnesses who described her walking on the ceiling
must be lying or deluded, but that there was no law against walking
on ceilings, was first published after his death and probably ranks
with George Washington's cherry tree as a benign invention. But it
is beyond question that Mansfield as a legislator supported the lift-
ing of the disabilities imposed by law on Protestant dissenters, and
that as a judge he made sure his juries acquitted Catholic priests
accused, usually by a professional informer, of celebrating mass—a
crime which under the Popery Act of 1698 carried a mandatory life
sentence.

The consequent accusations that Mansfield was a crypto-papist
were predictable and readily borne. Less easy to bear was the
destruction in the anti-Catholic Gordon riots of his townhouse in
Bloomsbury Square, which was targeted and burned to the ground
with its library and pictures (though the house, it is true, was rented,
and the Mansfields were safe at Kenwood). When troops finally put
down the disturbance and 25 of the rioters were tried and hanged,
Mansfield, speaking in the House of Lords in defence of the legality
of the troops' actions, said mournfully: 'I have not consulted books;
indeed I have no books to consult.'

Why was Mansfield, who was so intolerant on other matters, blasphemy included, so favourable to religious toleration? Poser is, I
think, justified in looking to his close friendship with Alexander
Pope. As a Catholic, Pope was debarred not only from owning land
but from attending mass, holding public office or living within
ten miles of London. The two men, although separated in age by
17 years, became close friends in the decade before Pope's death in
1744, Mansfield regularly visiting him at his home in Twickenham
and Pope as often coming to Mansfield's house in Lincoln's
Inn Fields and his chambers at 5 King's Bench Walk, where he
coached Mansfield in oratory. Among other admiring verses, one
of Pope's *Imitations of Horace* described Mansfield, still at the bar,

as 'his Country's pride'. For his part, Mansfield acted as counsel for Pope's publisher Dodsley in a copyright action to protect Pope's work from piracy, and Pope, in addition to making him an executor of his will, left him some valuable sculptures.

Mansfield had thus witnessed at close quarters the iniquity of the disabilities suffered by a Catholic whom he liked and admired, and who had shown him friendship and loyalty. He was also later to deal, as a judge, with the City of London's racket of nominating Protestant dissenters to posts they were disqualified by law from holding and then fining them for not filling them. It was not a long step from here to supporting religious toleration, and not a long step from there to being attacked as a Jacobite crypto-papist. The eighteenth century may have earned the sobriquet of the age of reason, but there may also be something in TH White's contention that at about its midpoint it became the age of scandal. Horace Walpole, who never liked Mansfield, excoriating him for supporting the execution of Admiral Byng, wrote: 'As it is observed that timorous natures … are generally cruel, Lord Mansfield might easily slide into rigour on this as he did on other occasions, when he was not personally afraid.' Perhaps after all the thin lips told a true tale.

33

Sir Thomas Morc

1478–1535

BEATIFICATION, WHICH FINALLY came to Thomas More in 1886, and canonisation, which had to wait until 1935, were only the icing on the commemorative cake. He had had, both during his life and since, a deserved measure of admiration as a scholar, a lawyer, a writer and a politician; for there is much in Robert Bolt's adulatory *A Man for All Seasons* which reflects what we know of More. But More was not simply a principled Catholic; he was also something of a fanatic. The Victorian historian JA Froude described him as a merciless bigot, and he described himself in his own epitaph as *hereticis molestus*. In ironic contrast to the religious toleration he described in *Utopia*, he advocated the execution of unrepentant heretics. 'When all allowances are made for the rancour of his Protestant critics,' the *DNB* says, 'it must be admitted that he caused suspected heretics to be carried to his house at Chelsea on slender pretences, to be imprisoned in the porter's lodge, and, when they failed to recant, to be racked in the Tower.'[1] He searched his friend John Petit's house for heretical literature and left him in prison, untried. He applauded the burning of a harmless leather seller called John Tewkesbury, noting: 'There never was a wretch, I wene, better worthy.'

And he was not, as it turned out, a man for quite all seasons. Henry VIII, whose faithful servant More professed to be and for the most part was, was a tyrant whose last resort against the papal refusal to sanction his divorce from Catherine of Aragon and his marriage to Anne Boleyn was to dethrone the Pope as head of the

---

[1] This review of *Thomas More's Trial by Jury* (2011), a collection of scholarly papers, prompted one of the editors to write to the *London Review of Books* pointing out that I had cited the first edition of the DNB and that the more recent edition no longer claimed that More had heretics tortured.

church in England. In this he had the counsel of the ruthless and crafty Thomas Cromwell.

More had in 1529 accepted the chancellorship left vacant by the impeachment of his patron Cardinal Wolsey, on condition that he would not be expected to support the annulment of the king's first marriage. He resigned the office in 1532 when the king succeeded in getting the clergy to acknowledge him as supreme head of the church in England 'as far as the law of Christ allows'. Two years after that, a complaisant Parliament passed the Act of Succession which required the king's subjects, on demand, to swear acceptance of Henry's and Anne's progeny as heirs to the throne. It was More's refusal, on religious grounds, to do this which led to his initial imprisonment in 1534. But the charge could only be misprision of treason, which was not a capital offence, and More resigned himself to a long stay in the Tower.

His undoing was the double-barrelled legislation that followed in November 1534. By the Act of Supremacy, Henry and his successors became—as the Queen still is—'the only supreme head in earth of the Church of England'. And by a concomitant statute it was made high treason not only to plot physical harm to the monarch or his heirs but also 'to deprive them of any of their dignity'. The act went on to make it treason to 'publish and pronounce, by express writing or words, that the King our sovereign lord should be heretic, schismatic, tyrant, infidel, or usurper of the Crown'; but the indictment on which More was tried did not charge him with accusing Henry of heresy or schism, for he had been careful to keep his counsel about this. It charged him with seeking to deprive the monarch of his new dignity as head of the Church of England. This too was an offence requiring malice, and it is on this that much of the debate about More's trial has for centuries turned.

More knew very well how he was being set up, and did what he could as a lawyer and as a theologian to evade it. Interrogated in the Tower in Cromwell's presence in early May 1535, he was asked—according to the indictment—whether he accepted that Henry was now the earthly head of the English church, and replied: 'I will not meddle with any such matters.' A letter More wrote to his favourite daughter, Margaret Roper, confirms that he had said this, and that he had also said that he would not 'dispute king's titles nor pope's, but the king's true faithful subject I am and will be'. His response was charged as malicious silence. So too was his refusal to answer when interrogated again in June. But the record of this interrogation, which survives, shows More describing the Act of Supremacy as a two-edged sword: if he accepted that it was good law, it was dangerous to the soul; if he asserted that it was bad law, it meant death to the body. In saying even this much, More had arguably gone beyond silence: he had admitted that his conscience forbade him to acknowledge the validity of the act.

Much of the rest of the indictment was taken up with More's correspondence with John Fisher, Bishop of Rochester, also in the Tower awaiting trial and execution; but the letters had been burned and interrogation of More, Fisher and the Tower staff yielded little about their contents. The indictment also, however, asserted that More, in the course of an interrogation about the lost letters, had incriminated himself to the Solicitor-General, Richard Rich. Urged by Rich to accept the new law, More had allegedly replied: 'Your conscience will save you, and my conscience will save me.' Rich had then, it seems, played the classic stool-pigeon's trick of disclaiming any authority to embark on the topic (today he would say 'Off the record, Tom ...') before asking More directly whether, if Parliament were to make Rich king, it would be treason to deny his kingship. More had replied that denial would be treason, since it would lie in his power to accept it. But if Parliament were to enact that God should not be God, More then asked in response, would resistance be treason? Rich, accepting that 'it is impossible to bring it about that God be not God', responded with the real question: why should More not accept that the king had been lawfully constituted supreme head on earth of the English church? The cases are not alike, More was said to have replied, because a subject can consent to Parliament's making of a king, but not to its making of a primate. In other words, the conferment of supreme spiritual authority lay beyond the powers of a temporal legislature.

This, if truly said, was deadly. In Bolt's play and in the eye of history it has become More's nemesis; and what appears to be a contemporaneous longhand note of the conversation, corresponding closely with the indictment, survives in the National Archives. But the records of the trial, such as they are, give no hint that this part of the indictment was proved in evidence. The first account of its having featured in More's trial is found in William Roper's biography of his father-in-law, written some two decades later and at second hand. But while the Guildhall manuscript, which is the nearest we have to a verbatim report of the trial, contains no sign of Rich's testimony, it is possible that Rich testified before the grand jury who found the indictment which set out his conversation with

More to be a 'true bill' fit to go to trial. *Thomas More's Trial by Jury* does not discuss this possibility, and since grand juries sat in private and may well have been able to indict without admissible testimony, it remains speculative. It is also distinctly possible that Roper simply took his account from the indictment.

What seems considerably less likely is the thesis which turned More scholarship upside down in 1964, when Duncan Derrett, in the face of much evidence to the contrary, suggested that the trial we know of was in fact a successful motion to quash the first three parts of the indictment, leaving the conversation with Rich as the sole basis for More's trial and conviction. This account (advanced some four years after Bolt's play) has a satisfactorily dramatic character, but Henry Ansgar Kelly, in his careful procedural review of the trial, is right to doubt it. Since Rich was Solicitor-General, and may have been in court as part of the prosecution team, it is conceivable that a decision was taken to go for a conviction without using his testimony.

The book, which is the work of many hands, includes a round-table discussion between three American judges and a British one about whether More had a fair trial. No one in the course of it mentions the nearest thing either country has had in modern times to a prosecution for withholding recognition of a question-able act of sovereignty: the contempt of Congress prosecutions brought against individuals who refused to answer the questions of the House Un-American Activities Committee. Here, as elsewhere, people may have been tried perfectly fairly for breach of an oppres-sive law. But one judge, the chief judge of the Fifth Circuit court of appeals, says of Rich's account: 'This cold record looks like "liar" to me.' I am not so sure. Certainly there is an air of *esprit d'escalier* in the parting shot which, according to Roper, Rich put into More's mouth: 'No more could the parliament make the king supreme head of the church.' But to say this was to say nothing that More had not already apparently said.

The problem with Thomas More scholarship, as this book illus-trates, is that his defenders oscillate between arguing that he did nothing unlawful and was framed, and asserting that he died a martyr for his loyalty to the papacy. More, I suspect, was well ahead of them in this regard. He knew quite well that he was one of the principal targets of the Act of Treasons, which had actually delayed its requirements until 1 February 1535 to allow him and others to adjust their consciences, and that his only hope lay in silence. Cromwell and his other accusers knew this too, and the trial therefore became—and has remained—a forum for argument about the evidential significance of silence.

The right not to incriminate oneself was a longstanding doctrine of the canon law, much honoured in the breach when treason and heresy called for torture, not least under More's own chancellorship. But there are numerous situations in which, without demanding that an accused person incriminate himself or herself, it is both lawful and reasonable to draw an inference from the fact that they have said nothing when one would expect them to say something. When in 1898 the law of England for the first time allowed accused persons to give evidence in their own defence, it also took away their privilege against self-incrimination once they entered the witness box. One of Michael Howard's unobjectionable reforms as Home Secretary was to change the law, and the police caution corresponding with it, in order to warn suspects that, while they were not obliged to answer police questions, failure to do so might count against them at trial.

More's silence, when faced with the simple question whether he accepted the Act of Supremacy or not, was eloquent, as he knew it must be. One defence, a somewhat artificial one, was that, since silence can imply consent, he should be taken as having consented to the Act of Supremacy—something he believed to be a sin, as we know from Reginald Pole's almost contemporaneous account of what More said once convicted: that the act was hostile to all law both human and divine. But his main defence was to fall back on the word 'maliciously' in the treason statute, arguing that there was no ill-will in his silence. As contributors to the book painstakingly explain, however, malice in law has for centuries been distinct from malice in fact. The latter signifies a requirement of ill-will, as it does frequently in libel. But used in criminal statutes it is ordinarily taken to mean 'deliberately', and that is the way it was read by the judges who sat to direct the jury who tried More.

The appendices to the book, which include the majority of primary sources for More's trial, conclude with an attempt, using these sources, to reconstruct the trial in dramatic form. The reconstruction adopts Pole's account that when the prosecutor urged that silence was itself proof of malice, the judges 'even though no one had any charge to make … nevertheless all cried out together "Malice! Malice!"' The docudrama accordingly has the judges at more or less arbitrary intervals croaking 'Malice!' It was without much doubt their ruling that malice required only intentionality and not ill-will that sent More to the scaffold for deliberately remaining silent.

But it was earlier, in mid-June, when Fisher was awaiting execution and More still awaiting trial, that Cromwell had made a chilling note of things needing to be done:

'Item to know [the king's] pleasure touching Maister More and to declare the oppynyon of the Jugges theron & what shalbe the kynge pleasure.

Item when Maister Fissher shall go to execucion with also the other.'

34

Lord Denning

1899–1999

THE DEATH AT the age of 100 of Alfred Thomas Denning (universally known as Tom) was the passing of one—perhaps the last—of a sparse succession of major judicial figures who have succeeded in shaping areas of the law into conformity with a strongly held world view.

Denning's most abiding and probably least deserved reputation was as a liberal. He adhered throughout his life to a conservative set of personal and public values, and he gave effect to them in his private life in rural Hampshire, in his judgments and in his numerous public pronouncements off the bench. It was these values which led him, as a newly appointed judge in the 1940s, to devise a legal doctrine which lawyers regarded as revolutionary but which performed the elementary moral task of holding people to their promises—something which the commercially oriented common law had found it expedient not to do.

His innovating continued with the deserted wife's right to salvage a home from the ruins of a marriage, and the liability of advisers for negligent advice. These were issues on which the law had got entrenched in indefensible moral positions, and it was a mark of Denning's greatness that he had the scholarship, the courage and the sense of opportunity to restore the credit of the common law when the chance came his way. By 1949, in spite of a prosecution of some Jewish businessmen in which his summing-up to the jury had given signs of unwholesome prejudice, he had been promoted to the Court of Appeal. He took with him his distaste for interference with individual enterprise, whether by the state or by trade unions, and his paternalistic (and sometimes simplistic) views on social questions.

These views had a long lineage. Sir Edward Coke's dictum in the days of the early Stuarts—'At the common law no man can be prohibited from working at any lawful trade, for the law abhors idleness, especially in young men'—repeatedly found echoes in Denning's judgments:

> 'Many a married woman seeks work. She does so …. to fill her time with useful occupation, rather than sit idly at home waiting for her husband to return. The devil tempts those who have nothing to do.'[1]

For four decades Denning went on to mould the law to his perceptions of private and public morality, rarely hesitating to torture precedent until it yielded the result he wanted. His enormous popularity was a combination of the appeal his pronouncements made to popular common sense, or at least to conventional wisdom, and the simple and comprehensible prose in which he couched them. His literary style, in fact, is perhaps his most underrated achievement.[2] While in his many books the simplicity is studied and sometimes embarrassingly overdone, Denning's judgments in case after case performed the feat, achieved by no other judge, of speaking directly and compellingly to ordinary people in well-constructed and lucid prose. Concepts which lawyers had struggled to articulate, clashes of doctrine which seemed insoluble, would emerge in his judgments as crystalline statements of principle. For all the professional smirks generated by his famous opening line in a judgment about an appalling motor accident ('It was bluebell time in Kent')[3] this accessibility was the rock on which his popularity and influence were built. When, not long after his retirement, he appeared in wig and gown on *Jim'll Fix It* and tried Little Noddy for knocking down PC Plod, what impressed was not the incongruity but the homogeneity of it: the same benign moralism as the legal profession had known for 40 years, in language begotten by Samuel Smiles upon Enid Blyton.

But Denning's simple language went with a penetrating mind. The son of a draper, born in Whitchurch, Hampshire, he was educated locally before going on to Magdalen College, Oxford. Of his four brothers, one became a general, another an admiral. After war service in France, where two of his brothers died, Denning began his university life as a mathematical scholar, took honours in that

---

[1] *Langston v AUEW* [1973] EWCA 7, [1974] 1 WLR 185.

[2] In a paper delivered in Lincoln's Inn in 2003 Denning's former colleague, Sir Martin Nourse, demonstrated how Denning's judicial prose, until his appointment as Master of the Rolls, had been conventionally complex and sophisticated. At that point it changed to the studied simplicity for which Denning became famous.

[3] *Hinz v Berry* [1970] 2 QB 40 (CA).

subject and then in law, and went on to shine at the bar. His 1929 edition of *Smith's Leading Cases* has become a collector's item.

Denning's compendious memory for law never deserted him. In judgment after judgment he would refer to authorities which counsel had not cited, sometimes predicating his decision on them. It led to some rancour, partly because it meant that cases were being decided on unargued points, but partly also because the cases he cited did not always support the propositions for which he invoked them. The result was always more important to him than how he got there.[4]

Denning's manner and image were part of his jurisprudence. The half-smile to be seen in every picture of him never left his face. People felt that they were in the presence of a benign judge with a ready ear for their problems. But while he could be readily influenced by the underlying agenda or the emotive side-issues of a case—'I just want to get the feel of it', he would say as he probed to and beyond the margins of legal relevance—he would rarely display his hostility towards those cases which, in his court at least, did not stand a chance. Instead he would help the destined loser to articulate his or her argument: 'I expect you'd say ....', 'Yes, you'd put it this way, wouldn't you?' Losers, especially litigants in person, would go away feeling that they had gained something, and Denning's court got through a lot more work.

But there were limits to his tolerance which became increasingly apparent. The hate-figures of the popular press—students, trade unions, squatters, prisoners—rarely if ever won their cases in Denning's court. His reputation was also damaged by his views on race, which finally precipitated his retirement in 1982 at the age of 83 (there was at that time no set judicial retirement age). A new book of his[5] contained derogatory remarks about black jurors. It was withdrawn and the passage rewritten. Denning expressed regret, but he had gone too far. His departure from the bench after 40 years as a judge, 20 of them as Master of the Rolls, took place under a shadow which lengthened in the succeeding years with further indiscretions.

Denning had been made a law lord in 1957. But he welcomed his transfer back to the Court of Appeal as Master of the Rolls five years later because in a three-judge court he needed only one ally

[4] For Marcel Berlins' astute parody of a Denning judgment, see S Sedley, *Ashes and Sparks* pp 203–204.
[5] *What Next in the Law.*

to secure a majority. Although the repeated oversetting of his judgments by the House of Lords became legendary, it is probable that Denning felt much freer to innovate and take chances, knowing that if his decisions were considered wholly impolitic it was the Lords who would incur the odium of upsetting them and his own standing would be undiminished.

Where he found himself without allies in his own court, his dissents sometimes won the day in the Lords, and even where they did not, some acquired their own legitimacy: for example his dissent giving priority to the right of peaceful protest over the rights of estate agents and property speculators.[6] (He happened to perceive the contest as charity versus trade. If he had been persuaded to see it as free enterprise versus political militancy, the outcome might well have been different.)

It would be as mistaken to remember Denning as a judicial Alf Garnett as it would to remember him as a beacon of judicial virtue. He was complex in his strategic views and in many ways a vigorous modernist. In the 1950s he helped to clear the path for the re-establishment of judicial review of public administration, a process which had become atrophied but has today changed the face of both law and government in Britain. It was Denning who coined the concept of legitimate expectation as a new shield for the citizen against the state. At times it seemed that such protection was for Denning the ultimate goal. Yet he was ready to abdicate in favour of an unaccountable executive where he believed the political stakes were too high. It was not uncharacteristic that in 1977, when he made this U-turn in the case of the American journalist Mark Hosenball, who was deported without being allowed to know or answer the case against him, he did so by asserting his faith in the infallibility of the security services:

> 'In some parts of the world national security has been used as an excuse for all sorts of infringement of individual liberty. But not in England.'[7]

Then came his judgment in 1980 on the attempt by the Birmingham Six to sue the police for the beatings they had suffered before five of them made confessions.

> 'If the six men win, it will mean ... that the convictions were erroneous. That would mean that the Home Secretary would either have to

---

[6] *Hubbard v Pitt* [1976] QB 142 (dissenting).
[7] *R v Secretary of State for the Home Department, ex parte Hosenball* [1977] 3 All ER 452 (CA).

recommend they be pardoned or he would have to remit the case to the Court of Appeal ... This is such an appalling vista that every sensible person in the land would say it cannot be right that these actions should go any further.'[8]

Seven other judges shared Denning's—as it eventually emerged—mistaken view; yet it is on him alone that history's unforgiving eye has come to rest. He could not complain, for this was what he constantly courted, and the peroration of his judgment in the Birmingham Six case—'This case shows what a civilised country we are'—remains an ironic epitaph not on them but on him.

At other times Denning's ends and his means coincided. In his 1963 report on the Profumo affair, a strongly authoritarian approach to public affairs marched with a rigorous view of private morality and a patrician attitude to individuals, as he chronicled the dealings of 'Mr Profumo' with 'Mandy' and 'Christine'.[9]

But neither xenophobia nor obscurantism obstructed Denning's response when, in 1974, the great issue on which his lead was awaited came before him (for Denning habitually diverted the most tempting appeals into his own court): was the new body of European law, overriding both the common law and the sovereignty of Parliament, going to be welcomed and assisted by the judges or cribbed and confined by restrictive judicial interpretation? Denning surprised everybody who thought they knew his foibles. In a judgment which ranks among the great passages of English judicial prose, he avoided both grudging acquiescence and overt welcome by adopting the image of the great forces of nature which an island people had traditionally faced and coped with:

'The Treaty is like an incoming tide. It flows into the estuaries and up the rivers. It cannot be held back.'[10]

Faced with the great issues of political power, Denning was a realist in his stewardship of the law. Later, as a crossbench peer, he proclaimed himself a traditional constitutionalist and tried vainly to stem the same tide as he saw it threatening to burst the banks of Westminster.

---

[8] *McIlkenny v Chief Constable of West Midlands Police Force, Hunter v Chief Constable of Lancashire Police Force* [1980] QB 283 at 323 (CA).

[9] Viz Christine Keeler and Mandy Rice-Davies, the latter credited by the press with the immortal riposte 'Well he would, wouldn't he?'—but cf Ivan Lawrence QC, *My Life of Crime* (Book Guild, 2010) p 51.

[10] *HP Bulmer Ltd v J Bollinger SA* [1974] Ch 401 at 418 (CA).

If there is a label for Denning's stance as a lawgiver, it is arguably radical conservatism. The emergence of just this, in Denning's
later years, as the dominant mode of the political state is some
confirmation of his status not only as a judge but as a historic figure
of lasting importance.

35

Lord Sumption and Public Law

I retired from the bench in April 2011. Later that year, shortly before taking his seat in the Supreme Court, Jonathan Sumption QC delivered a public lecture in which he excoriated the judiciary for trespassing into politics. This response was published in the London Review of Books. *The controversy was conducted without rancour, and we subsequently sat amicably together as members of the Judicial Committee of the Privy Council.*

ALTHOUGH IT IS unusual, there is nothing novel about a member of the bar being appointed directly to the UK's highest court. When the highest court was the appellate committee of the House of Lords, appointments to it were occasionally made in this way, sometimes to good effect. Among the last, now more than half a century ago, were James Reid QC, a Scottish Tory MP who, as Lord Reid, became one of the best judges of the postwar years, and Cyril Radcliffe QC, a distinguished public servant[1] and barrister.

The legislation which in 2009 took final appeal in the UK out of the legislature and into its own space, and which populated it with judges who, although titular lords, no longer had to be peers, made provision for appointment to the new Supreme Court to be open to any lawyer of more than 15 years' standing. (It failed to take the opportunity to make leading legal academics eligible—a gateway which, for example, gave Canada one of its greatest chief justices, Bora Laskin.) The first beneficiary of this dispensation, Jonathan Sumption QC, a noted historian as well as a leading lawyer, was sworn into office in January 2012.

The previous November, after he had been appointed but before he had taken office, Sumption delivered one of the law's more prestigious annual lectures[2] to a packed audience in Lincoln's Inn.

---

[1] I say nothing here about Radcliffe's role in the partition of India in 1947.
[2] The 2011 FA Mann Lecture, which should be read alongside this chapter. It can be readily found online.

Entitling it 'Judicial and Political Decision-Making: The Uncertain Boundary', he used the lecture to reprove the judiciary which he was about to join for failing to keep out of the political arena. As the audience filed out, someone said: 'At last we have our own Scalia.'

Like Justice Scalia of the US Supreme Court, Sumption felt able to characterise the constitutional debate in America between originalists and their opponents as 'fundamentally a debate about the permissible limits of judicial lawmaking in a democracy, where the law as declared by the Supreme Court would not necessarily have obtained congressional or electoral endorsement.' This is how originalists have sought to present the issue, purporting to restrict lawful interpretation to the framers' original intent and denouncing liberals who treat the constitution as a living instrument for using interpretation to make new law. But now that they dominate the Supreme Court, the judicial ideologues who purport to draw the originalist line, Scalia prominent among them, are making law for all they are worth. Among many instances, they have recently made unsolicited use of a lawsuit about democratic representation in order to declare unconstitutional all legislative restrictions on corporate election funding. What can be said, as Sumption suggests, is that the US, with a judicial power to strike down primary legislation, stands at one end of a spectrum of judicial interventionism. What cannot be said, as he then suggests, is that France stands at the other.

France, Sumption asserts, was 'the first country in the world to develop a coherent scheme of public or administrative law'; yet, he says, 'successive French constitutions from 1799 to 1958 have been characterised by a persistent hostility to judicial interference with the two other branches of the state.' If this is literally the case, it is simply because judicial oversight of public administration is entrusted by the constitution to the Conseil d'Etat, which is formally a part of the administration and not a court. Sumption, acknowledging this, seeks to advance his thesis of British exceptionalism by asserting that 'the *section du contentieux*, which deals with public law litigation, remains a great deal more deferential to the policy-making organs of the state than English judges are.' Having sat both with the *section du contentieux* and with a regional *tribunal administratif*, and having talked and worked with their judges (for that is what they are), I can say for certain that this is not the case where policy-making spills over into law. As long ago as 1873 the Conseil d'Etat took a step the UK courts have never taken, by holding the state liable to pay damages for serious abuses of power.

The leading British commentary, Brown and Bell, holds that 'the surprising feature' of French administrative law, given its Napoleonic origin, is the fact that 'it has survived to provide one of the most systematic guarantees of the liberties of the individual against the state anywhere in the world.'[3] I know of no French commentary which takes a different view. Sumption cites the well-known remark of one of the architects of the Napoleonic Code, Jean-Etienne-Marie Portalis, 'Juger l'administration, c'est aussi administrer' as if it were a warning against judicial review. In fact, Portalis was arguing for a specialist court to supervise the legality of public administration— something both France and Britain now have. None of this gives support to any suggestion that France has a domesticated poodle where Britain possesses a junkyard dog.

How far, Sumption then asks, can judicial review go before it trespasses on the proper function of government and legislature in a democracy? The question, he tells us, 'has never troubled practitioners, and rarely features in the judgments of the courts'. In consequence, he concludes, 'English public law has not developed a coherent or principled basis for distinguishing between those questions which are properly a matter for decision by politicians answerable to Parliament and the electorate, and those which are properly for decision by the courts.'

It is as difficult to know where to begin answering these assertions as it is to know what they are based on. Like a good many other public law practitioners, academics and judges, I have spent my working life thinking about and dealing with little else. But one thing we have not done is to conflate government and legislature, as Sumption does in order to suggest that both ought to be equally immunised by their democratic credentials from judicial oversight. The courts go to considerable lengths to respect the constitutional supremacy of Parliament; Sumption gives no serious instances to the contrary. It is the executive—the departments of state over which ministers preside, along with quangos and local government—which is subject to public law controls. That is because executive government exercises public powers which are created or recognised by law and have legal limits that it is the courts' constitutional task to patrol. When I argued the leading case of *M v Home Office* in the Court of Appeal[4] (the case went on to the House of Lords, which confirmed

---

[3] LN Brown and J Bell, *French Administrative Law* (Oxford University Press, 1998).
[4] *M v Home Office* [1992] QB 270 (CA).

the liability of ministers for contempt of court in the discharge of their offices), I proposed a formulation which Lord Justice Nolan adopted in his judgment and which has been accepted as correct by our unreflective and atheoretical profession: 'The proper constitutional relationship of the executive with the courts is that the courts will respect all acts of the executive within its lawful province, and that the executive will respect all decisions of the courts as to what its lawful province is.'

So one returns to Sumption's lecture to see what it is that Britain's judges have been doing that they ought not to have been. He cites Lord Justice Laws's distinction of principle between 'macro-policy', which with rare exceptions is a matter for ministers and not for the courts, and policy as it affects individuals, which is the stuff of judicial review. But the principle, while 'never overtly rejected', is according to Sumption not consistently applied: 'The tendency of the courts to intervene in the making of "macro-policy" has become more pronounced.' Indeed 'many of the decisions of the courts [on fundamental rights] have edged towards a concept of fundamental law trumping even parliamentary legislation.'

His main evidence for these categorical assertions, couched as they are in the language of the present, consists of four cases decided respectively in 1995, 1996, 2000 and 2002. The first of them is the case in which the High Court struck down a £234 million subvention to Malaysia which, while directed to the construction of the Pergau Dam, was tied to kickback orders for the British arms industry, and had in any event been condemned by the government's own advisers as a waste of money. The ground on which the court intervened was that the grant was not authorised by the statute under which Douglas Hurd, the Foreign Secretary, had purportedly made it, because it was not capable of fulfilling the statutory purpose of promoting development. In other words, the court was doing its job of testing the legality of executive action against the relevant statutory power. It was not, as Sumption openly suggests it was, substituting its own view of policy for the Foreign Secretary's. We don't know if the High Court got it wrong, for example by reading 'development' as meaning 'sound development', because the Foreign Secretary (who had failed to obtain advice from his own lawyers) didn't appeal and instead took the short cut of using different funds for the same purpose. That was in 1995.

In 1996, a split Court of Appeal struck down social security regulations which took all benefits away from asylum seekers who had not claimed asylum on entry to the UK. The court applied to the executive's power to regulate benefits Lord Ellenborough's ruling in 1803 that the exclusion of impoverished foreigners from the system of poor relief was contrary to 'the law of humanity, which is anterior to all positive laws, [and which] obliges us to afford them relief to save them from starving.' But the story did not end there. When in 2002 the Home Secretary, David Blunkett, slipped into a bill a provision expressly empowering such action, the Human Rights Act required him to include a safety-net provision that the use of the power was not to result in inhuman or degrading treatment of the destitute. Mr Justice Collins, a conscientious and experienced High Court judge, who tried to take a principled approach to the problem of hungry and ill asylum seekers on our streets, was rewarded with public abuse by a Home Secretary who appeared to have a shaky grasp of the separation of powers; but he was vindicated by both the Court of Appeal and the House of Lords which, duly applying Parliament's own legislation, held that it did not authorise executive action that would render the treatment of the already destitute inhuman or degrading. One might have considered this something to be proud of; but Sumption considers it to be evidence of judges failing to read Parliament's intentions accurately—in this case an intention contained in an act of 1993 which neither expressly nor implicitly conferred any such extreme power.

Sumption's third example of judicial incoherence is the *Alconbury* case, which he describes as 'one of the most remarkable instances in recent times of an attempt by the judiciary to transfer decision-making out of the democratic arena'. A challenge to a central pillar of the town and country planning system succeeded at first instance on the ground that cases 'called in' by the Secretary of State were being denied the judicial determination to which they were entitled. It was decided at first instance by a presiding judge whose experience lay not in public law but in commercial law, and it was overset on appeal—not on the ground that such decisions were the sole province of ministers but that ministers were themselves subject to judicial review. Its real interest is not, however, as a short-lived aberration which the courts themselves corrected. It is that the government accepted that its minister was neither independent nor impartial on planning policies—how could he be?—but won the case on the ground that his decisions were subject to judicial review which *was* independent and impartial. What the *Alconbury* case contributes to a critique of current public law jurisprudence, apart possibly from an own-goal, is hard to discern.

The fourth illustration is a case in which the Court of Appeal had to decide whether a regime which imposed swingeing penalties on hauliers who were considered not to have done enough to prevent clandestine immigrants using their vehicles involved an unfair process and a disproportionate interference with property rights. The Human Rights Act required the court to answer this question, and it was divided about the answer. Sumption is entitled to his view, which others share, that the minority judgment upholding the scheme as legitimate was correct. But he is mistaken, here as elsewhere, in his conflation of delegated statutory powers, which these were, with executive policy, which this was not. Delegated powers have to be matched against the wording and the purpose of the statute that creates them, and sometimes of other statutes too. Policies are there to secure consistency and direction in the exercise of discretionary powers which would otherwise tend to be used inconsistently and arbitrarily but which need to retain a measure of flexibility.

An argument that collapses this elementary distinction gives cause for concern. So does the allegation, which Sumption repeated in an interview with *The Times* on the day he was sworn in, that the courts have gone outside the legitimate region of reviewing the application of policy to individuals and have embarked on the review of policy itself. Let me illustrate why these are not necessarily discrete categories. A young couple fall in love and marry. She is British; he is Chilean. Because they are both under 21, immigration rules, which set out Home Office policy, forbid him to settle here with his wife, who has a university place and a promising career ahead. The purpose of the rule is to inhibit the importation of spouses by forced marriage. Forced marriage is a serious matter meriting determined government action, but there is nothing to link the vast majority of young couples affected by the rule with it. The young couple bring judicial review proceedings. The impact of the rule on their right to marry and to live as a family is manifest. The rule itself has a lawful purpose, but the Home Office accepts that it has no bearing on them. How could the courts decide whether the impact on the couple was legitimate without considering in detail the justification for the rule itself? That is what both the Court of Appeal and the Supreme Court did. Had they not done so, the Home Secretary's case would have gone unheard. All but one of the judges decided that the impact on the individuals before them was out of proportion to the policy objective. The result was not to stifle policy initiatives designed to inhibit forced marriages; these remain a matter for government alone. It was to ensure that such initiatives conformed to the law by not impacting disproportionately on individuals. This is a critical linkage which recurs in the now well-developed law of legitimate expectation, which sometimes requires government to honour its promises even when its policy has legitimately shifted.

When exiguous evidence is presented in support of a thesis, it can start to look as if there is something wrong with the thesis. But, however poorly substantiated, critiques of this kind offer encouragement to sections of the media which are out to get the judges. Last December, at one of the Lord Chief Justice's press conferences, a tabloid journalist asked: 'The new member of the Supreme Court, Mr Sumption, has made it clear that he believes that judges, using mainly processes of judicial review and human rights, have delved too far into the everyday decision-making in politics—my examples being the recent cases involving Sefton and the Isle of Wight, and the High Court has told local councils what cuts they may or may not make. Do you agree with Mr Sumption?' 'I am very sympathetic with Mr Sumption and the views he has expressed,' Lord Judge said. He then explained that judges have to enforce the law, that local authorities too have responsibilities, and that the court's decisions occasionally but inevitably had an impact on 'administration for which others are responsible'. All perfectly correct, but not what Sumption had been saying, and not a ground for criticising any of the decisions the journalist had fed him. The Isle of Wight case, for example, required a complicated analysis of the parliamentary legislation and statutory guidance governing the duty of local authorities to provide care for severely disabled adults. Mrs Justice Lang's careful decision, holding that the council had not gone about this lawfully, was clearly correct and has not been appealed. Such cases may well—in fact frequently do—arise from an honest error in a pressured and under-resourced area of administrative law. But one asks what the critics of such decisions want. That local authorities should be able to break the law without redress? That courts whose job it is to apply the law should abdicate? That councillors or officials should be allowed to dispense with the law if they think fit?

An uninstructed reader would gain little notion from Lord Sumption's lecture of the extensive body of judicial authority recognising the inadmissibility of adjudication on political issues. They would find no reminder that when, at the last minute, the government produced national security as its reason for banning trade unions at GCHQ, its surveillance headquarters, in 1984 the courts backed off without demur. They would learn that when the *Alconbury* case reached the House of Lords,[5] Lord Hoffmann reminded us that what is in the public interest is for legislatures and ministers to judge, but not that he also said that 'when ministers or officials make decisions affecting the rights of individuals, they must do so in accordance with the law.' Nor would they find Lord Bingham's nuanced and classic account, in the *Belmarsh* case, of the relationship of the system of justice to the system of government:

> 'The more purely political (in a broad or narrow sense) a question is, the more appropriate it will be for political resolution and the less likely it is to be an appropriate matter for judicial decision ... Conversely, the greater the legal content of any issue, the greater the potential role of the court, because under our constitution and subject to the sovereign power of Parliament it is the function of the courts and not of political bodies to resolve legal questions.'[6]

Instead, there is a repeated insinuation that judicial interference in the political process regularly occurs: 'The judicial resolution of inherently political issues is difficult to defend.' It is not only difficult to defend; it does not happen. I can recall in 1995 refusing to permit judicial review of a white paper on night flights at Heathrow which I had found to be 'a farrago of equivocation'. I did so on the ground that its deviousness was a matter for political debate, not for adjudication. Robert Stevens in his book *The English Judges* comments that my decision did not endear me to ministers, but I doubt that allowing judicial review to proceed would have been more likely to earn their gratitude.

Judges who sit in the administrative court could give scores of other examples. Here is one from *R (Wheeler) v Office of the Prime Minister*:

> 'Whether the differences are sufficiently significant to treat the Lisbon Treaty as falling outside the scope of an implied representation to hold a referendum in respect of a treaty "with equivalent effect" must depend primarily, as it seems to us, on a political rather than a legal judgment. There are, as Mr Sumption submitted, no judicial standards by which the court can answer the question.'[7]

As the press conference episode illustrates, the effect of the kind of critique advanced in this lecture is not neutral. It harms the

---

[5] *R (on the application of Alconbury Developments Ltd) v Secretary of State for the Environment, Transport and the Regions* [2001] UKHL 23.

[6] *A v Secretary of State for the Home Department* [2004] UKHL 56 at [29].

[7] *R (Wheeler) v Office of the Prime Minister* [2008] EWHC 1409 (Admin) at [34].

standing of the judiciary and confidence in the law, just as it would do if a judge, naming no names and citing no instances, were to deliver a public lecture on the perils of judicial corruption. Smoke, in the public mind, means fire. Nobody who knows the history of English public law would deny that there have been decisions which smack at least as much of politics as of law: the condemnation of the Poplar councillors in 1921 for paying men and women equal wages, for example. But that is a long way from the charge that modern public law judges, lacking any jurisprudential compass, routinely cross the boundary separating law from politics.

There is more in the lecture: a critique of the European Court of Human Rights for trying to make one size fit all—a problem the court itself is well aware of and has been grappling with for decades—and a perfectly tenable argument that the modern growth of public law has been stimulated by a perceived deficit in the democratic process. But there is a possibility that the central allegation of repeated judicial intrusion into the business of government will be seen as a political incursion into the business of adjudication. One leaves the lecture reflecting that if we had parliamentary confirmation hearings for new judicial appointees (something Sumption rightly opposes), this is the kind of manifesto we would get and that politicians would probably applaud. What would happen to a candidate who stood up for the integrity of modern public law and for judicial independence within the separation of powers is anybody's guess.

36

Bob Dylan

These historical curiosities are reviews of Bob Dylan's first two London concerts. In those years, reading for the bar left time for other things, which in my case included being Tribune's *folk music critic. In 1962 I had played an impromptu session with the then little-known Dylan at the Troubadour folk club in Earl's Court. By 1964 he was a celebrity; by 1965 he was a star. Both reviews display an embarrassing loftiness; but I wonder whether in their time and place they were not on the whole right.*

I

THERE IS A folksinger's lament written by Shel Silverstein, complaining that he wants to sing about chain gangs, freight trains and coalmines—'But what can you do if you're young and white and Jewish … And your mother says it's dirty down the mine.' The answer, if Bob Dylan is anything to go by, is that you can do all right. The Festival Hall audience at his first British concert certainly thought so.

Dylan's main harbinger, his all-purpose protest song *Blowin' in the wind*, which has topped the charts, is a fair sample of his work: full of agitated awareness, asking questions rather than thumping tubs. He couldn't possibly have happened before the sixties, but he has learnt his craft largely from the great Okie ballad-maker of the thirties, Woody Guthrie. In some ways, as his detractors unceasingly point out, he is just striking Guthrie-like poses. Where Guthrie bummed round the country because he would have starved in the Dustbowl, Dylan has done it simply because he has ants in his pants. When I first heard him, a bit more than a year ago, he was also affecting Guthrie's strangled intonation, which he seems mercifully to have dropped now.

But the important thing is that Bob Dylan has an even better ear than Guthrie had[1] for the poetic possibilities of everyday language,

---

[1] Woody Guthrie was still alive (he lived until 1967), but he had been chronically disabled for some years by Huntington's disease. Dylan was among the few people to visit him in hospital.

together with a feeling for rhetoric that enables him to jolt his audience in its seats. On paper most of his songs are riddled with faults—clumsy phrases, absurd rhymes, badly thought-out melodies—and technically neither his guitar nor his harmonica nor his voice are anything more than average. Yet he is a real artist, with his well-timed throwaways and his shy grin, with the pushing intensity of his delivery, and with the seething live images that run through his songs. He often aims too high and comes a cropper; but he barely ever commits the deadly sin of cliché.

Two of his songs I would say are masterpieces. One is *Who killed Davey Moore?*, a shattering reworking of the old *Cock Robin* idea.[2] The other is *Don't think twice, it's all right*, practically the only outstanding song about love produced by the folk revival.

If he can keep his omnivorous mind off easy pop formulas (the weakest of his songs at the RFH was a self-pitying love song full of damp relative minors that put you in mind of Roy Orbison) and can go on learning from the genuinely popular American tradition, and if the American folk establishment will stop kowtowing to him and bully him occasionally, Dylan may in time become the great figure they are already cracking him up to be. At 23 he still has plenty of time.

29 May 1964

II

When Bob Dylan was here a year ago, this column took its hat off to him and to his genuineness and real talent, in spite of his flaws as a songwriter. Certainly the Bob Dylan who has caught everyone's imagination in the last two years had fire in his belly, and at his packed Albert Hall concert this week it was still his earlier songs that shone—*The lonesome death of Hattie Carroll* in particular (a harrowing account of a young white landowner's wanton killing of a Negro[3] maid a few years ago) and even *With God on our side* (which to tell the truth is not much more than doggerel buoyed up by passion).

But ever since he arrived on the scene the American folk establishment has been lying on its belly in front of him, and it really looks as though his talent is being killed with kindness. Some of

[2] Davey Moore was a young professional boxer killed by a blow to the head.
[3] In 1965 this was the politically correct synonym for black.

his new songs, no kidding, sounded as though he'd been borrowing ideas from the wretched Donovan, Britain's own instant painless Dylan.

Then again, take his new *Gates of Eden*—another of his shelves of serried images. Where the string of seemingly random images in *A hard rain's gonna fall* had a blaze of real fear to light it up (the Cuba crisis in point of fact, but it could as easily have been Korea or Berlin or Vietnam), *Gates of Eden* just doesn't connect with experience. It's a handsome stack of phrases, but there's no edifice, no structure.

If Dylan had been intelligently criticised early on by the people he was ready to listen to he would still be trying to write better songs. As it is, he's in effect given up the effort. Much of his new material is cliché-ridden. Only his wry treatments of the battle of the sexes are still alive and kicking. He doesn't even make the effort to be likeable on stage any more—and why should he bother? The touts were getting £10 for tickets to see him.[4]

There's no doubt that he's still a very considerable artist. If this article has sounded disappointed, that is because he was even better in the past. It's not that he's sold out. Not even that he's running out of ideas, though the Rolling Stones-type R&B material he's recently been producing doesn't sound too original. I think the real trouble is the universal acclaim that now follows him—the applause drowns the opening lines of half his songs, and the admiration wraps him in cotton-wool.

How can you keep protesting hotly when everyone within earshot is busy agreeing with you, especially the people who are making money out of you? The songs sounded different, and Dylan's whole approach was different too, in the days when he had to shout 'For Christ's sake, listen!' and didn't know if people were going to.

14 May 1965

---

[4] £10 in 1965 was half a week's wages.

37

Ewan MacColl

1915–1989

EVERYTHING EWAN MacCOLL did was theatre. His performance of a single song in a pub back room was as calculated
an event as the Radio Ballads with which he and Charles
Parker created a new genre in sound (and won the BBC its first
Italia Prize). As an actor he had had a reputation as a ham, and as
a dramatist he belongs to a self-confident phase of political history
that is long gone. As a folklorist and scholar, he was ready to let
inspired assumptions fill gaps in his knowledge. Yet out of activities
at which he did not excel he created an art-form which was his own:
part tradition, part composition, part observation, part invention,
part documentary, part drama, part music, part speech.

His own singing style was a good example. No one who had
watched him would forget the elbow propped on the chair back,
hand over ear, eyes closed, head tilted back, the fine baritone carefully crumbling into a rusty *tremolo* at the line's end. No known
traditional singer has sung in this style, yet a whole generation
of listeners came to believe that this was the true oral tradition.
In fact it was one of Ewan's brilliant artefacts, deliberately combin-
ing the classical strengths of his own delivery with a Brechtian
coarseness that echoed the voices of the old men and women (his
mother Betsy Miller among them) in whose mouths the tradition
still lived.

It was in the same eclectic and synthetic way that he composed
many of his finest works, the thematic songs which he made largely,
but not only, for the Radio Ballads. Often he would work from
scraps of taped dialogue, singing the fragments and ideas together
on to a running tape until a whole song was formed. There was
always a political pulse, for Ewan's engine was his political passion
(a passion which gave his songs power and depth but which took his

own politics down the cul-de-sac of Maoism[1]); the dignity of gipsies under endless persecution: the endurance and pride of the herring fishermen; the deep culture and strength of the miners. Ewan's was a heroic male view of a man's world, and to that extent a limited view. But it was articulated and sung with a flair that stood squarely in the tradition of English radical poetry. There is a striking parallel between songs like Ewan's 'Big Hewer'–

> I've worked in the Hutton, the Plessey, the Brockwell Seam, go down!
>
> The Bensham, the Busty, the Beaumont, the
>
> Marshall Green, go down!
>
> I've lain on my back in the old Three-Quarter
>
> Up to the chin in stinking water,
>
> Hewing the coal, away in the hole, go down!

–and passages of Milton and Blake where place names are similarly piled into great monuments.

Like Georges Brassens, who realised as a young man that he could either be a mediocre poet or a very good songmaker, MacColl created a genre that displayed his enormous talents for melody, rhetoric and performance, whether in rendering traditional songs or in making new ones. I will remember not the waspish protectiveness with which he dismissed any challenge, however tentative, to his own aesthetic, but the electric silence in which his singing of a song like 'The Bonnie Earl Of Murray' held us. And I will remember his drama documentary for International Co-operative Day 1964, a presentation very much of its time—jazz musicians, actors, soloists, massed choirs, celebrating the achievements and the enduring ideals of co-operation:

> 'Who remembers us?' asks one of the Rochdale pioneers. 'We who were born hungry and who died hungry, we who planted trees in a forest of stone?'
>
> 'All of us remember' say the children. 'Yours the seed and ours the fruit.'

As the curtain falls, a ragged man in the aisle calls out to the cast:

> 'Do you remember a mechanic from the Chatham dockyard who tried and failed in 1760? That was me, friends. There was a weaver, one of

---

[1] His 'Ballad of Stalin', circa 1950, is best forgotten.

many, who was gaoled for debt after the collapse of the Oldham Cooperative Supply Company in 1795. That was me … I greet you in the name of all the failures … Only do not forget the idea, the dream behind it all. If you do, then our lives will have been without purpose, our deaths without significance. Remember that.'

The triumphalist age of the world socialism, waning in Ewan's lifetime, is over. That his melody and rhetoric can still give you gooseflesh is evidence, not only of his enduring flair, but of the persisting need for a sense of tradition and purpose of those who continue to trudge down a road lit now by the flames of burning palaces of culture.

Occasional Pieces

38

A Commonplace Book

These memoirs of cases I had argued at the bar were written down at intervals in the course of a year (possibly 1982—I'm now unsure). I have resisted the temptation to make more than marginal alterations.

I

THE HOUSE OF Lords: five old men as dry as tinder, solemn as owls. I am on my feet and on my own, a junior without a leader. Until now, this was the path of glory; now it is the valley of death. For some quirky reason, two Lord Chancellors are sitting, one current, one ex. For some even quirkier reason, they both appear to be on my side. Since my client is the egregious Erin Pizzey and the bone of contention her Chiswick refuge for battered women, this surprises me until it dawns that these crusty old Tories have even less time than she has for local authorities who claim the power to decide how many people may occupy a house.[1]

'If the council sets a limit and then a son comes home from service abroad', Dilhorne barks at me, 'they say they can prosecute the head of the household, do they?'

What is this? The question supports my argument, but how can anyone who speaks to you so rudely be on your side? In the microseconds for which I battle with this conundrum, my back goes: a pain like a bullet travels up my spine, the herald of a working lifetime of back trouble. I grab the edge of the lectern to keep myself upright. If their lordships have noticed anything they do not show it. Propping myself on my elbows, I soldier on.

After a while we seem to have followed the white rabbit down the burrow.

'Can it be a household if it has no head?' says one.

---

[1] When occupied by more than one household.

'Is a regiment a household?' says another.

'How about the Household Cavalry?' asks Hailsham.

'Why not?' I reply hopelessly.

'Suppose,' says Hailsham, leaning suddenly forward and looking hard at Dilhorne, 'suppose my noble and learned friend invites me to his country house for the weekend. Do I become a member of his household while I am there? Do I cease to be the head of my own?'

I am stumped, not so much for an answer as for a clue to what this is all about. At lunchtime John Griffiths, the veteran law reporter, tells me: Dilhorne has never invited Hailsham to his country house, and Hailsham has left Dilhorne in no doubt that he resents it. This morning's case had been as good an opportunity as any to ventilate the grievance.[2]

II

Some years later I am waiting to weigh into the argument about Colonel B.

John Melville Williams QC is leading for the National Union of Journalists, whose journal has jeopardised national security by revealing that Colonel B[3] is Lieutenant-Colonel Johnstone, whoever *he* may be. I am waiting to come in and stitch up the argument with a few sparkling submissions for the Leveller magazine and Peace News, who revealed it first. John is waiting for me to come in and screw up what he has achieved so far.

The House of Lords are cross. The magistrates' gagging order was a mess and they are going to have to allow the appeal. But it goes against the grain to have to do it for a bunch of bolshie journalists, radicals and conchies. So they spend the morning doing the music-hall knockabout act. One of them puts a point; John starts to answer it; another of them interrupts him and demands to know why he's wasting their time; while John is explaining, the first one asks him if he'd mind sticking to the point.

At lunchtime one of the Leveller collective ('What is a collective?' their lordships asked in chorus at 10.31 this morning) asks John what it's like being dragged up a blind alley and finding four heavies there waiting to put the boot in.

---

[2] I admit having recounted some of this in *Lions Under the Throne* Ch 1.
[3] The pseudonym under which the Tottenham magistrates had allowed him to testify.

III

The Commission for Racial Equality is investigating a textile mill. It is in the Halifax area and has not a single Bengali worker. The management say they'd be glad to have some but the union won't let them. The union says it has no colour bar but management won't have Bengalis.

Today it's the turn of the mill-owners to give the Commissioners an account of themselves. The managing director and the company's shrewd old solicitor are there. They have pulled a stroke on the Commission: they have briefed a Bengali barrister to represent the company.

He opens their case. He produces a photograph of an electrical switchboard with several switches on it. He begins to explain that this is a high-technology industry and that the local Bengalis are peasants who will burn the place down if turned loose on equipment like this. They are illiterate, he says, and untrustworthy. They go home on holiday and do not come back for six months. This is why they are not employed at the mill. It has nothing to do with prejudice. Indeed there is no racial prejudice in Halifax. Counsel himself has represented National Front members on criminal charges in the area: would he do that if race relations were anything but good there?

We listen with open mouths. Counsel's exposition ends and it is my turn to ask questions for the Commission. What can I ask? What can he say? I ask if the company's case really is that Bengalis as a group are unsuitable for employment in the mill.

The solicitor and managing director are not leaving this one to chance. As their counsel opens his mouth to replace his foot in it, they chorus 'No!' He is not permitted to speak another word.

IV

This is going to be one of those cases. I have come to Winchester to get damages for a fitter who fell off a ladder while repairing a lorry. However, it is not that simple. The engineering expert whose evidence we are relying on takes me aside and tells me that if pressed (as he certainly will be) he would have to say the accident was chiefly our client's fault. I send him home. The orthopaedic surgeon who fixed the broken femur then tells me that, if pressed, he would have to say that our client is fit for work and is malingering. I get my opponent to agree the medical reports and send the surgeon home.

After a conference which has started to resemble the Farewell Symphony, we rejoin my client's wife in the waiting area. 'My God,' she says to him, 'You're not going into the witness box, are you? It'll all come out about you lot repairing your mates' cars instead of working.' My heart in my boots, I enter court with a client, no witnesses, no wife (she won't have anything to do with it) and a superb x-ray photograph of his femur which looks like one of his own engineering jobs, all plates and bolts and undoubtedly worth a few quid in damages.

He tells his story to the judge, who seems bored. My opponent opens his cross-examination with his twenty-one-pounder: 'Where were you in the habit of taking your lunch?'

'In the Bournemouth Conservative Club,' says my client. The judge sits up and starts to take an interest.

'And how much did you drink with your lunch on the day of the accident?' asks my opponent.

This is it. On a day like this, in a case like this, it has to be. The silly sod had fallen off the ladder because he was drunk. But there's nothing about this in the written defence. I shoot to my feet: 'My lord, If this is intended to found an allegation of drunkenness, it's not pleaded.'

'Quite right,' says the judge. He beams at the plaintiff. 'You needn't answer that question.'

I come out of court with a judgment for £30,000. My client is pleased. Even his wife is relieved.

'I don't know anything about the law,' he says to me, 'but I'm a good fitter and I know a skilful job when I see one.'

On the whole it seems better to accept the compliment than to suggest that where you drink may matter more.

V

Early days. My personal injury practice is getting off the ground, and here I am at Bow county court with a case from the London docks. What has happened to my client lacks the romance of either sail or steam. He was hit by a shower of shit from the bilges of a moored freighter as he pulled his lighterman's punt round her hull. As it is unlawful for moored ships to use their bilges rather than the shore toilets, his allegations are strenuously denied by the only man on board, the ship's mate, whose name happens to be Longbottom.

The shipowners are represented by another young and eager barrister named Beloff, newly emerged from the chrysalis of the presidency of the Oxford Union. He puts it to the plaintiff that his tale is a tissue of lies. It turns out that something similar has happened to the plaintiff before, and he has collected a few pounds in compensation for it.

'Where there's muck there's brass,' suggests Beloff.

'It's happened before because they're all too bloody lazy to close their bilges in port,' says the plaintiff.

I call a witness—his foreman, who was on the deck when the plaintiff came dripping up the Jacob's ladder and who now recounts how he fell about laughing and said 'Wotcher, shitlegs.'

Beloff pounces: 'Shitlegs? The plaintiff told us he was hit in the face.'

'It's just an expression,' says the foreman. 'If a bloke works Sundays, I call him Sunday-face. If a bloke works during a strike I call him a blackleg. It's got nothing to do with his face or his legs.'

Mr Longbottom goes into the witness box and swears he religiously used the shore toilets. My client tugs my gown: 'What hit me was so runny he'd never have made it to the shore toilets.'

My nerve fails. I am unable to put my client's case. Still, the judge, who has handled the whole proceeding with complete impassivity, finds in his favour. He then criticises my client for burning his clothes instead of washing them, and gives him £13 damages. A famous victory.

VI

Even earlier days—practically my first personal injury case to come to trial. My client, the plaintiff, was working in a brewery. His job was to catch the metal casks as they were rolled, full, down a ramp on to a concrete floor which they had pitted so badly that a steel plate had been laid over part of the pit. The floor was awash with beer because the casks leaked and the drains were blocked.

My client had been issued that day with size 12 wellies because they were all the stores had left. He stepped forward to catch a cask, caught the protruding end of his boot under the edge of the steel plate, slipped over in the lake of beer and was run over by a succession of barrels as he struggled to liberate his trapped foot.

I get to court in a state of nerves. A witness has not turned up. My particulars of claim suddenly look totally inadequate. I must amend them. We need an adjournment. My client reassures me: we can manage without the witness, and the pleadings are fine. He is a Nigerian law graduate and a member of Lincoln's Inn. Sure enough we win.

VII

As a teenager, Alice Jefferson worked in Acre Mill, the asbestos factory in Hebden Bridge. There was loose asbestos all over the place: they skylarked and made wigs out of it. Now in her early forties she has mesothelioma, the asbestos cancer, and she is dying. John Pickering, her solicitor, has broken all records and got her case to court within a few months of issuing the writ. He wants a judge to see what happens to the victims, not just to read about it when it's all over bar the dependency.

It takes Alice Jefferson ten minutes to get up the steps of the courthouse. Every movement is pain. She ought to have died by now, says the physician who has come to give evidence for her. We talk a little with her. Even with her sunken face and unnaturally bright eyes she is a handsome person. She has kept all her remaining energy to tell her story to the judge, and she does it with clarity and determination. Whatever they say, she does not intend to die. She has a teenage son and a little girl of four. The boy can cope, though he says he doesn't mind how ill she is if she'll only live. The girl—her husband does his best, but he won't be able to do her hair properly for school. Sitting behind my leader, the gentle and able David Turner-Samuels, I am blind with tears. Nobody must see.

The judge gives her every penny he can, but it's nothing. Alice isn't a lawyer or a surgeon. Her loss of earnings is limited to a few years' wages as a part-time cleaner. And what price can anyone put on the pain in her side and in her heart?

Three months later Alice is dead. Yorkshire TV have made film about her. When it is shown, 'Alice, a fight for life' moves a lot of people and spurs the campaign to ban the use of asbestos. But the title has been changed by the lawyers: the working title was 'Getting away with murder'.

39

Under Milk Wood *Lost and Found*

A short piece from the London Review of Books *blog.*

A DECADE AFTER Dylan Thomas's death, a lawsuit was brought by Caitlin Thomas on behalf of his estate to recover the manuscript of *Under Milk Wood* from Douglas Cleverdon. It was Cleverdon who had produced the play for BBC radio and had now put the manuscript on the market. The claim failed: the judge, Mr Justice Plowman, accepted Cleverdon's case that Thomas had made him a gift of the manuscript.

The story as it emerged at trial was this. The play had been commissioned in the middle of the war, but by 1946, when Cleverdon took over responsibility for it, very little of it had been written. After much cajoling Thomas delivered a completed text on Thursday 15 October 1953, four days before he was due to fly to the US to give readings of the play—the trip on which he died. Cleverdon had his secretary, Miss Fox, type it on to a set of stencil skins. On the Saturday she returned the original to Thomas—'and,' said the judge laconically, 'he lost it'. The result was that on the Monday Thomas found himself at Victoria air terminal, about to leave for a reading tour of the US without a copy of his text.

But he had phoned Cleverdon at home at the weekend in panic, having realised that the manuscript had been mislaid. On the Monday Cleverdon got Miss Fox to run off three copies from the stencils and took them in a taxi to the terminal. Thomas told him that he had saved his life. Cleverdon, however, was still concerned at the loss of the original. '[Thomas] said if I could find it I could keep it. He told me the names of half a dozen pubs, and said if he had not left it there he might have left it in a taxi.'

'Mr Cleverdon,' the judge drily held, 'got possession of this manuscript from the Soho public house in which it had been left by Dylan Thomas. That, in my judgment, is sufficient delivery to perfect a gift in Mr Cleverdon's favour.'

Finding the manuscript, however, had not been entirely straight-forward. Cleverdon had to go on a pub crawl. In an account published privately a few years later,[1] he described how he finally found it in the Swiss Tavern in Old Compton Street:

'I asked the barmaid whether anyone had found a script by Dylan Thomas (who was a fairly regular habitué). She looked under the counter, said "Here it is", and gave me the manuscript in its rather tattered folder.'

What would the chances be today of the manuscript being neither purloined nor binned?

---

[1] *Under Milk Wood: account of an action to recover the original manuscript*, Introduction by Douglas Cleverdon (Guernsey, Toucan Press, 1969).

40

Getting It Wrong

One of the numerous pleasures of being an ex-judge is being invited to give a talk, usually after a dinner, to an audience of law students. I have sat through enough self-congratulatory homilies about the law to be determined never to deliver one myself. Hence the talk below, given in variant forms at Gray's Inn and Queen's College, Oxford.

ANY ADVOCATE CAN get it right. It just takes application, learning and judgment. What requires inspiration and an occasional a touch of genius is getting it hideously and irretrievably wrong: not just losing, which all advocates do half the time, but screwing up big time.

Dickens, in his days as a lawyer's clerk, had seen how readily it could happen. In the course of the lawsuit for breach of promise of marriage brought against the gentle Mr Pickwick by his landlady Mrs Bardell, Mrs Bardell's leading counsel, Serjeant Buzfuz, has let his junior, Mr Skimpin, call one of Mr Pickwick's friends, Mr Winkle, to give some unimportant corroborative evidence. When Mr Skimpin has concluded his short examination in chief, Mr Pickwick's junior counsel, Mr Phunky, decides he will take advantage of the opportunity to cross-examine a friendly witness by pressing Mr Winkle for a testimonial to Mr Pickwick's moral probity.

He makes the classic mistake of going one question too far:

'You have never known anything in his behaviour towards Mrs Bardell, or any other female, in the least degree suspicious?' said Mr Phunky, preparing to sit down; for Serjeant Snubbin [his leader] was winking at him.

'N-n-no,' replied Mr Winkle, 'except on one trifling occasion, which, I have no doubt, might be easily explained.'

Now, if the unfortunate Mr Phunky had sat down when Serjeant Snubbin winked at him, or if Serjeant Buzfuz [Mrs Bardell's counsel] had stopped this irregular cross-examination at the outset (which he knew better than to do; observing Mr Winkle's anxiety, and well knowing it would, in all probability, lead to something serviceable to him), this unfortunate admission would not have been elicited. The moment the words fell from Mr Winkle's lips, Mr Phunky sat down, and Serjeant Snubbin rather hastily told him that he might leave the box, which Mr Winkle prepared to do with great readiness, when Serjeant Buzfuz stopped him.

'Stay, Mr Winkle, stay!' said Serjeant Buzfuz, 'will your lordship have the goodness to ask him, what this one instance of suspicious behaviour towards females on the part of this gentleman ... was?'

'You hear what the learned counsel says, sir,' observed the judge, turning to the miserable and agonised Mr Winkle. 'Describe the occasion to which you refer.'

'My lord,' said Mr Winkle, trembling with anxiety, 'I—I'd rather not.'

'Perhaps so,' said the little judge; 'but you must.'

Amid the profound silence of the whole court, Mr Winkle faltered out, that the trifling circumstance of suspicion was Mr Pickwick's being found in a lady's sleeping apartment at midnight; which had terminated, he believed, in the breaking off of the projected marriage of the lady in question, and had led, he knew, to the whole party being forcibly carried before George Nupkins Esq, magistrate and justice of the peace, for the borough of Ipswich.

'You may leave the box, sir,' said Serjeant Snubbin.[1]

With a bit of experience, Mr Phunky's gaffe might have been avoided. But some forensic elephant traps are unavoidable.

Law Latin has always been pronounced as if it were part of the English language: a prima facie[2] case for certiorari,[3] and so forth. But towards the end of the nineteenth century Latin teaching in schools adopted a new and supposedly authentic pronunciation: *veni vidi vici* became 'wayni weedy weechy'. Inevitably the new usage found its way into the legal profession, with the kind of result recorded in AP Herbert's misleading case, *R v Venables*:[4]

'Extraordinary confusion prevailed this morning in the Lord Chief Justice's court when Mr Ambrose Wick applied for a writ of certiorari to issue to the Petty Sessional Bench of Chimney Magna.

Mr Wick, a young advocate appearing in the High Court for the first time, said: My Lord, in these proceedings I ask for a rule *neessee* of *kairtiorahree*—

---

[1] Charles Dickens, *The Pickwick Papers* (1837) Ch 34.
[2] Pronounced 'prim-er fay-she'.
[3] Pronounced 'sir-shore-air-eye', except in the Republic of Ireland, where legal pronunciation follows church Latin and the writ is known as 'chairtsiorahree'.
[4] AP Herbert, *Misleading Cases in the Common Law* (1935) Ch 56.

The Lord Chief Justice: I beg your pardon?

Mr Wick: Kairtiorahree. I am going to submit, my Lord, that an order of the Chimney Magna justices was *ooltra weerayze*—

The Lord Chief Justice: I hope you will do nothing of the sort, Mr Wick. ... What do you mean by "*ooltra weerayze*" and "*day yooray*"? Are they patent medicines or foreign potentates?. ...

Mr Wick: My Lord, *ooltra weerayze*— "beyond the powers"—

The Court: Can it be that you have in mind the Latin expression *ultra vires*?

Mr Wick: No, my Lord; I never heard that expression before.'

If Mr Wick's problem was that he knew too much, it's also possible for counsel to know too little. Sir Thomas Inskip QC when he was Attorney-General (he went on to become Lord Chancellor and then Lord Chief Justice) had to argue a case on the Gaming Acts before the House of Lords. In the course of his opening he informed the Appellate Committee that roulette was played with cards.

"Balls" said the presiding law lord.[5]

We've all wanted to say that from time to time, but the opportunity rarely presents itself.

A near-contemporary of AP Herbert was Theo Mathew. His *Forensic Fables*, published pseudonymously between the wars, contain numerous examples of how to get it magnificently wrong.

'The Circuiteer and the Nice Old Buffer[6]

A Circuiteer, Recently Elected to the Bar Mess, Determined to Try his Luck at the Assizes. Arriving at the Railway Terminus Rather Late, he Just had Time to Fling himself into a Carriage as the Train Steamed Out. It was Occupied by an Elderly Party, whom the Circuiteer Diagnosed as a Nice Old Buffer. He had a Rug over his Knees and he Wore a Top Hat. He was Smoking an Excellent Cigar. The Nice Old Buffer Appeared to be Rather Surprised at the Circuiteer's Intrusion; but the Latter, being of a Chatty and Affable Disposition, Soon Put Him at his Ease. Before Long the Nice Old Buffer had offered the Circuiteer a Cigar and they were Getting on Like a House on Fire. The Circuiteer Told him about his University Career, his Uncle Thomas, the Man he had Read With in Chambers, and a Lot of Other Things.

Turning to the Object of his Travels, he Mentioned to the Nice Old Buffer that he was Going to the Assizes; that Mr Justice Stuffin was the Presiding

[5] See (1934) 50 LQR 276.
[6] 'O' (Theo Mathew), *Forensic Fables* (1926) p 9.

Judge; but that the Profession did not Think Much of him. Stuffin, said the Circuiteer, would never have got a Judgeship on his Merits; but he had Married a Woman with a Good Deal of Money and had a Safe Tory Seat. He was just Going to tell the Nice Old Buffer what the Court of Appeal had Said the Other Day about One of Stuffin J's Judgments when the Train Arrived at its Destination. There were Javelin-Men and Trumpeters on the Platform, together with the High Sheriff of the County and his Chaplain. They had Come to Meet the Judge. ...'

Please don't let me discourage you from developing innovative arguments. It is sometimes worth running the risk of the kind of comment delivered by Mr Justice Maule in 1852:

'The last point is perfectly new, and it is so startling that I do not apprehend that it will ever become old.'[7]

If there is a moral, it's don't try it on—but do by all means try it out. This does not, however, include cracking jokes. For my generation of barristers, one way of getting beaten to death in open court was to crack a joke in Lord Justice Megaw's court. Cracking jokes is the prerogative of the bench.

There is, however, a caveat even for the judicial humourist:[8] if you are going to get a gale of sycophantic laughter from the bar, it has to be apparent that you are actually making a joke. I learnt this some years ago when my court was shown a nineteenth century case concerning the business activities of a peer called Lord Mayo. When someone asked who Lord Mayo was, I suggested that he must have been a relative of the Earl of Sandwich. This was met with the total silence it deserved by both bar and bench.

It's not only as a jurist, of course, that you can get your foot wedged in your mouth. In one of my other incarnations, as a book reviewer, I try to keep in mind what happened many decades ago when, for no reason anyone has ever discovered, a review copy of a clandestine edition of *Lady Chatterley's Lover* was sent to the editor of a country life journal. The editor passed it on to his regular book reviewer, who filed the following copy:

'Although written many years ago, *Lady Chatterley's Lover* has just been reissued by Grove Press, and this fictional account of the day-to-day life of an English gamekeeper is still of considerable interest to outdoor-minded readers, as it contains many passages on pheasant-raising, the apprehending of poachers, ways to control vermin, and other chores and

<hr/>

[7] *Whitaker v Wisbey* (1852) 12 CB 44, 58.
[8] Anathematised by WS Gilbert, *The Mikado*, Act I, Pt Va.

duties of the professional gamekeeper. Unfortunately, one is obliged to wade through many pages of extraneous material in order to discover and savour these sidelights on the management of a Midland shooting estate, and in this reviewer's opinion this book cannot take the place of J.R. Miller's *Practical Gamekeeping*.'

***

There's no talisman against getting it wrong, except getting it right. Getting it right, however, doesn't necessarily mean winning. Possibly the hardest thing to achieve in legal practice is losing a case well. By this I don't mean going down with flags flying, guns blazing and band playing. I mean leaving court knowing that you couldn't have done more: if you can get that right, you won't be getting much wrong.

Afterword

A DIFFERENT CAT

At the first sign of spring
the cat would uncurl
go out to taste the air
and leave

With the first frost she'd reappear,
sleep like a teenager through the lifeless days
and when the land warmed leave again

When in her eighteenth autumn
the air turned sharp and no cat came
we knew she'd not be coming

Later the teenagers stretched and left, returning
at the first sign of frost, until one autumn
they found the house shuttered
the eaves dripping
a different cat on the doorstep

Index

las Casas, B de   44
Law Commission   58, 59, 205,
    206, 208
law courts   25–6
Law Latin   274–5
Lawrence, S   207
Laws, J   7, 8, 250
'law's whiteout'   18–20
Lawton, Lord Justice   110
Leavis, Dr   3
legitimate expectation   244, 253
Lemon, D   207
Leopard, The   59
Leveller   266
Levin, B   185
Levy, L   153
Lewis, T   15, 231
libel
  internet
    libellous posts   95, 96
  Lord Mansfield, and   229, 230
life peerages   25
Lilburne, J   230
Little Red Schoolbook   66, 67, 69
Little White Book   66, 67, 69
Liversidge, R   63, 145, 148, 149
Livingstone, K   208
Locke, J   44, 83, 167
London Docks   268–9
Longbottom (ship's mate)   268, 269
Loreburn, Lord Chancellor   31
lorry fitter   267–8
losing a case well   277
Loughlin, M   164, 165, 166
Ludlow, E   19
Lukes, S   49
Lyndhurst, Lord   24

MacColl, E   259–61
Mackay, Lord   181, 208, 216, 220
Macpherson, W   207
Madison, J   83, 118, 167
Magna Carta   4, 150, 164, 166
Maharaj, R   88
Malone, J   64, 65, 166–7
Mansfield, Lord   13, 15, 16, 17, 26,
    39, 40, 61, 63, 225–34
  Dido Elizabeth Belle   232, 233
  libel, and   229, 230
  religious liberty   233
  slavery, and   230–31, 232–3

Mao, Chairman   69
margin of appreciation   68, 70, 71,
    72, 73, 97, 100
Marks, L   90–91
Marris, R   127, 128
Massey   116, 117
Mathew, T   86, 275–6
Maule, Justice   270
May, T   179
Maynard, Justice   117
Mayo, Lord   276
McCardie, Justice   113
McCluskey, Lord   208
McCormick, D   144
McEwan, I   10
McVitie, J   125
Meese, E   153
Megaw, Lord Justice   276
Miller, G   135
Miller, J R   277
Miller, Judith   94
ministerial power   13, 14, 15, 60,
    61, 62, 63, 64, 65
miscarriages of justice   209
Mitchell, F   125
Mitterrand, F   76
Mobil Oil   182
Monitor   61
Montesquieu   83, 167
Moore, J   76
More, Sir Thomas   235–40
Morning Herald   228
Mortimer, J   67
Mosley, O   147, 148
Mount, F   82
Mullan, J   90
Mundella, A   27

Napoleon I   176
Narayan, R   191–3
National Union of Journalists   266
National Union of Students   177
Neuberger, Lord   138
New Statesman   91
New York Times   94
New Yorker   155
Newton, I   54
Nhu, Madame   178, 179, 183
Nicklinson, T   127, 128, 129
Night Jack   93
Nolan, Lord Justice   250